Cambridge First Certificate Handbook

With Answers

Helen Naylor and Stuart Hagger

CAMBRIDGE
UNIVERSITY PRESS

PUBLISHED BY THE PRESS SYNDICATE OF THE UNIVERSITY OF CAMBRIDGE
The Pitt Building, Trumpington Street, Cambridge, United Kingdom

CAMBRIDGE UNIVERSITY PRESS
The Edinburgh Building, Cambridge CB2 2RU, UK
40 West 20th Street, New York, NY 10011–4211, USA
10 Stamford Road, Oakleigh, VIC 3166, Australia
Ruiz de Alarcón 13, 28014 Madrid, Spain
Dock House, The Waterfront, Cape Town 8001, South Africa

http://www.cambridge.org

First published 1999
Reprinted 2001

Printed in the United Kingdom at the University Press, Cambridge

ISBN 0 521 62919 5 Student's Book ('With Answers' edition)
ISBN 0 521 62918 7 Student's Book ('Without Answers' edition)
ISBN 0 521 66658 9 Self-study Pack
ISBN 0 521 62917 9 Set of 2 Cassettes

Thanks and acknowledgements

The authors would like to thank colleagues at The Swan School, Oxford, and London School of English for their comments and encouragement.

The authors and publishers would like to thank the following teachers and advisors who trialled and commented on the material and whose feedback was invaluable.

Christine Barton, Greece; Tony Bayley, Spain; Fredericka Beets, France; Henny Burke, Spain; Sarah Ellis, Italy; Jane Hann, UK; Jenny Mills, UK; Annette Obee, Greece; Anne Prince, UK; Shona Read, UK; Anna Sikorzynska, Poland; Marite Stringa, Argentina; Liz Tataraki, Greece; Clare West, UK; Gaynor Williams, Greece; Philippa Wright, UK; Alison Vahle, UK.

The authors and publishers are grateful to the following for permission to reproduce copyright material. It has not always been possible to identify the sources of all the material used and in such cases the publishers would welcome information from the copyright owners.

James Kirkup and the Salzburg University Press for p. 16: 'The Only Child: An Autobiography of Infancy', published in 1997 as a combined edition with 'Sorrows, Passions and Alarms: An Autobiography of Childhood' in a volume entitled *Child of the Tyne*; The Reader's Digest Association Limited for pp. 21, 29, 114, 118–120, 122, 125, 128, 151–152 and 175 from *The Reader's Digest Did You Know?*, © 1990; *The Guardian* for pp. 25–26: 'A Game of Too Many Halves', © The Guardian; *The Independent on Sunday* for p. 31: 'Alternative Vets Try Acupuncture' by John Arlidge; for pp. 34–36: 'For the Gorilla with Everything' by Matthew Sweet; for p. 44: 'Feng Shui Reaches DIY Store' by Graham Bell; and for p. 53: 'What the Fruitarian Ate One Day Last Week' by Susie Miller; The Telegraph Group Limited for pp. 31–32: 'Noise Pollution', © Rita Carter, 1995; for p. 43: 'Hard Life', © Jane Dowle, 1995; for pp. 55–56: 'First Person' series, © Margaret Rooke and Ruby Milligan, 1994; and for pp. 172–173 'Hard Life', © Jonny Beardsall, 1995; *Top Sante* for pp. 33–34: 'The Truth About Lying'; *Focus* for p. 37: 'Wire Walking the Thames'; for p. 124: 'Inventions'; for p. 151: 'Action Academy'; and for p. 164 'Who'd Win the Insect Olympics?'; The Agency (London) Limited for p. 38: *Waiting and 20 Pieces of Sliver* by Stan Barstow, reproduced by permission of The Agency (London) Limited, © Stan Barstow. First published by John Farquarhson Limited. All rights reserved and enquiries to The Agency (London) Limited, 24 Pottery Lane, London W14 LZ. Fax: 0171 7279037; Michael Joseph for p. 40: *Kiss Kiss* by Roald Dahl; *Radio Times* for the adapted article on p. 42: 'My Kind of Day', *Radio Times* 1–7 November 1997; Macmillan for p. 43: *The Serpent of Paradise* by Dea Birkett; *Sunday Telegraph* for p. 46: 'The Science of Sod's Law' by Robert Matthews, © Robert Matthews, *Sunday Telegraph*, 17 March 1996, Review Section, page 2; *Daily Mirror* for p. 46: 'You're not the person you thought you were' by Gill Swaine; *Time Out* for p. 54: 'Singles' by Brix; and for p. 58: 'Film Review'; Geoff Tibballs and Guinness Publishing Limited for p. 156, adapted from *The Guinness Book of Oddities*, © 1995; *The Times* for p. 160: 'Pet with the Lion Heart' by Jack Crossley, © Times Newspapers Limited.

The authors and publishers are grateful to the following illustrators and photographic sources.

Illustrators: Rachel Decon: pp. 14, 44–45, 154, 177; Nick Duffy: pp. 65, 66, 71, 161, 179; DTP Gecko: pp. 60, 72, 90, 124, 146, 197, 198, 200; Phil Healey: pp. 46, 62, 131, 134, 138, 139, 153, 155; Rosalind Hudson: pp. 16, 67, 69, 89, 116; Amanda MacPhail: pencil icon; Mark Mclaughlin: p. 23; Andrew Quelch: pp. 17, 40, 64, 85, 87, 92, 111; Tracy Rich: pp. 11, 27, 47, 58, 78, 157, 175, 185; Peter Visscher: pp. 164; Katherine Walker: p. 189.

Photographic sources: Action Plus: p. 26; Britain on View: p. 195 (tl); British School of Motoring: p. 93; John Birdsall Photography: pp. 97, 167; Bruce Coleman Collection: pp. 160, 182; Collections: pp. 30, 51 (bl, br), 52 (b), 100, 121, 181; Colorific!: pp. 50, 51 (tr); The Ronald Grant Archive: pp. 128, 156; Sally and Richard Greenhill: p. 105; The Image Bank: pp. 28, 31, 193 (l); Magnum Photos Ltd: p. 35 (b); Paul Medley, DTP Photography: pp. 70, 191, 194 (tl); Oxford Scientific Films Ltd Photo Library: p. 125; J. D. Phillips, Ridge Pottery: p. 194 (bl); Pictor International Ltd: pp. 51 (bm), 77, 81, 145, 172, 194 (tr); Popperfoto: p. 177 (l); Powerstock/Zefa: pp. 51 (mm), 53, 114, 148, 194 (br), 195 (tr, br); Rex Features Ltd: pp. 36, 37, 55, 177 (r); Frank Spooner Pictures Ltd: p. 151; Tony Stone Images: pp. 34, 35 (t), 51 (ml, mr), 52 (t), 75, 84, 99, 107, 119, 186, 193 (r), 195 (bl); The Travel Library: pp. 158, 178, 190.

(t) = top, (b) = bottom, (m) = middle, (l) = left, (r) = right

Freelance picture research by Mandy Twells.

Text permissions by Fiona Donnelly.

Book design by Gecko Limited.

Cover design by Tim Elcock.

The cassettes which accompany this book were produced by Martin Williamson, Prolingua Productions, at Studio AVP, London.

Contents

General introduction   vi
Vocabulary introduction   vii

Chapter 1 *Reading*

Section A: Reading and understanding

UNIT 1	Dealing with difficult words	12
UNIT 2	Phrasal vocabulary	18
UNIT 3	Key words	22

Section B: Reading and answering exam questions

UNIT 4	Multiple matching (main points) *Paper 1 Part 1*	28
UNIT 5	Multiple choice *Paper 1 Part 2*	38
UNIT 6	Gapped text *Paper 1 Part 3*	46
UNIT 7	Multiple matching (specific information) *Paper 1 Part 4*	54

Chapter 2 *Writing*

Section A: Ways of writing

UNIT 1	Writing about events	62
UNIT 2	Describing	68
UNIT 3	Writing about ideas	73
UNIT 4	Writing personally	78
UNIT 5	Language for letters	81

Section B: Writing exam answers

UNIT 6	Transactional letters *Paper 2 Part 1*	84
UNIT 7	Writing a story *Paper 2 Part 2*	91
UNIT 8	Discursive writing: compositions and articles *Paper 2 Part 2*	96
UNIT 9	Reports *Paper 2 Part 2*	102
UNIT 10	Set books *Paper 2 Part 2 Question 5*	107

Chapter 3 *Use of English*

UNIT 1	Multiple choice cloze	114
	Paper 3 Part 1	
UNIT 2	Open cloze	122
	Paper 3 Part 2	
UNIT 3	Key word transformation	129
	Paper 3 Part 3	
UNIT 4	Error correction	145
	Paper 3 Part 4	
UNIT 5	Word formation	150
	Paper 3 Part 5	

Chapter 4 *Listening*

Section A: Listening and understanding

UNIT 1	Improving your understanding	158
UNIT 2	Identifying and using the context	162
UNIT 3	Keeping a clear head	164

Section B: Listening and answering exam questions

UNIT 4	Short texts with multiple choice	166
	Paper 4 Part 1	
UNIT 5	Gap filling	171
	Paper 4 Part 2	
UNIT 6	Multiple matching	176
	Paper 4 Part 3	
UNIT 7	Two- or three-option answers	179
	Paper 4 Part 4	

Chapter 5 *Speaking*

Questions and answers about the Speaking Test	186
UNIT 1	Socialising	189
	Paper 5 Part 1	
UNIT 2	Individual long turn	191
	Paper 5 Part 2	
UNIT 3	Two- and three-way discussion	196
	Paper 5 Parts 3 and 4	

Appendices

APPENDIX 1	Word + preposition combinations	201
APPENDIX 2	Preposition + word combinations	203
APPENDIX 3	Model answers for Writing chapter	204
APPENDIX 4	How to show your answers	206
APPENDIX 5	Tapescripts	207
APPENDIX 6	Answers	220

General introduction

The *Cambridge First Certificate Handbook* is for students preparing for the Cambridge First Certificate in English exam, either individually or in groups, with or without a teacher. It is based on the principle that you need to build up your knowledge and understanding methodically before attempting exam questions.

The aims of *Cambridge First Certificate Handbook* are:

- to build up general skills in reading, writing, listening, speaking and language use, which will give a solid base from which to do the exam
- to give help and practice in tackling all the different exam questions

Organisation

The five chapters of the book correspond to the five papers of the exam:

Chapter 1: Reading
Chapter 2: Writing
Chapter 3: Use of English
Chapter 4: Listening
Chapter 5: Speaking

The **Reading**, **Writing** and **Listening** chapters are each divided into two sections, A and B. The units in **Section A** build up the knowledge and confidence you need for all parts of the paper. The units in **Section B** (exam units) continue this work, dealing with each part of the paper in turn.

The **Use of English** and **Speaking** chapters are divided into units according to the different parts of the exam. They are all exam units and are directly related to what is tested in the exam.

There are six **Appendices** at the end of the book: reference lists of word and preposition combinations (Appendices 1 and 2), model answers for some of the writing tasks in Chapter 2 (Appendix 3), information about how to show your answers on the special answer sheets (Appendix 4), tapescripts (Appendix 5) and answers (Appendix 6).

Special features

Exam overviews before each chapter give details of what each paper consists of, the timing and the marks awarded.

Information boxes at the beginning of each exam unit contain relevant information about each exam question: the format of the question, what is being tested and what you need to do to answer the question well.

The first exercise in the exam units in Chapters 1, 3 and 4 is a **Familiarisation exercise**, a shorter and simpler version of the real exam question.

Summary boxes tell you what you have done in the unit so far, and what you are going to do next.

Towards the end of the exam units you'll find **Suggested approach boxes**; these provide a step-by-step procedure for tackling each exam question.

Each exam unit ends with an **Exam practice exercise** similar to what you can expect to face in the exam itself.

In the Writing and Speaking chapters there are 'banks' of phrases which you can refer to and use in your own work. These are marked with a dotted green line.

In the Writing chapter, texts marked: can be used as models for your own writing.

We hope you'll enjoy using the book and that you'll do well in the exam.

Helen Naylor

Stuart Hagger

Vocabulary introduction

Increasing your vocabulary is one of the most important parts of your preparation for the exam. You 'know' vocabulary in two different ways:

1 The words you **use** when you speak or write English (your 'active' vocabulary). You need to have enough words to write and speak about a variety of topics in an interesting way (Papers 2 and 5).

2 The words you **understand** when you read or hear them (your 'receptive' vocabulary). You need to recognise a large number of words and phrases to help you in the Reading and Listening papers (Papers 1 and 4), and to prepare you for Paper 3, Use of English. Your receptive vocabulary will always be much wider than your active vocabulary, in your own language as well as in English.

Improving your vocabulary: single words

You can increase your active vocabulary by finding the words for common, everyday things and actions. If you were asked to describe the room you are in now or the street you live in, how many of the necessary words would you know in English?

Exercise 1

The topics covered in the exam include:

> People (living conditions, social relations, family relationships)
> Occupations
> Education, study and learning
> Free time activities (sports, hobbies)
> Entertainment (cinema, theatre, restaurants, music, the arts)
> Travel and tourism
> Shopping and consumer goods
> Food and drink
> The media
> The weather
> The environment
> Science and technology
> Health and fitness
> Services (e.g. banks, post offices)
> Transport
> Places
> Fashion
> Crime

Choose a topic from the list and explore it with the help of your dictionary.

For example, Family relationships:
Do you know what relations the following people are to you?
– the son of your mother's sister
– your sister's husband
– the parents of your grandparents

Do the same with one or two other topics from the list. The aim of the exercise is to build up your knowledge of everyday words.

Phrasal vocabulary

A great deal of English vocabulary consists of groups of words which must be understood or used together. **Phrasal vocabulary** describes all those cases where two or more words make one unit of vocabulary. Examples are:

Word + preposition combinations:
He insisted on coming.
She is incapable of dishonesty. (see Appendix 1)

Preposition + word combinations:
It happened by chance.
The car was out of control. (see Appendix 2)

Phrasal verbs (where the meaning of the individual words may not help you to understand the word combination):
He took up fishing at the age of 50.
  (= he started a new activity or hobby)
Let's give up and go home. (= stop what we are doing)
When will you get round to repairing the car?
  (= finally do it, after a long time)

Collocations (words which 'belong' together):
To do your homework (*make* is not possible)
To make a complaint (not *do*)
A golden opportunity (not a *silver* or *precious* one)

Idioms:
I'm feeling a bit under the weather. (= ill)
I'm at a loose end. (= I haven't got anything to do)
They jumped at the chance of going to Australia. (= they were happy to be able to go)

Other word combinations which don't fit the categories above:
Straight away (= immediately)
Above all (= most importantly)
For the time being (= temporarily)

In this book we have described all the above types of word combinations as **phrasal vocabulary**.

Collecting vocabulary

Look at the simple words below.

head foot finger hand chair room door book

All of them have more than one meaning; most of them can have more than one grammatical function; many of them can form part of a piece of phrasal vocabulary. For example:

What's your new head of department like? (= your boss)
When we last saw them, they were heading for the coast. (= going there)
Dinner there will cost you about £50 a head. (= for each person)

Exercise 2

Use one of the words in the list on the previous page to fill the gap in each sentence.

1 There isn't enough _____room_____ for 12 students in here.
2 Please don't _____ the fruit unless you're going to buy some.
3 He walked out of the café and left me to _____ the bill.
4 Could you _____ me those papers, please?
5 We've asked Professor Plum to _____ the meeting.
6 You'll have to _____book_____ early or there'll be no tickets left.
7 I don't much like the people who live next _____door_____ to me.
8 With your _____ for figures, you ought to be an accountant.

The answers are at the bottom of the page.

Because so many words in English work in this way, you need to have a system for recording new vocabulary which allows you to see different uses of each word. Here is a suggested way of doing this:

	Words	Examples	Notes, translation etc.
Noun [a/the/some]	a light some light the lighter	*Can you give me a light?* *There's not enough light in here.*	*Hast du Feuer?*
Adjective	light (*not dark*) light (*not heavy*)	*She's got light brown hair.*	
Adverb	lightly (*not hard*)	*She tapped me lightly on the shoulder.*	
Verb	to light to lighten	*a cigarette*	
Compound	a lighthouse		
Opposite	dark heavy		
Phrasal vocab	see things in a different light		*= differently, in a different way*

Reading

The Reading chapter is in two sections.

Section A Reading and understanding
teaches general reading skills which you'll need
for all parts of the exam.

**Section B Reading and answering exam
questions** applies these skills to the Paper 1 exam
format. In this section you'll get help and practice
in tackling the four parts of this paper.

SECTION A

Reading and understanding

Unit 1 Dealing with difficult words

Unit 2 Phrasal vocabulary

Unit 3 Key words

SECTION B

Reading and answering exam questions

Unit 4 Multiple matching
        (main points)

Unit 5 Multiple choice

Unit 6 Gapped text

Unit 7 Multiple matching
        (specific information)

EXAM OVERVIEW   PAPER 1 READING (1 hour 15 minutes)

Paper 1 has four parts:

PART 1	Multiple matching 6 or 7 questions	2 marks per question
PART 2	Multiple choice 7 or 8 questions	2 marks per question
PART 3	Gapped text 6 or 7 questions	2 marks per question
PART 4	Multiple matching / Multiple choice 13–15 questions	1 mark per question
Total:	35 questions	

Dealing with difficult words

When you are reading a text without the help of a dictionary and there is a word which you don't know:

- look at the **function** of the word in the sentence
- look at the **context** of the word in the sentence and the text

What function does the word have in the sentence – what work is it doing?

Is it a **noun**, an **adjective**, a **verb** or an **adverb**? Identify the nouns, adjectives, verb and adverb in this sentence:

Daniel quickly put the old sepia photograph in the drawer.

Aim of Exercises A1–A4: to practise identifying some different sorts of nouns, adjectives, verbs and adverbs.

Exercise A1

Put each of these **nouns** into **two** correct columns in the table below. First decide if you can or can't see each one and then decide if you can or can't count each one. The first three nouns have been done for you as examples.

luggage suitcase happiness problem firefighter furniture finger plastic love family flower water cow blackbird back factory beef advice pencil wool musician Marxism steel beetle oxygen

1 Can see	2 Can't see	3 Can count	4 Can't count
luggage	happiness	suitcase(s)	luggage
suitcase			happiness

Now put each noun into one of the categories below. The first one has been done for you as an example.

Collective word *luggage*   Person   Thing   Animal/Insect/Bird   Plant   Part of person   Building
Liquid/Gas   Other material   Food   Abstract idea

Exercise A2

Put the **adjectives** below into **one** of these different categories. The first one has been done for you as an example.

Age/Time *new*   Colour   Material   'Positive'   Shape   Origin   Size   'Negative'

~~new~~   round   attractive   green   generous   Chinese   glass   careless   long   stupid   last   dark
lovely   little   square   wooden   exciting   elderly   impatient   clever   satisfied   destructive
silk   cream   artificial   former   oval   priceless   wide   unimaginative

Exercise A3

Verbs can work:

– with a direct object	James cut the bread.
– without a direct object	Please sit down.
– with or without a direct object	Can you sing this song?
	I can't sing very well.

Put these **verbs** in **one** correct column in the table below. If you're not sure, try adding *it* after the verb and decide if it sounds right. The first three verbs have been done for you as examples.

~~cut~~   ~~sit~~   ~~sing~~   know   smile   hit   sleep   carry   fly   find   eat   laugh   read   ring
discuss   surprise   lie   talk

I cut it – Sounds OK, so 'cut' takes a direct object.

I sit it – Doesn't sound right, so 'sit' doesn't take a direct object.

1 Usually with direct object	2 Usually without direct object	3 With or without direct object
cut	sit	sing

Exercise A4

Put the **adverbs** below into one of these different groups. The first three have been done for you as examples.

How? *tidily*   Where? *forwards*   When? *often*

~~tidily~~   ~~forwards~~   ~~often~~   away   late   carefully   backwards   fortunately   soon   here   well
fast   recently   yesterday   outside   badly   finally   upstairs

13

Aim of Exercises A5–A7: to decide the function of words in sentences.

Exercise A5

Sometimes a familiar word can be used in an unfamiliar way. For example, you might know what an 'arm' is, but do you know what an 'arms salesman' does or what 'to arm the rebels' means?

Look at these sentences, and decide whether the words in green are working as nouns, verbs or adjectives. The first one has been done as an example.

1 Who is going to head the government enquiry?
   verb
2 You can buy souvenir walking sticks in the village shop.
3 A lot of factory workers will probably lose their jobs.
4 As a child Tanya had so many dislikes that I never knew what to give her to eat.
5 I love that bit in the film where Kevin hands the teacher a dead rat.
6 When Camilla left him to return to Finland, Spencer felt very lonely.
7 Sarah has been appointed chair of the education committee.
8 If we're going there on Saturday, we'd better book first.
9 Clive originally met his wife in a shoe shop.
10 Although it was very cold, we stood on the platform as the waiting room was so dirty.
11 Empty buildings could be used to house homeless people.
12 Do you remember the days when you had to wind watches every day?
13 There's some building work going on in our office, so it's very noisy.
14 Who'll captain the team, with Adams injured?
15 Unless you have been there, you can't really picture the Grand Canyon.

Exercise A6

Look at how the word *sprill* is being used in the sentences below. (*Sprill* is not a real English word.) First, decide what work (noun, adjective etc.) *sprill* is doing in each sentence. Remember:

the or *a* tell you that it is a noun
she, him etc. indicate a person
-s could be a verb or a plural noun
-ed or *-ing* could be a verb, an adjective or a participle
-ly is probably an adverb

Then write two real words that you could put in its place.

1 I'm glad to see you looking so sprill today.
   It must be a positive adjective because of 'I'm glad'. You could put 'happy' or 'well' in its place.
2 Scientists used to visit the island in large numbers to study the many unusual kinds of sprills living there.

3 The children were sprilling in the playground.
4 I met a very friendly sprill on the train to Cambridge, and we had a nice chat.
5 It was such a sprilling film that it kept us all on the edge of our seats.
6 Marianne began to talk sprillily about her visit to Tibet.

7 I sprill Tom every time I see him.
8 Sprill is cheap and easy to get to for holidays.
9 Dr Dalmore is a very sprill man with a long nose and short legs.
10 We enjoyed visiting the local sprill yesterday.
11 Everybody is capable of sprill.
12 Oh dear! What's that? Sprill?

13 Unfortunately it was written very sprillily and nobody could understand it.
14 Sprill should be at work, shouldn't he? What's he doing here?
15 If you have a sprill about our service, please write to the Managing Director.
16 Craig spends every Saturday night alone at home, sprilling.

Exercise A7

In each of the following sentences one word has been missed out. Decide what **kind** of word should fill the gap in each case, and then write **two** words which could logically go in the space.

1 I hate _people/customers_ who speak impolitely to me. *noun – plural – person: people, customers*
2 Shaun was _____ along the street, singing happily.
3 Petrina opened the door very _____ .
4 Pass me that _____ , please.
5 Chris is not a person with much _____ in his life.
6 It was an absolutely _____ day, one which I just want to forget.

7 I don't really like _____ much; my stories never seem to interest her.
8 The floor was covered in _____ . I wondered whose job it would be to clear it up.
9 They entertained us _____ all evening, and we went home in a good mood.
10 Sally ran out of the house, _____ .
11 The forest was full of _____ , which ran away when we approached.
12 More and more of them arrived, until by 4 o'clock there was a large _____ of them in front of us.

Look at the context of the unknown word in its sentence and in the text

Aim of Exercises A8–A9: to work out the meaning of unknown words from the context.

The words before and after an unknown word can help you to discover its meaning. You probably do not know these words:

grip   steer   puncture   pursuers

However, in the context of the story below, it is easy to guess the meanings.

Grip must be a verb meaning *hold* – what else can you do with both hands to the wheel in a car?

Steer must be what you do to make a car go in a certain direction.

A *puncture* makes a car difficult to steer, and means you have to change a wheel: it must be what happens when a hole in a tyre causes the air to escape.

If *pursuers* got nearer to them when they stopped, the word must mean people who follow somebody.

I *gripped* the wheel as hard as I could with both hands, and tried to *steer* the car in the direction of the farm. But it was no use: we kept going to the left, and I knew we must have a *puncture* in one of the front tyres. We would have to stop and change the wheel, which would give our *pursuers* enough time to get nearer to us.

CHAPTER 1

READING

Exercise A8

The story below describes a childhood memory of an exciting ride at a funfair. Read the text once and look at the words in *italics*. If you don't know the meaning of a word, remember to ask yourself:

- what kind of word is it? (what is its function?)
- what other information (before or after) can help you decide its meaning?

WE PAID OUR MONEY at the ticket office, and got in a little blue cabin heavily decorated with shining *brass* and upholstered in deep red, soft material: we were the only ones in a cabin made to
5 take six people. As we waited to start, I tried to make myself comfortable on the seats, but they were so high and *vast* that I could only sit on the edge with my legs *dangling* and my hands tightly *clutching* the brass safety *rail* in front: I felt very small.
10 The operator pulled an oily *lever* and the little cabin, after a sudden *jerk*, slowly began to climb the noisy ratchet railway to the top. We passed huge, *wobbling* wheels, and lots of other machinery,
15 which was making a terrible *din*. I *peeped* over the side of the cabin – the whole town seemed to be gathered in the square below, watching our ascent. As we *crawled* higher and higher my
20 spirits sank lower and lower. Below us, some seagulls were flying about among the *struts* of the structure: after that, I did not dare look over the edge of the cabin again.

A childhood *memory*

Look at the items below, and in each case decide which of the four choices given is closest in meaning to the word in the passage. Circle the correct answer. The first one has been done for you.

1 brass (line 3)	A cloth B wood C paper (D) metal	3 dangling (line 8)	A running B hanging C walking D standing	5 rail (line 9)	A door B net C exit D bar
2 vast (line 7)	A small B hard C big D soft	4 clutching (line 8)	A touching B holding C feeling D tasting	6 lever (line 10)	A machine B wheel C button D handle

7 jerk (line 11)	**A** movement **B** cry **C** explosion **D** light	9 din (line 15)	**A** product **B** movement **C** thing **D** noise	11 crawled (line 19)	**A** moved **B** fell **C** started **D** wanted
8 wobbling (line 13)	**A** moving **B** speeding **C** breaking **D** stopping	10 peeped (line 16)	**A** fell **B** went **C** looked **D** spoke	12 struts (line 22)	**A** people **B** legs **C** feelings **D** water

Are there any other words in the passage you don't know? If there are, use the context to help you decide their meaning.

Exercise A9

Read the passage below once, **without** stopping to think about the words you don't know, and answer these questions.

1 About what time of the day or night was it?
2 Why were the two people in the forest?
3 How did they feel about the world of nature at the end of their expedition?

Now read the passage again, and write a short explanation for the words in *italics* **without** using a dictionary. The first one has been done for you.

a ~~badger~~ **b** kneel **c** shriek **d** scurrying
e sett **f** mournfully **g** soggy **h** dense
i tripped **j** mud **k** poked **l** tottered
m haven **n** thoroughly

badger: must be a noun ('the'), and probably an animal ('it'); it seems to be active at night, lives in the woods, is quite shy, and is rare enough for people to go out specially to see; it has a black and white head.

If there are any other words that you don't know, use the context to help you decide their meaning.

The *badger* moved slowly out from the trees into the open ground. From where we lay, I could see its black and white head clearly in the moonlight. Unfortunately my friend chose that moment to *kneel*
5 on a very sharp piece of wood, and his *shriek* of pain immediately sent the badger *scurrying* back to the safety of its *sett*. Simon looked at me *mournfully*. I tried hard to give the impression that I didn't mind what had happened, but probably failed.
10 'I don't suppose it'll come back now,' he said unhappily. 'We might as well give up and go home.'
So we walked quietly back through the forest. It had started to rain, the ground under us was getting more *soggy* by the minute, and to cap it all the moon
15 was suddenly covered by such *dense* cloud that it became impossible to see the way. Simon *tripped* over a fallen tree and fell flat on his face in some *mud*, which did not improve his appearance, and I nearly had my eye *poked* out by a low branch. By the time we
20 *tottered* back to the *haven* of our hotel, we were both so *thoroughly* fed up with the world of nature that not even the thought of our fishing trip later that morning could cheer us up.

Badger Watching

CHAPTER 1

READING

It is possible to know all the individual words in a sentence, but not understand the meaning of what you are reading. This may be because the sentence contains 'phrasal vocabulary' (see Vocabulary introduction, page viii) which is new to you. In such cases you need to:

- identify which words go together
- think of these words as one idea, and deduce the meaning from the context

Phrasal vocabulary: which words go together?

Aim of Exercises A1–A4: to become more aware of what sort of words go together.

Exercise A1

Match each of the phrases in green on the left (1–5) with one of the explanations on the right (a–e). The phrases all come from the text about badger watching on page 17.

1	'We might as well …	**a**	to make a bad situation even worse
2	… give up and go home'	**b**	we had had quite enough experience of …
3	… to cap it all, a cloud covered the moon	**c**	make us feel happier
4	… we were fed up with the world of nature	**d**	stop what we are doing
5	… not even the thought of our fishing trip could cheer us up	**e**	the best thing for us to do is to …

Exercise A2

There may seem to be no logical reason why certain words go together to make an expression with a particular meaning. With no context to help you, the following exercise is a 'guessing game', but it will make you more aware of the **kind** of phrase which can cause problems in your reading. Match the two parts of some common expressions to give the meanings shown on the right.

1	put up	**a**	of the past	=	it's no longer true, doesn't exist now
2	make	**b**	the battle	=	you've solved 50% of the problem
3	it's got nothing	**c**	in your notice	=	say you intend to leave your job
4	hand	**d**	with something	=	tolerate something
5	for the time	**e**	in the right direction	=	a (small) improvement
6	a thing	**f**	a mess of it	=	do something very badly
7	that's half	**g**	time off	=	be away from work
8	pick up	**h**	to do with me	=	I have no interest or responsibility
9	take	**i**	where you left off	=	start again in the same situation
10	a step	**j**	being	=	temporarily

Exercise A3

In each of the following sentences, <u>underline</u> the phrase which could be replaced with the words shown below it in green. The first one has been done for you as an example.

1 Let's hope that by the beginning of the next decade pollution will <u>be a thing of the past</u>.
no longer exist

2 I'm not sure what tonight's programme is called, but I think it's got something to do with Indian regional cookery.
a connection

3 Have you any idea what has become of Harry since he left the company so suddenly all those months ago?
happened to

4 Des told me that the thing he really couldn't stand about being unemployed was sitting around all day with nothing to do.
hated

5 Jane's away today, so I'll have to ask you to stand in for her.
replace

6 Look at the weather! It's ten to one half the staff will decide to stay away from work today!
probable

7 By the time he'd finished telling me about all the difficulties and dangers I would face on the journey, he'd managed to put me right off going.
discourage me from

8 Only somebody born and bred in New York can really understand the reasons for the strong emotions which are sometimes publicly expressed in that city.
from

9 That report you sent me was just the job: it made it impossible for the directors to refuse to give me all the money I had asked for.
perfect

10 A lot of people object to the idea that before a company sells a new product they can try it out on animals to see if it is harmful.
experiment

Exercise A4

Read the following article about James Garfield, who collects phone-cards.

James Garfield started collecting phone-cards without really noticing it. When a card was *finished*, instead of throwing it away, he kept it. One day, *he realised* that he had *enough to start* a collection. That was ten years ago
5 and now what was once a hobby *dominates* his life. He spends *much* of his time on the phone to other enthusiasts trying to *find* cards to add to his 5,000-strong collection. "The other day I *heard about* a very early Japanese one. That particular one is very rare so I

didn't want to *expect* too much. I discovered it was   10
owned by another collector but I was able to offer him one that he wanted; *I wasn't certain whether the deal would succeed or not* for 24 hours, but in the end we reached a satisfactory agreement."
    And what does James's wife think of his obsession?   15
"He's mad, but at least he can laugh at himself still! And to be honest, his enthusiasm is beginning to *affect* me – I was really excited when he got the rare Japanese one."

Now look at the ten items of phrasal vocabulary below. Match each phrase with one of the words or phrases in italics in the text. Make sure each one fits grammatically.

1 used up *finished*   2 build up my hopes   3 it dawned on him   4 a good deal   5 got news of
6 the makings of   7 rub off on   8 track down   9 has taken over   10 it was touch and go

Deducing the meaning from the context

Read the following conversation, which contains some phrasal vocabulary that you may not know.

Cindy

> Hello there, Ian. I haven't seen you for ages! What are you up to these days? You must have plenty of time on your hands, now you don't have to go to work every day.

> Yes, I wanted to keep healthy rather than sit and watch TV all day, so I've taken up golf. Difficult at first, but now I'm beginning to get the hang of it and I'm really enjoying it. You ought to give it a go yourself!

Ian

Now look at the steps which will help you to find the meaning of the phrasal vocabulary.

Step 1 Identify the words that go together.

> Hello there, Ian. I haven't seen you for ages! What are you up to these days? You must have plenty of time on your hands, now you don't have to go to work every day.

> Yes, I wanted to keep healthy rather than sit and watch TV all day, so I've taken up golf. Difficult at first, but now I'm beginning to get the hang of it and I'm really enjoying it. You ought to give it a go yourself!

Step 2 Think of the words as one idea.

> Hello there, Ian. I haven't seen you for ages! What are you .... these days? You must have plenty of time .... , now you don't have to go to work every day.

> Yes, I wanted to keep healthy rather than sit and watch TV all day, so I've .... golf. Difficult at first, but now I'm beginning to .... and I'm really enjoying it. You ought to .... yourself!

Step 3 Fill in the gaps with simple words.

> Hello there, Ian. I haven't seen you for ages! What are you doing these days? You must have plenty of time free, now you don't have to go to work every day.

> Yes, I wanted to keep healthy rather than sit and watch TV all day, so I've started to play golf. Difficult at first, but now I'm beginning to learn how to do it better and I'm really enjoying it. You ought to try it yourself!

Exercise A5

Aim: to decide the meaning of phrases, using the context to help you.

Read the following text, and choose the best of the three alternatives A, B, or C to explain each of the phrases in *italics*. Remember to think of each group of words as one 'idea', and try to decide for yourself what meaning it has before you look at the choices.

Short holiday breaks

Most people (1) *take it for granted* that if they have two weeks' holiday it automatically means spending the whole fortnight away from home. However, it can be just as satisfactory to have short breaks (2) *now and again* rather than using up all your holiday (3) *in one go*. Here is a selection of current 'breakaways'.

Food, wonderful food

Two weeks of eating wonderful food could (4) *play havoc with* your weight and figure, but only a limited amount of damage can be done in a few days! So, if you want to (5) *tuck into* a full cooked breakfast, or (6) *work your way through* every dessert on the menu, a short break is the time to do it. You could either book accommodation (7) *within easy reach of* a favourite restaurant, or choose a hotel which is known for its good food.

Spending sprees

Some people actually enjoy last-minute Christmas shopping, but most of us don't: if you're working, you (8) *don't have any say in* when you are free, so we all find ourselves shopping at the same time on December 23rd. Instead of having to put up with the crowds, how about booking a late-autumn two- or three-day break in your favourite shopping city – Edinburgh, London, Paris or New York – and shop (9) *to your heart's content*. Or why not (10) *head for* Germany during December, when the traditional Christmas markets in towns such as Köln or Rüdesheim will be (11) *getting into full swing*.

Learning breaks

Most people have often thought they'd like to (12) *try their hand at* something new, such as a sport or craft, but it is hard to get going. Study Centres are starting points for all sorts of exciting skills, where people can find out more about their chosen subject. The social side is (13) *every bit as* important, bringing together people with shared interests, making these breaks (14) *just the thing* for anyone who is holidaying alone.

1 take it for granted
   A decide
   B hope
   C believe

2 now and again
   A now
   B sometimes
   C again

3 in one go
   A at the same time
   B at different times
   C going away

4 play havoc with
   A not damage
   B damage a little
   C seriously damage

5 tuck into
   A cook
   B refuse
   C enjoy

6 work your way through
   A systematically eat
   B travel slowly through
   C thoroughly study

7 within easy reach of
   A at
   B near
   C within

8 don't have any say in
   A don't know
   B can't choose
   C don't say

9 to your heart's content
   A as much as you like
   B as little as you like
   C as late as you like

10 head for
   A leave
   B forget
   C visit

11 getting into full swing
   A getting too many visitors
   B starting to become busy
   C becoming less busy

12 try their hand at
   A learn
   B teach
   C buy

13 every bit as
   A not
   B equally
   C almost

14 just the thing
   A unsuitable
   B perfect
   C only

21

This unit concentrates on a variety of features that you'll meet when reading:

- ► reference words – what does *it* refer to?
- ► 'missing' words
- ► the same thing said in a different way
- ► the use of negative structures
- ► key words that help you predict
- ► main points and subsidiary points

What does 'it' refer to?

Exercise A1

Aim: to understand how words such as *it, this, so* etc. work in sentences.

So I bought it even though it cost £100.

Unless you find the rest of this letter, you can't understand what *it* is – you need to see an earlier sentence.

Read the following sentences. Use arrows to show the connection between the words in **green** and what they refer to. Underline the key word or phrase. The first one has been done for you.

1 There are huge numbers of trainers on the market nowadays, and perhaps because of that, finding the perfect ones is not easy.
'that' refers to the fact that there are huge numbers of trainers on the market

2 Half a century ago, scientists knew very little about dreams. They could not even say what proportion of the night they occupied.

3 Animals which feed at night can eat food that is also eaten by daylight-feeding animals, but without coming into direct contact with them.

4 People who eat breakfast tend to be slimmer than those who don't have it. Perhaps this is because if you miss food early in the day it leads to mid-morning 'snacking'.

5 Many of us have felt dizzy when climbing a ladder or looking down from the top of a high building. We usually blame it on a 'fear of heights'. But this is not necessarily the reason.

6 The economists – not to mention the shopkeepers – were disappointed with Christmas. Normally shops can expect to make record profits at that time, but last year didn't come up to their expectations.

7 It's the opening of New York's Fashion Week and Karl Lagerfeld and his team are everywhere. So are his clothes.

'Missing' words

Certain words can be 'missed out', usually to avoid repetition.

That day was one of the busiest of the year.

days has been left out

Sometimes a word is missed out because it is structurally unnecessary.

The wall I built fell down.

that or *which* has been left out

Exercise A2

Aim: to understand what is being expressed, even when some words are missed out.

Read the following sentences and answer the questions. The first one has been done for you.

1 Many thousands of people pass through the main airport during the summer months, with most concentrated in the middle two weeks of August. What word could follow 'most'? *people*

2 Of all the changes we've experienced over the past 50 years in our daily lives, the development of shopping has been one of the most remarkable. 'Remarkable' what?

3 The elegance of Dublin's 18th-century streets would be a good reason to visit Ireland's capital. The city's pubs would be too; people there talk to you simply for the pleasure of making conversation. Combine the two, and you have a city that should appeal to any visitor.
  a 'Would be' what?
  b What word or phrase could follow 'two'?

4 The Grand Theatre is really worth a visit. Although once in danger of being pulled down, it was lovingly restored in the 1980s; its bar is now the place fashionable people go to be seen.
  a What two words could come before 'once'?
  b What word could come after 'place'?
  c Does 'to' belong to 'go to', or 'to be seen'?
  d What two words could be added before 'to'?

5 Forget your roller-blades, this year's fashionable means of transport is the motor scooter. Not bad for a 50-year-old invention.
What is 'not bad'?
  a the motor scooter
  b the fact that it is fashionable this year

Saying the same thing in a different way

Exercise A3

Aim: to identify when and how a writer repeats something, but uses different words.

Read the following sentences and answer the questions.

1 *Flora Britannica* by Richard Mabey. The result of five years of intensive research, this unique work of reference is a comprehensive guide to Britain's wild plants which combines Richard Mabey's own knowledge with that of people around the country.
  a What is 'this unique work of reference'?
    'Flora Britannica'
  b What two words could be used instead of 'that'?

2 Richard Attenborough's star-packed film about the life of Charlie Chaplin tells the story of the diminutive comic's journey from poverty to riches.

Who is 'the diminutive comic'?

3 The flowering of the giant titan arum last week at Kew Gardens in London attracted world attention, but in its wild home in Indonesia, the plant is under threat. The monster flower is often cut down because it is believed – wrongly – to attract malarial mosquitoes.

What phrase in the second sentence tells you what a giant titan arum is?

4 The Spanish don't eat a great deal of mustard. The rest of the world, however, loves this hot, yellow spice. Over half of all the ready-made condiment is manufactured in Dijon, making it the global capital of mustard.

a What two phrases are used in order to avoid repeating the word 'mustard'?

b What does 'it' refer to?

5 For 400 years or more, military doctors knew that maggots could help to heal soldiers' wounds. They found that wounds covered with these insects healed much faster than those that weren't.

a What are maggots?

b What does 'those' refer to?

c What phrase could follow 'weren't'?

Some negative structures

Exercise A4

Aim: to understand how some negative structures are used.

Read the following sentences and answer the questions. The first one has been done for you.

1 It wasn't because Jeremy disliked tennis that he gave up playing.

Do we know why Jeremy gave up tennis? *No, but it was nothing to do with disliking it.*

2 For the previous six months Rebecca had spent most weekends going to parties and discos, so it was hardly a big surprise to anyone but herself when she failed her exams.

Who was surprised at her failure?

3 Giant ants are the insect equivalent of the blue whale or the elephant. But, unlike big animals, big insects attract very little international effort to conserve them.

How much attention do big animals receive?

4 If there is one thing we should be worried about in the English-speaking world it is not that we are doing badly at learning other people's languages but that we increasingly pay so little attention to the correct use of our own.

a What does 'own' refer to?

b What is 'the one thing we should be worried about'?

5 Around 1450 the German inventor, Johannes Gutenberg, created a means of mass-producing books and in doing so gave the world a way of taking knowledge out of the control of the few and putting it into the hands of the many. No other invention has so radically changed the spread of knowledge.

a What was Johannes Gutenberg's invention?

b What makes this invention unique?

Key words

Exercise A5

Aim: to predict what comes next by recognising some key words and phrases.

Often there will be some kind of **contrast**.

For some pop bands, success is to be on the front cover of 'Rolling Stone' magazine; for others, just being paid for playing in public is enough.

Sometimes the key words can help you to predict an **explanation**.

With more and more people moving to the cities, the economy of the countryside is being threatened.

Sometimes key words can introduce **additional information**.

Baseball caps, often worn with the peak facing backwards, were once the fashion from San Francisco to Tokyo.

Complete the sentences in any way that makes sense, with either a contrast, an explanation or additional information.

1 With regard to pollution, the fact is that while some rivers are improving, others *are getting worse* .

2 Although the rain brought a smile to the face of the farmers, the holidaymakers ....

3 It would be much more useful to spend the money on something we really need rather than ....

4 Education is not just a question of doing well in exams, ...

5 The reason Monday is not a good day to go to the fish shop ....

6 Top sports people are often criticised because they are paid a lot of money. However, ...

7 There is very little relationship between success at school ....

8 Steve had learned French when he was younger and thought he would have no problems when he was in Paris. In fact, ...

9 The Chinese made the first maps in 1155, but for centuries they were based more on the rich imagination of travellers than ....

10 Never having played golf before, I ....

Main and subsidiary points

Exercise A6

Aim: to distinguish between the important and the subsidiary points in paragraphs.

Read the text on page 26 about the health of footballers. The questions that follow each paragraph focus on finding the main point and identifying the sentences that support the main point (i.e. explain, illustrate or give examples). There will be some words that you don't know, but this shouldn't stop you from understanding the general sense.

The Health of Footballers

FOR SUCCESSFUL footballers the season is becoming longer, sometimes extending to 40 weeks a year, and the game has become faster and more competitive.

The chance of being injured has also increased. It is now almost impossible for a player to get through a season without missing at least one game through injury. Every year the game loses 50 players permanently. Injuries to the knee ligaments, ankle fractures, torn Achilles tendons, groin and pelvic injuries and chronic back pain are the most common complaints. In later life, footballers can suffer from arthritis in their hips and knees.

1 What are all these problems examples of? (In other words, what is the main sentence of this paragraph?)

Health care for footballers has improved, with all clubs employing physiotherapists and having doctors at every match. The Professional Footballers' Association has a rehabilitation centre which takes care of injured players, helping them to recover their fitness and also giving necessary psychological support.

2 Underline the main point which the second sentence in this paragraph supports.

But top footballers have an extra pressure put on them by their clubs. Often the club has paid a lot of money for the player and therefore wants to see its investment earning his salary. Players return to the game before they are fully fit. There are stories in the game of strikers running before their broken legs are fully mended and goalkeepers playing with broken toes.

3 Summarise in your own words the main point of this paragraph.

In England, teams do not have very long between seasons to recover and rest. This year the season finishes in May and pre-season training begins in July, so there's just time for a quick holiday before it all starts again.

4 Which is the main point, and which is the supporting point?

And it's not just physical rest that's important. Sports psychologists are busier than ever helping players to cope with all the mental difficulties of being a sporting hero. The football world is a very macho one; it's not easy for players to talk about emotional problems. Some managers would be deeply worried if they knew any of their players had had therapy and would probably drop them from the team; other more open-minded managers, on the other hand, actually direct their troubled players to see a psychologist, particularly for help with loss of confidence and an inability to concentrate.

5 Which two words support 'it's not just physical rest'?

6 Which point is more important in this paragraph: the work of footballers **or** the work of psychologists?

So next time you see a £10m player rolling around, holding his leg, have some sympathy for him. He may not be pretending.

Exercise A7

Aim: to revise all the work of this unit.

Read the text below and answer the questions which follow.

SALT IS EXTREMELY IMPORTANT.
Life depends on *it* as much *as* on water
or oxygen. Human beings and animals
need salt for the proper functioning of
their bodies. But it is strange to think
that a *mineral* as cheap and commonplace as this
has played such an exotic and dramatic role in
history. Salt sparked off wars in 250 BC; it
caused North American Indians to hand over
land and furs to European settlers; and in Tibet,
Ethiopia and Rome it was so highly valued that
it became a form of money.

However, people were not aware of just how much they
needed salt until they discovered that it had a very
practical use. If meat or fish could be kept in a barrel of
salt, or brine, the food could be stored for months
without *it* going bad. *So* salt became very valuable, and
demand began to exceed supply. For Julius Caesar, the
news that there was salt in Britain provided a good
reason for invading *the country*. And Roman soldiers
were even paid in salt —
the origin of the
word ‚salary‛.

It is hardly a great surprise, then, to find that salt —
like gold — acquired *magical* properties, and stories and
superstitions grew up around it. Primitive people put it
on the head of an animal that was about to be
sacrificed to the gods; babies in medieval Europe were
washed in salt water and *children made* to wear little
bags of the *stuff* around their necks to keep them from
harm. Even today, in many countries, the accidental
spilling of salt still makes people throw
a pinch of the spilt salt over the
shoulder to counteract bad
luck — just in case
there‚s some truth
in it.

(line numbers in margin: 5, 10, 15, 20, 25, 30, 35)

1 What does *it* (line 2) mean? Salt
2 What two words could follow the second *as* in line 2?
3 What is the *mineral* (line 6)?
4 What practical use did people discover and why is this introduced by *however* (line 13)?
5 Which words in lines 14–15 express the main point of this paragraph?
6 What is *it* in line 17?

7 *So* (line 17) means *As a result of this.* What is *this*?
8 What is *the country* (line 20)?
9 Does the writer think it is surprising that salt was thought to be *magical* (line 25)?
10 What word could come between *children* and *made* (line 29)?
11 What is the *stuff* (line 30)?

Points to remember

- Words like *it*, *this* and *so* must refer to something in another part of the text.
- When words are missed out, you can often understand better if you decide what the missing words are.
- An idea may be expressed in a different way to avoid repetition.
- Negative meanings need to be identified.
- Some words such as *however* and *so* can help you predict what you're going to read.
- Not all sentences have the same importance – some are in the text to support the main point.

UNIT 4 *Multiple matching* (main points)

Paper 1 Part 1

INFORMATION

In Part 1 of the Reading paper, you are given **either** a number of summary sentences, **or** some phrases in the form of headings or titles, which you have to match to the appropriate paragraph in a text. There are six or seven questions in this part.

- There is always an extra choice which does not match anything in the text.
- You are being tested on whether you can understand the main idea of each paragraph (see Unit 3 Exercise A6).

Familiarisation exercise

You are going to read part of an article about San Francisco. Choose the most suitable heading from the list **A–F** for each part (1–4) of the article. There is one extra heading which you do not need to use. There is an example at the beginning (0).

A Where it is
B Why it became famous
C Natural disasters
D Growth of the city
E Who lives there
F When it all began

SAN FRANCISCO

0   **F**

The city of San Francisco was founded by the Spanish in 1776.

1

It grew in size and importance when gold was found in California in 1848, and again in 1869 when the railway from the east was built.

2

The city lies on a piece of land between the Pacific Ocean and San Francisco Bay.

3

It was partly destroyed by an earthquake and fire in 1906, and further earthquakes have occurred since then.

4

In the 1960s, San Francisco became well known throughout the world as the home of 'flower power' and the hippy culture.

The exercises in this unit give you practice in:

▶ identifying the most important idea in a paragraph, and
▶ matching it with a summary sentence or heading

In the exam, you may be given either sentences or headings to match, so the exercises give practice with both.

Exercise B1

Read the following paragraph from an article about money.

Banknotes and coins are now used throughout the world as money, but this was not always the case. In 1642 the General Assembly of Virginia in the USA passed a law stating that tobacco was to be the only accepted currency. Tobacco was the basis of Virginian currency for over 100 years, and in other parts of the world such things as dogs' teeth, tigers' tongues, tea, shells and stones have all been used to pay for goods and services.

In order to find the general theme of the paragraph, ask yourself:

What is the paragraph about?
Money, which used to be in different forms.
What else is included?
Examples of things that were used as money – tobacco etc.

Now answer the following questions.

1 Which one of these three sentences best summarises what you have read? Remember that the sentence should summarise the general theme, not the details.
   A There was a law about tobacco in Virginia.
   B Many different things have been used as money.
   C Tobacco was once a valuable product.

Check that you have chosen the correct answer by looking at the bottom of this page. The other two choices only relate to part of the paragraph, not the overall topic.

2 Which one of these three headings is most suitable for the paragraph? Again, look for something that summarises the whole paragraph.
   A Ways of paying
   B Virginian currency
   C Coins and notes

Now do the same with a different paragraph – this time the subject is supermarkets. Read the paragraph first, then ask yourself what's the **main** information and what is example, illustration or supporting information.

Most supermarket customers do not use shopping lists, but know what they intend to buy when they enter the store, and also where to find it. What the supermarket manager wants, however, is for them to buy things they didn't know they needed. One successful way of achieving this is to change the positions of items from time to time, moving slower-selling products to places where shoppers expect to find the basic things they want.

3 Which one of these three sentences best summarises what you have read?
   A Shopping lists are often not needed in supermarkets.
   B Some items in supermarkets sell more slowly than others.
   C Supermarkets sell more by moving the position of goods.

4 Which one of these three headings best summarises what you have read?
   A Some basic needs
   B Spend more than you intend
   C No more shopping lists

The answer to Question 1 is B.

CHAPTER 1

READING

Exercise B2

You're going to read an article about an animal doctor (a vet) who uses homeopathic medicine on his 'patients'. (Homeopathy is an alternative method to traditional Western medical treatment.)

What to do:

- Look at the pairs of summary sentences below.
- Read the text once.
- Tick (✓) which of the two sentences is best as a summary for each paragraph (¶). Remember, the summary sentence will use different words from those in the text to express the point.

Summary sentences

Paragraph 1: A Alan Robb is one of a growing number of alternative vets. ✓
B Britain has only 13 qualified alternative vets.

Paragraph 2: A He was treated by his own doctor with homeopathic methods.
B He adapted his own experiences to his treatment of animals.

Paragraph 3: A He has a large number of remedies.
B The results are more important to him than the reasons.

Paragraph 4: A After a slow start, his business is doing well.
B Farm animals are now among his animal patients.

Paragraph 5: A The owners of animals have to pay for the treatment.
B Results are often better than the owners expect.

A Homeopathic Vet

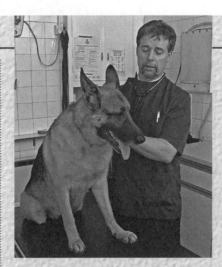

¶1 ALAN ROBB is a vet who not only treats animals in the usual way but also uses alternative remedies like homeopathy on his patients. Although there are only thirteen qualified alternative vets in Britain, the number of self-taught practitioners such as Mr Robb is increasing rapidly.

¶2 Mr Robb, who works in Scotland, decided to apply the principles of homeopathy to animals after he was treated by a homeopathic doctor. 'When I began working, I became dissatisfied with certain conventional treatments and I started thinking about my own experiences of alternative medicine. If homeopathic medicine had worked for me, I thought, surely it would work for animals too.

¶3 I started using three or four homeopathic remedies I learnt from a book and the results were very encouraging. Now I have almost 1,000 different treatments. Many of them I use to treat myself.' He admits that he does not know why the remedies he uses work, only that they do. 'I am not a clinician and, frankly, it does not bother me that I don't know. The whys and the hows remain a mystery. All I know is, it works.'

¶4 When he first advertised his homeopathic remedies, the local people were slow to come to him, but over the last few years there has been a big rise in the popularity of alternative medicine for humans. This has encouraged pet owners to consider the same kind of treatment for their animals. So Alan Robb's list of patients has steadily increased. He now treats some 250 dogs, cats and farm animals, including cows and horses, each week for everything from broken hips to psychological disorders.

¶5 Alan Robb also uses acupuncture (sticking the ends of needles into bodies at particular places to stimulate the nerve impulses) and laser treatment. He insists that the animals are not frightened by these methods. The only people who sometimes express doubts are the owners. People come to him with their sick animals and when he mentions one of his alternative treatments they realise they are being asked to pay for something they do not understand. 'Most people are pleasantly surprised at the results,' says Mr Robb.

Now look at **headings** for the same text and choose which one of each pair is appropriate. Remember, the heading should **summarise** the paragraph.

Headings

Paragraph 1: A Qualified vets
B A different kind of vet ✓

Paragraph 2: A How it all began
B How to treat animals

Paragraph 3: A How it works
B Success he can't explain

Paragraph 4: A Farm animals are treated
B Growth of alternative treatments

Paragraph 5: A Animals don't mind
B Owners unsure at first

Exercise B3

You're going to read an article about noise. Beside each paragraph there is a question or questions to answer. The questions focus on the main point of each paragraph.

1 What's the topic of this paragraph?
unwanted noise

2 Name two facts about this topic.

3 What's the most important piece of information about our ears?

4 What kind of noise can ruin people's home lives?

5 Which sentence in this paragraph is the most important?

Noise Pollution

¶1 *Unwanted noise is everywhere – and getting worse. It can make people ill with migraines, stomach upsets, skin problems and can even lead to terrible things, including murder. It is a public health problem which is not going to go away.*

¶2 Our ears act as our warning signals. They are designed to tell us about danger, and they never turn off. Even in sleep, if someone calls your name, your brain will register the sound. So unwanted noise is like a continuous alarm that never lets us relax.

¶3 If it comes from neighbours, you will feel angry and probably trapped. Victims of noisy neighbours who don't complain are likely to get depressed, while those who do make their feelings known are often accused of being neurotic. Most people, however, do not end up murdering their neighbours, they simply move away.

¶4 Long-term exposure to loud noise (levels above 90 decibels which is the equivalent of being in a noisy factory) can lead to hearing loss. But certain sounds are attention-grabbing, regardless of decibel level, and it is these sounds that are the most difficult to shut out.

6 Why is the human voice a very distracting sound?

¶5 Research is being done on the effect of background noise on people's ability to concentrate, and it has been found that the most distracting noises are those which vary a lot in rhythm, frequency and speed. In fact, the human voice is one of the most distracting sounds.

7 How does a third person make a difference?

¶6 The sound of two people talking can reduce concentration by 30%, but if a third person joins in, producing a more constant babble of noise, the reduction in concentration is less. For this reason, people often work better in a big, crowded office than in one which they share with just one or two others.

8 What's the purpose of piped music?
9 Why doesn't it work?

¶7 Another background noise which some people find irritating is so-called 'piped music' – the music used by supermarkets and airports, for example, which is supposed to put people into a dreamy state of mind. A recent survey found that 80% of people do not notice the music in the background and the other 20% hated it. As a result, one of London's airports has dropped it.

10 What are therapy, pain relief, and increased IQ, examples of?

¶8 But other kinds of music are used as therapy to help people relax, and pain clinics sometimes use it to relieve pain. Other types of music make people feel active and full of energy. American scientists recently claimed that listening to Mozart can increase your IQ by 15 points.

The message from all this is that when we can choose the sounds we hear, then all is well; it is unwanted noise that can lead to disaster.

Now look at the following **headings** and choose the most suitable one for each paragraph of the text about noise pollution.

A Always on duty	**E** Voices break concentration
B Three are better than two	**F** Noise from next door
C A threat to health	**G** Sounds you can't ignore
D Various benefits	**H** Pointless music

You have:
- practised identifying the most important idea in paragraphs
- matched summary sentences and summary headings to paragraphs, with the help of questions

You are now going to:
- do more matching but without any help – in other words, you have to decide what is the main point of the paragraph
- identify the extra sentence or heading which is not needed, as you will have to in the exam

Exercise B4

The following magazine article about lying has ten paragraphs. Before the first five paragraphs is a list of five summary **sentences A–E**. Before the next five paragraphs is a list of five **headings F–J**.

What to do:

- Read the A–E choices first, then the first five paragraphs.
- Choose the most suitable summary sentence for each paragraph and <u>underline</u> the words or phrases in each paragraph that helped you make the match. The first one has been done for you.
- Follow the same procedure for headings F–J.

A Adults have their own rules about what is acceptable.
B Lying can be put into different categories.
C Adults don't always make clear what children should do.
D Most people lie regularly for social reasons.
E As soon as it's learnt, it's forbidden.

The truth about lying

0   **D**

Can you imagine a whole day without telling lies? 'Yes, of course', most people would answer, but then they've probably forgotten all those little lies that are said so easily – 'This is delicious.' 'You look lovely in that shirt.' 'I'd love to come with you.' etc. <u>Lying is a way of making life run more smoothly</u>.

1

We are told not to lie from the moment we learn how to do it. According to psychologist Richard Wiseman, this is at the age of about four when children realise they can deceive people. We are not born liars.

2

In childhood, the line between imagination and lying is often not clear. Children are praised for creative imagination but generally criticised for hiding the truth.

3

As adults we have definite ideas about which kind of lies are OK and which are not. Very often the reason for the lie is the important thing in accepting or rejecting the lie.

4

Generally speaking there are three types of lies, and liars. The first sort of liar wants to please people, the second wants to protect him or herself, the third sort doesn't care about other people and lies to get what he or she wants.

F The worst kind?
G Both sides benefit
H How to hear lies
I Visual signs
J Not your responsibility

5

If someone is fishing for compliments and you tell them what they want to hear, you probably think it's a 'kind' lie. However, you get something as a result of this lie – affection, friendship, peace and quiet.

6

When you lie for self-protection, the reason is clearer. To explain your lateness, you tell your boss the train was cancelled, not that you overslept. You cannot be blamed for being late, because you are not responsible for the 'behaviour' of the train and the consequences.

7

The third sort of lie could be more dangerous. It is, for example, the kind that people tell in order to climb up the ladder at work, without caring who gets hurt in the process.

8

But what about being lied to? Can you spot when someone is telling you a lie? Apparently there are some verbal clues – lots of ums and ahs – and liars take longer to answer a question. They also speak faster but don't always give the right amount of detail.

9

And then there's body language. Experts say there are certain things that can help identify someone who's not telling the truth. Speaking through their fingers and putting the hands over the face is one. Playing with their hair or clothes and being unable to stay still for any length of time is another.

But the truth of the matter is that we all lie at some time, and if anyone tells you they don't, they're lying.

Exercise B5

The following seven sentences (**A–G**) summarise the seven paragraphs of an article about gorillas. Read the sentences, and then match them to the paragraphs of the article, 1–6. <u>Underline</u> the word or phrase in each paragraph that helped you make the match. There is an example at the beginning (0).

A Watching TV became a favourite activity for them.
B A zookeeper had an unusual problem with two gorillas.
C Their TV habits are very similar to human ones.
D They like a variety of programmes.
E They became bored while in quarantine for six months.
F TV may be a substitute for the company of other gorillas.
G They stay outside all day, and watch TV at night.

For the gorilla with everything

0   **B**

'What can we do to stop gorillas in zoos from getting bored?' <u>Not a question that is uppermost in most people's minds</u> *but one that Ian Turner, keeper at Longleat Safari Park, had to think about with Samba and Nico, two West African lowland gorillas in his care.*

1

Fifteen years ago when the two gorillas arrived in the UK from a zoo in Switzerland, they had to spend a period of six months in isolation, or quarantine as it is called. Ian and the other keepers at the safari park realised that Samba and Nico were suffering from boredom.

2

Ian remembered a TV programme he had seen about a gorilla in Columbus Zoo, USA, whose stress levels had been reduced by putting a TV in his enclosure. So Samba and Nico were given a TV for their six-month isolation period. When this period ended, the two gorillas proved to be very keen on their new entertainment – so much so that they refused to eat and made noisy protests when their TV was temporarily removed.

3

During the day, Samba and Nico wander around their island on a lake in the safari park, searching out the fruit and nuts left each morning by the keepers. At night, they return to their small 'house' and watch TV.

4

They are fond of sports coverage and animal programmes, especially anything with chimpanzees or gorillas. Ian says that at the moment they are particularly keen on an advert for tyres which features some orang-utans. Nico also goes for cartoons because of all the funny noises.

5

The keepers, many of whom have worked with the gorillas for 15 years, are convinced that Samba and Nico can see exactly what we see. When Planet of the Apes was shown again on TV recently there was an enthusiastic response from the inhabitants of gorilla island. 'Nico was rushing around. He collected a load of food and sat down in front of the TV and ate it, just like we do,' says Turner.

6

Gorillas have extremely large brains. Their lives in the wild, however, are simple – just eating, playing and sleeping. It is believed that the greater part of a gorilla's brain is used in social activities with other gorillas. Samba and Nico don't have a large group within which to explore these possibilities and, like many humans, seem to use their TV for their social life and sense of community.

Look again at the article about gorillas, and match the headings below (**a–h**) to the most suitable paragraph. There is one **extra** heading which you do not need to use.

a A daily routine	**e** A species in danger
b Television addicts	**f** A curious problem
c Like human behaviour	**g** TV helps their social life
d Bored during isolation	**h** Their favourite programmes

SUGGESTED APPROACH FOR PART 1 OF THE READING PAPER

1 Read the instructions so you know what the text is going to be about.
2 Look briefly at the list of headings or sentences.
3 Read the text once all the way through.
4 Look at the headings or sentences again. Cross out the one that has been given as an example in paragraph 0.
5 Match an easy item to a paragraph, and continue to match, doing the ones you are certain of first. Remember to look for a 'match' between different ways of saying the same thing, and check that your choice reflects the main idea of the paragraph.
6 Cross them off the list as you do them. Remember, there is an extra one that doesn't fit.

Exercise B6 Exam practice

You are going to read a magazine article about two men who walked across a river on a tightrope. Choose the most suitable heading from the list **A–I** for each part (**1–7**) of the article. There is one extra heading which you do not need to use. There is an example at the beginning (**0**).

A A question of luck
B Keeping it steady
C Their lives at risk
D Entertaining the crowd
E More pleasure than pain
F Nearly a disaster
G A dream come true
H Making the connection
I A drink to celebrate

WIRE-WALKING THE THAMES

0   I

Two men stepping past each other on a highwire isn't usually considered a newsworthy event – but when they're drinking champagne 50 metres above the River Thames, that's a different matter. On 15th September 1997, in front of a 10,000-strong crowd, Didier Pasquette and Jade Kindar-Martin sipped their bubbly midway along the 1,200-foot long, one-inch wide steel cable strung between the river's north and south banks. It took them just half an hour to complete the crossing, but the stunt took a lot longer than that to plan.

1

Organiser Adrian Evans, who thought up the stunt years beforehand, watched as his dream became a reality. 'I've known Didier for about nine years, and we used to talk about one day attempting a two-man Thames crossing. In the world of tightrope walking it's difficult to think of a more romantic and spectacular walk.' Evans finally got to stage it as publicity for the Thames Festivals which is intended to stimulate interest in London's riverfront.

2

One of the river's widest points in London was chosen for the attempt and in the early morning the banksides were closed to traffic. The first job was to get the wire into position. A motor launch crossed the river, unwinding the steel wire behind it into the water. Each end of the wire was then attached to two twin cranes either side of the river which then began hoisting it into the air. The cranes ensured that the wire was set absolutely level – vital for a safe crossing.

3

Getting the rope into exactly the right position was an extraordinary feat in itself. It took until 4 pm to get this right, leaving just three hours for the wire to dry. The wire had also to be set into position, to prevent potentially dangerous 'lateral swing' which could be caused either by wind or the movements of the walkers themselves. Nylon ropes were slung over the wire and below, 34 people on the bankside or in boats grabbed hold of the rope ends and held them tight – a low-tech solution to the problem.

4

Weather was the one factor that the team had no power to control. 'We were extremely lucky,' says Evans. 'It was a beautiful day. If there had been a blowy, gusty wind we would have had to postpone the crossing, and the same would have been true of any rain above the level of a gentle drizzle. The tightrope would have been far too slippery and hazardous.'

5

At 7 pm, as the sun went down and spectators gathered, the tightrope walk began. Pasquette and Kindar-Martin had no safety net below them or safety harnesses around them. One false move and they could hit the water at 60mph, more than enough force to kill. The only assistance the pair had were their silk shoes and a pair of 30-foot-long balancing poles.

6

Pasquette crossed from the north bank, Kindar-Martin from the south. They quickly demonstrated their confidence with a series of crowd-pleasing moves – standing on one leg, kneeling and even lying down on the wire. The biggest cheers were reserved for the heart-stopping moment at the mid-way point when the two men crossed each other's paths. Pasquette sat sideways on the wire while Kindar-Martin stepped over him.

7

After successfully making it to safety, Pasquette revealed to the waiting press that the walk wasn't quite as effortless as they had made out. He'd had painful cramps in his arm towards the end of his walk. But overall, he'd had the time of his life. 'It was beautiful, it felt wonderful. I wasn't frightened – I do this for my living. We never think about falling, we thing about going, going, going.'

CHAPTER 1

READING

Paper 1 Part 2

> ### INFORMATION
>
> In Part 2 of the Reading paper, you are given a text followed by seven or eight four-option multiple choice questions. The questions test detailed and general understanding.
>
> * Four possible answers are given and it is important to remember that three of the answers are **wrong**. You need therefore to understand the text before looking at the questions and the four choices. If you don't, you may misread the text because you have three wrong pieces of information in your head.
> * There may be questions such as 'What is meant by …?' or 'What does *it* refer to?' which test your understanding of language as well as ideas.
> * The questions come in the order of information in the text but one question (probably the last one) may test understanding of the whole text.

Familiarisation exercise

You are going to read part of a story about a family. For Questions 1–4, choose the answer (**A, B, C or D**) which you think fits best according to the text.

Old Thompson was seventy-four the winter his wife died. She was sixty-nine. They would have celebrated their golden wedding the following summer, and they were a quiet and fond couple.

Bob, the Thompsons' younger son, and his wife Annie were living in the house in Dover Street when Mrs Thompson died. The Thompsons had had four children. The elder son was lost at sea
5   during the war; one daughter married and went to Australia, and a second daughter, Maud, fifteen years older than Bob, lived with her family in another part of the town.

Bob and Annie had not known each other long before they became eager to get married; Bob because he liked Annie and she (though she was fond of Bob in her own way) because she could at last see a life away from her coarse family. When Mrs Thompson suggested that they marry and
10 live with them in Dover Street until they could get a house of their own, Annie hesitated. Her idea of marriage had been to gain a husband and an orderly, well-furnished home at the same time. But she soon saw the advantages in this arrangement. She would, first of all, escape from her present life into a house which was quiet and efficiently managed, even if it were not hers; and she would be able to go on working so that she and Bob could save up even more quickly
15 for their own house. She would also get Bob, a good enough husband for any working class girl; he was kind and pliable, ready to be bent her way whenever it was necessary for her intentions.

1 How many people were living in the house just before Mrs Thompson died?
 A two
 B three
 C four
 D five

2 Annie hesitated about going to live in Dover Street because
 A she wanted to get away from her present life.
 B she really wanted a house of her own.
 C she would have to give up her job.
 D she had not known Bob for very long.

3 What is meant by 'this arrangement' (line 12)?
 A getting married and living with the Thompsons
 B buying a well-furnished home
 C being able to do the housework efficiently
 D getting away from the house to go to work

4 'it' in line 13 refers to
 A her life.
 B her marriage.
 C the house.
 D the arrangement.

The exercises in this unit give you practice in:

▶ checking general and detailed understanding
▶ dealing with multiple choice questions
▶ checking what 'it' refers to (see also Unit 3 Exercise A1)

Exercise B1

Read the following paragraph two or three times until you feel you understand Sonia's feelings and action.

Sonia left home not so much because she was unhappy, but because she wanted to live independently; and although she found that living alone had its ups and downs, she was on the whole a lot happier.

Check that you understand how Sonia felt about living at home and why she left.

She wasn't unhappy at home. She wanted to be more independent.

So, how did she feel about living on her own? Complete this sentence in your own words.

She felt ...

Now look at the four multiple choice answers to the same question. Remember only one is correct. Which of them is nearest to your own answer?

A unhappy
B very happy
C more satisfied
D lonely

Check at the bottom of this page to see if your answer is right. If you've made the wrong choice, look at the text again. You might, for example, have chosen 'B'. But the text says 'a lot happier' which is not the same as 'very happy'.

Exercise B2

You're going to practise the procedure from Exercise B1, but this time with a longer text.

What to do:

- Read the four paragraphs on page 40 about a man called Mr Boggis.
- Think what kind of business Mr Boggis was probably involved in.
- Look at the five questions which follow the text.
- Read each paragraph again and underline the part which the question refers to.
- Answer the question in your own words.

The answer to Exercise B1 is C.

¶1 During the past few years, Mr Boggis had achieved considerable fame among his friends in the trade by his ability to produce unusual and often quite rare items with astonishing regularity. Apparently the man had a source of supply that was almost inexhaustible, a sort of private warehouse, and it seemed that all he had to do was to drive out to it once a week and help himself. Whenever they asked him where he got the stuff, he would smile knowingly and wink and murmur something about a little secret.

¶2 The idea behind Mr Boggis's little secret was a simple one, and it had come to him as a result of something that had happened on a certain Sunday afternoon nearly nine years before, while he was driving in the country. He'd gone out in the morning to visit his old mother, and on the way back the fanbelt on his car had broken, causing the engine to overheat. He had got out of the car and walked to the nearest house, a smallish farm building about fifty yards off the road, and had asked the woman who answered the door if he could please have a jug of water.

¶3 While he was waiting for her to fetch it, he happened to glance in through the door of the living-room, and there, not five yards from where he was standing, he spotted something that made him so excited the sweat began to come out all over the top of his head.

It was a large oak armchair of a type that he had ¶4 only seen once before in his life. Each arm, as well as the panel at the back, was supported by a row of eight beautifully turned spindles. The back panel itself was decorated by an inlay of the most delicate floral design, and the head of a duck was carved to lie along half the length of either arm. 'Good God!' he thought. 'This thing is late fifteenth century!'

(Paragraph 1) What impressed Mr Boggis's friends?
(Paragraph 2) How did Mr Boggis discover his source of supply?
(Paragraph 2) Why did Mr Boggis go to the farmhouse?
(Paragraph 3) Why did he start sweating?
(Paragraph 4) What was special about the armchair?

You have already thought about your own answers to the questions. Now look at four possible multiple choice answers and decide which of them corresponds most closely to what you said.

1 What impressed Mr Boggis's friends?
  A He had a private warehouse.
  B His supply of items was secret.
  C He had a regular supply of items.
  D His fame was considerable.

Which of the above four choices fits best? Look at how the right answer is arrived at.

A: No, we don't know he had a private warehouse; it just seemed to his friends as if he had.

B: Well, yes it was. He didn't tell them where he was getting his items from but this wasn't what impressed his friends, so it's not the answer to the question.

C: It says in the text that he produced 'unusual and often quite rare items with astonishing regularity', and it was that fact that led to him becoming so famous among his friends.

D: Yes, his fame was considerable among his friends; but it wasn't his fame that impressed them.

So C is closest to what I thought, and is the right answer.

Do the same with the following four questions. Make sure you go through each choice one by one to find the one closest to the answer you gave in your own words.

2 How did Mr Boggis discover his source of supply?
   A through nine years of driving in the country
   B by chance
   C by having a secret idea
   D by looking for it for more than nine years

3 Why did Mr Boggis go to the farmhouse?
   A to visit his mother
   B because he was thirsty
   C to get a new part for his car
   D to get some water for his car

4 Why did he start sweating?
   A because he was afraid of something
   B because it was so hot in the house
   C because of what he saw
   D because there was something on top of his head

5 What was special about the armchair?
   A It was very old.
   B It was supported by eight spindles.
   C It was carved in the form of a duck.
   D It was the only one of its kind.

Now read the rest of Mr Boggis's story and answer the multiple choice questions which follow. Wherever possible, think about your answers to the questions before you look at the choices.

Mr Boggis poked his head in further through the door, and there, by heavens, was another of them on the other side of the fireplace! He couldn't be sure, but two chairs like that must be worth at least a thousand pounds up in London. And, oh, what beauties they were!

When the woman returned, Mr Boggis introduced himself and straight away asked if she would like to sell her chairs.

Dear me, she said. But why on earth should she want to sell her chairs. No reason at all, except that he might be willing to give her a pretty nice price. And how much would he give? They were definitely not for sale, but just out of curiosity, just for fun, you know, how much would he give?

Thirty five pounds.

How much?

Thirty five pounds.

Dear me, thirty five pounds. Well, well, that was very interesting. She'd always thought they were valuable. They were very old. They were very comfortable too. She couldn't possibly do without them, not possibly. No, they were not for sale but thank you very much all the same.

They weren't really so very old, Mr Boggis told her, and they wouldn't be at all easy to sell, but it just happened that he had a client who rather liked that sort of thing. Maybe he could go up another two pounds – call it thirty seven. How about that?

They bargained for half an hour, and of course, in the end Mr Boggis got the chairs and agreed to pay her something less than a twentieth of their value.

6 Mr Boggis liked the chairs because
   A they were very beautiful.
   B they looked very comfortable.
   C he was curious about them.
   D he hoped to sell them for a profit.

7 The woman thought her chairs were
   A extremely valuable.
   B less valuable than they really were.
   C worth a thousand pounds in London.
   D not worth selling.

The next kind of question might come as the last in a series of questions. It is a test of general understanding, not detail. It's a bit like someone asking you about a book you're reading: 'What's it about, then?' The best choice of answer will be one that catches the meaning of the whole text, not just part of it.

8 What do you think would be a good title for this text?
   A Where Mr Boggis found his source of supply
   B Mr Boggis's day out
   C An unexpected find
   D Why Mr Boggis likes driving

SUMMARY

You have:
• worked with a logical approach to multiple choice questions
• answered questions that test general understanding

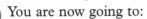

You are now going to:
• focus on questions that ask for a more detailed understanding

---

Exercise B3

Read the following four texts (Extracts 1–4) and answer the questions, which test your understanding of phrasal vocabulary and reference words (see Units 2 and 3).

Extract 1

I'm a huge fan of colour, and our end-of-terrace Edwardian house in London has been transformed since we moved here in January. We took out all the horrible modernisations and I was able to *start again*
5 *from scratch*, so I painted all the rooms using a palette of seven colours, including copper, silver and gold leaf.
   I spent a year on my back in a white room with a white ceiling after a car accident and *that*, I can assure you, would put anybody on to colour. It doesn't have
10 to *cost the earth* – I believe in style *on a shoestring*, in fact I've done up the whole house for less than £5000.
   I originally came to London wanting to be a hair stylist. I got *taken on* as a junior in a very fashionable salon, and by the time I was 17 I was working as a
15 stylist with lots of famous clients. Then came the car crash, and the serious injury to my back which put me in bed for a year. *It* obviously wasn't going to stand up to the physical demands of hairdressing any more, so I turned to interior design and an unexpected new
20 career in TV.

1 What is meant by 'I'm a huge fan of colour' (line 1)?
   I like colours very much.

2 What is meant by 'start again from scratch' (lines 4–5)?

3 What does 'that' refer to (line 8)?

4 What does the writer mean by 'cost the earth' (line 10)?

5 What is meant by 'on a shoestring' (line 10)?

6 What does the writer mean by 'taken on' (line 13)?

7 What does 'it' refer to (line 17)?

Extract 2

It was my first night on Pitcairn Island. A storm had cleared the air and I could hear palm fronds rustling like grass skirts and the sea washing the rocks. They were familiar sounds. I had heard them in my mind back in England as I stared at *the ink smudge* on my wall map and
5 prepared for this trip to the world's remotest island. Then, the knowledge that Pitcairn was little more than a square mile of land, *lost in the blanket of the ocean*, was worrying. Now that I was here, *the same thought* was comforting. It would make getting to know the island and the islanders simple.

8 What is 'the ink smudge' (line 4)?
9 What does 'lost in the blanket of the ocean' make you feel about the island (line 7)?
10 What is 'the same thought' (line 8)?

Extract 3

In the earliest athletic competitions in Olympia, around 800 BC, the only race on foot was the sprint along the length of the stadium. *This* soon developed into two lengths, but as the
5 track wasn t circular a pole was placed at one end and competitors had to run round *it* before heading back for their second length.

11 What does 'This' refer to (line 3)?
   A the stadium
   B the track
   C the race
   D the Olympics
12 What does 'it' refer to (line 6)?
   A the stadium
   B the pole
   C the track
   D the length

Extract 4

I suppose being a tea-taster is an unusual job. Sometimes it would be much easier to say I'm an accountant, especially at parties. Strangers constantly say, "how interesting, now what's the best tea to buy,
5 what's your favourite, and what's the best way of making a good cup?" *It* gets a bit boring sometimes.

13 What does 'it' refer to (line 6)?
   A talking about his job
   B his unusual job
   C going to parties
   D making tea

SUGGESTED APPROACH FOR PART 2 OF THE READING PAPER

1 Read the text carefully – you may need to read it, or parts of it, twice.
2 Look at the first question.
3 Look back to the text and underline the part which the question refers to.
4 If you have time, think how this information might be rephrased (or how you would answer the question in your own words).
5 Look at the choices and either choose the answer that you think is right or eliminate the ones you know are wrong.
6 Check against the text.

Exercise B4   Exam practice

You are going to read an extract from a newspaper article. For Questions 1–7, choose the answer (**A, B, C** or **D**) which you think fits best according to the text.

ON THE FACE OF IT, there is little to connect the oriental art of Feng Shui with the world of hammers, power drills and paint. But the ancient Chinese philosophy, which involves changing the design of your living or working space to improve your fortune, is proving to be a big hit in the world of 'Do-It-Yourself' stores, where people go to buy building materials and tools.

Two vast new DIY superstores have been designed in the UK following Feng Shui guidelines, and their business is booming. Both store managers maintain their success is due to the positive energy that has been channelled into their shops by Feng Shui experts, who were called in for advice before the final decisions were made about the design of the new buildings.

"I first encountered Feng Shui when I went to the opening of our company's first store in Taiwan. Everyone there takes it so seriously you cannot fail to be impressed," said David Ingliss, store manager.

Mr Ingliss's hosts in Taiwan told him of the Hong Kong millionaire who relocated his business empire into a new skyscraper. However, soon after the move, the business began to go down. In desperation the businessman called in the Feng Shui experts, who said that because his new office block was round it was like a huge cigarette, and all the energy was burning off through the roof. They said the only thing he could do was to build a swimming pool on the roof, which he did. And to this day there is an office block in Hong Kong with a swimming pool 40 floors up which no one ever uses, but there is a successful company underneath it.

"Some people may think Feng Shui just mystical rubbish and I must

38

1 What did the Feng Shui experts do for the UK stores?
   A They gave some advice about business.
   B They taught the managers their philosophy.
   C They made suggestions about design.
   D They helped to build the stores.

2 What impressed Mr Ingliss in Taiwan?
   A the people's attitude to Feng Shui
   B the opening of a new store
   C how serious everyone seemed
   D the amount of business there was

3 What does 'it' (line 38) refer to?
   A a cigarette
   B the building
   C some energy
   D the roof

4 Why was the swimming pool built?
   A to provide somewhere for the employees to relax
   B to stop the building from falling down
   C to make the building safer in case of fire
   D to stop the building's energy from being lost

5 What does Mr Ingliss think about Feng Shui?
   A It is superstitious rubbish.
   B It can give you more energy.
   C It can help your sales.
   D It doesn't tell you anything new.

6 What is meant by 'a DIY Disneyland' (line 65)?
   A a very large building
   B a place which is enjoyable to visit
   C somewhere for all the family
   D a store where there are lots of things to do

7 What do Mr Ingliss's and Mr Dorsett's stores both have?
   A successful garden departments
   B long opening hours
   C leisure areas
   D lots of space for customers

admit there is a superstitious element to it," said Mr Ingliss. "But much of it is just common sense and has a direct relevance to good selling. Experts believe that things should not be messy and crowded together – it interrupts the flow of positive energy – so we made a policy of keeping the aisles between the shelves wide, clear and welcoming, and generally followed the Feng Shui principles for positioning various departments and activities." Mr Ingliss's store, with a floor area greater than two football pitches, has been described locally as 65 a DIY Disneyland, which he takes as a great compliment. And it has also been one of the most successful in its first year of any of the chain of stores.

Jon Dorsett, manager of a sister store, also sticks to the policy of wide, uncluttered aisles and even goes so far as to order all restocking work to be done outside opening hours. "We paid close attention to advice on colour, lighting and especially on the distribution of indoor plants," said Mr Dorsett. "We trained them to grow around the entrance to the garden centre and installed wind chimes. Wind chimes by doors help weaken negative energy and bring in positive opportunity. The department is now among the top five in the company."

"I'm not sure that I believe in the magical side to it but I did move a mirror at home that was facing the front door – that is very unlucky apparently – but it actually just looks better in its new place," said Mr Dorsett.

Paper 1 Part 3

> ℹ️ **INFORMATION**
>
> In Part 3 of the Reading paper, you are given a text from which six or seven sentences or paragraphs have been removed; these have been put in a mixed-up order after the text. The task is to decide **where** in the text the sentences or paragraphs have been taken from.
>
> - There is one extra sentence or paragraph which does not fit anywhere in the text.
> - It is important to be able to follow the 'flow' of a text, and to understand how parts of a text are connected (see Unit 3 Exercise A5).

Familiarisation exercise

You are going to read an article about Murphy's Law. Four sentences have been removed from the article. Choose from the sentences **A–E** the one which fits each gap (**1–3**). There is one extra sentence which you do not need to use. There is an example at the beginning (**0**).

Murphy's Law

Named after an American, Edward A. Murphy, this 'law' is used to describe situations in which if something can go wrong, it will go wrong!

Everyone has them: days when we would have been better off just staying in bed. At breakfast, our toast slides off our plate and lands on the floor – butter-side down. Getting dressed, we spend ages looking through a drawer full of socks, and fail to find a single pair that match. At the supermarket we queue up at the checkout, and find that our queue doesn't move while the queue next to us zooms through. **[0 | E]** Murphy's Law – 'if something can go wrong, it will' – is at work in the universe. But science can show that there is some truth behind these popular beliefs.

Take falling toast which lands butter-side down. A BBC science programme set up an experiment to find out if the popular belief really was correct. **[1 |]** And the result was 148 butter-up landings, and 152 butter-down – an almost 50:50 split which goes against Murphy's Law.

But I now realise that this experiment was unrealistic. **[2 |]** When toast does land on the floor, it's usually after it has slid off or been knocked off a plate. And as my simple experiment shows, this produces very different results from throwing it in the air. Try it for yourself.

Get a paperback book and put it face-up on the table. Now slowly push it over the edge to simulate the effect of toast sliding off a plate. **[3 |]** But it doesn't spin fast enough to come face-up again by the time it hits the floor. So there you are, the book – or toast – will end up face-down more or less every time. And you've got a scientific explanation based on the forces of gravity.

A Throwing toast up into the air is not exactly common practice at the breakfast table.
B The butter-down effect has nothing to do with the toast itself.
C The producer persuaded a group of people to throw buttered toast into the air 300 times.
D As it goes over the edge, it starts to tip over and spin.
E If you have always suspected that such happenings are not accidents, I have good news for you.

The exercises in this unit give you practice in:

▶ moving around a text, seeing how sentences and ideas belong in a particular place
▶ using key words to help you follow the sequence of a text

In the exam, you may be given **either** sentences **or** paragraphs to match, so the exercises in this unit give you practice with both.

When you read, people and ideas are introduced or defined and then referred to in different ways. For example, when you read about a person, at some stage in the text she will be named, and in other parts she will be referred to as 'the woman' or 'she' etc. When you're reading, your eye will meet 'she' and your brain will tell you 'Oh yes, that's the same woman I read about in paragraph 2.' Sometimes, your eye has to go back (or ahead) to check the connection.

Niki walked in the door and up the stairs without saying a word to her husband; she'd had a tiring day and didn't want to talk to him yet.

Exercise B1

Read the following article about the discovery of a new star sign, and then answer the questions that follow. The aim of this exercise is to make your eyes (and your brain) move around a text, checking references and repetition.

You're not the person you thought you were

¶1 SO YOU THOUGHT YOU WERE A SAGITTARIAN – lively, attractive and optimistic. But if you were born between November 30 and December 17 you are actually Ophiuchus, 13th sign of the zodiac, forgotten by astrologers for nearly a century.

¶2 The world of astrology has been thrown into confusion by astronomer Dr. Jacqueline Mitton, spokesperson for the Royal Astronomical Society, who says that the signs of the zodiac are completely wrong.

¶3 Dr. Mitton was surprised at the anger her announcement had caused. Avoiding a large number of phone calls, photographers and requests for TV and radio interviews, she said: "It's amazing how much passion I've caused. I'm astonished that people care so much about astrology."

¶4 Her pronouncement, nevertheless, has brought chaos to the whole system of zodiacal signs. Sagittarians are not alone in wondering who they're supposed to be this morning. Pisceans turn out to be Aquarians, Virgoans were mostly born in the sign of Leo, and Taureans are in Aries.

¶5 But Dr. Mitton is not going to apologise. All she has done, she says, is point out what astronomers have known for ages – that astrologers have been using the wrong dates for when the sun passes through the groups of stars that make up the zodiac.

¶6 Dr. Mitton, 46, born on July 10 and once a Cancer (careful, home-loving, introverted), but now found to be a Gemini (impatient, enthusiastic, lively-minded) thinks astrology is "complete nonsense".

¶7 But she still reads her stars. "We all want something mysterious in life. And we all look for guidance from something outside ourselves. I'm fascinated by astrology. There are bits of good advice in it for everyone."

¶8 So, how will people manage now? How will they search for their perfect astrological partner? Dr Mitton doesn't care. "Labels don't make any difference," she said. "Either people found their characteristics fitted them, or not. Personally, I think I'm more Gemini than Cancer.

¶9 "More importantly, I hope people will discover the science of astronomy about real stars. It's far more interesting than zodiacal predictions."

Read the paragraph indicated, and answer the questions. You will have to look at different parts of the text to find the answers.

Paragraph 2: In which two later paragraphs do you read about the two worlds of astronomy **and** astrology?

paragraphs 5 and 9

Paragraph 3: Which two paragraphs tell us what her 'announcement' was?

Paragraph 4: How is her 'pronouncement' previously referred to?

Paragraph 4: Where is the first reference to Sagittarians being confused?

Paragraph 5: In which previous paragraph can you find a summary of what Dr Mitton has pointed out?

Paragraph 7: What is 'But' in contrast to?

Paragraph 8: What doesn't Dr Mitton care about?

Paragraph 8: What are the 'labels'?

Paragraph 8: Where is there a previous reference to Gemini and Cancer which explains this sentence?

Paragraph 9: In which previous paragraph does she show her belief that astronomy is better than astrology?

Exercise B2

In this exercise, some sentences have been removed from the text.

What to do:

- Read the following magazine article about the connection between a dream and the British National Lottery. At certain points, two alternative sentences are shown. One of them is the sentence which was removed, the other does not fit the context.

- Identify the key words or phrases which will help you decide which sentence fits the context. These words may be in the **sentences** themselves or in the **text**, either before or after the sentence.

My dream numbers

The twice weekly National Lottery in Britain seems to produce a steady stream of stories of happiness, frustration, disappointment and disaster. And the latest is the story of Sally Ferguson's dream.

1a She was very lucky in her choice of numbers for the lottery.
1b She woke up four days before the draw with six numbers fixed firmly in her mind.

When it came to filling in her husband, Jim's, National Lottery playslip, she simply used the numbers that she'd dreamt about. Sally, who's 44, didn't think much more about it.

2a Her husband was not with her at lunchtime …
2b In fact, she didn't even see the draw …

because she was working in a restaurant near her home in Devon.

1 key words: *'dream' in the text, 'woke up' in the sentence.*

correct sentence: b *(the other sentence is wrong because it doesn't have any connection with dreams)*

2 key word(s):
....
correct sentence: ☐

One of her colleagues told her three of the numbers that had come up. 'I was quite calm about it really,' Sally remembers.

'I said to my boss, Fiona: "All I need now is another three and I'm a winner." Fiona replied: "Dream on, honey."'

It wasn't until the next day, when a customer read all the numbers out loud at lunchtime, that Sally realised she'd selected five of them – plus the bonus number. She went to the local supermarket where Jim had paid for the entry.

3 key word(s): ....
correct sentence: ☐

3a There she overheard the manager, George White, talking about an 'unknown' local person who was a big winner.

3b The manager, George White, was congratulating her husband and talking about an 'unknown' local person who was a big winner.

'I said to Mr White, "What do you have to do when you get six numbers right?"' He jumped over the shop counter, checked my ticket and said:

4 key word(s): ....
correct sentence: ☐

4a 'You're the mystery winner!'
4b 'You've won £630,000 in the Lottery!'

They found out later that she'd won £630,000 but, like everybody in similar situations, she says it won't change her life – except, perhaps, for a world cruise, a new car for Jim and flying lessons for herself.

Sally's dream was obviously very good news for her but how often does this kind of thing happen? Research shows that around four percent of dreams concern things which will happen. Some people think it's wrong, and in some cases dangerous, to use information that comes to you in dreams:

5 key word(s): ....
correct sentence: ☐

5a so Sally was right to use the numbers she dreamt about.
5b however, Sally would have been mad not to use the numbers to try to make this dream come true for her.

SUMMARY

You have:
- seen how, as a reader, your eye and brain have to refer to other parts of a text
- seen how key words can help decide the correct sentence for the context

You are now going to:
- get more practice in putting the missing sentences or paragraphs into the gaps, making sure they fit with the information that comes before and after

CHAPTER 1

READING

Exercise B3

Read the following article about the changing lifestyle of the nomadic Tuareg people of northern Africa. Look at the four **paragraphs (A–D)** which have been removed from the article – there is no 'extra' paragraph.

What to do:

- Underline any words or phrases in the text and in the paragraphs that seem to refer **backwards** or **forwards** – words like *they* or *but*.
- Now read the article again, from the beginning, and choosing the **simplest** first, decide which paragraph fits in each space.

- If you find this difficult, look at the example on the next page, which shows the whole thought process for the first missing paragraph.

The Tuaregs

Nearly one and a half million Tuaregs live in and around the Sahara Desert of northern Africa in some of the most inhospitable conditions in the world.

1 _____

The desert itself is as large as the US without Alaska. To outsiders, it looks like an impossible place to live, but the Tuareg have learned how to adapt. They are mainly nomadic, that is they move around with their animals between dry- and wet-season camps.

2 _____

Nature has forced the Tuareg to be nomadic. Rainfall is uncertain and grass or pasture for the animals is uncommon, so they have to move in order to find food. In the long dry season, families have to camp near a well of water, to which the animals must return every day or two.

3 _____

Changes are, however, taking place in this traditional way of life. Since 1969 they have suffered from seasons of little or no rain. Animals and humans have died of starvation.

4 _____

As a result of these changes, many young Tuareg men are making long journeys to northern African countries in search of salaried jobs. And without their young men, the future for the Tuareg way of life doesn't look hopeful.

A Three to five families camp together in leather tents, which are dyed reddish brown with earth pigment. The tents are comfortable inside with mats or carpets on the ground, and flaps which are raised or lowered, according to the time of day, to control the temperature.

B And political changes have affected them, too. The Tuareg people were used to wandering freely across the land. But their world has been broken up by the creation of newly-independent countries whose politicians do not like the nomadic habits of the Tuareg.

C They are descended from the original inhabitants of northern Africa, and speak a Berber language which has its own alphabet. The Tuareg have a tradition of oral and written poetry, and rock inscriptions can be seen throughout the Sahara.

D But once the first rains come, the animals are free to wander widely for a few months, eating well and putting on the weight they lost during the dry season. And as the animals wander, so do the families.

The Tuaregs: example for the first missing paragraph

The first sentence of the text introduces <u>Tuaregs</u>, the <u>Sahara Desert</u> and its <u>inhospitable</u> <u>conditions</u> – we're obviously going to read more about these things.

Having read through the paragraphs A–D, we notice that paragraph C begins with <u>They</u> (could refer to the Tuaregs), and at the end of the same paragraph we see <u>Sahara</u> (without the word 'Desert', which suggests that we already know about it).

The next piece of text starts with <u>The desert</u>. So it seems as if paragraph C could fit in position 1 (need to check again when we've done a few more).

Exercise B4

This is a kind of 'jigsaw' exercise, where you have to put pieces together to make a complete picture. You do this by identifying the words and ideas that connect the sentences together.

You're going to read three sets of sentences about six different forms of transport in cities on page 52. Read the first set of sentences on the left (A–F), and to each one add a sentence from Set 2 and then a sentence from Set 3. There are no extra sentences to deal with. Before you start, look at an example of what to do:

- Read sentence A about buses. Underline what you think the key phrase is, that is the phrase which can help you get an idea of what might come next.
  key phrase: 'The great advantage'
- Think what information the next sentence could contain.
  It could be another advantage, or it could be a contrast – a disadvantage.

- Look at Set 2, and choose which sentence follows on best.
  Sentence ii because it introduces a contrast. Sentence i almost looks right because this is a disadvantage too, but the word 'also' tells me that the first sentence should have contained a negative piece of information.
- Now look at Set 3, and choose which sentence completes the sequence.
  I must look for a sentence that connects to or contrasts with the fact that buses are powered by diesel and are noisy and smelly. Sentence d mentions power and introduces a contrast to diesel.

Follow this process with the remaining sentences. Look carefully at the key words and phrases to make sure you build up a logical sequence of sentences.

Set 1	Set 2	Set 3
A The great advantage of **buses** is that they can carry a large number of people.	i) They also contribute to the pollution of the city air through their exhaust fumes.	a) On the other hand, they do not enable you to take very much with you, or to travel with friends.
B **Taxis** can, of course, only carry a small number of people at a time.	ii) Unfortunately, however, most of them are powered by diesel, which makes them noisy and smelly.	b) Where this is the case, and where the streets are relatively free of other vehicles, this is an attractive and convenient method of transport.
C **Private cars** are generally agreed to be the worst form of urban transport – by all, that is, except those who use them.	iii) If the latter were forbidden, this would be an excellent way for individuals to get about.	c) Parking is always a problem, and one which is going to become worse and worse.
D **Underground railways** have the great advantage of being unheard and, apart from their station entrances, unseen from the street.	iv) They are, unfortunately, extremely expensive to build, and the few cities that already have them also face huge maintenance costs.	d) This is a problem which is being overcome in many cities by the introduction of electrically-powered vehicles.
E The rails of **tramcars** were once a common sight in most city streets.	v) Some cities have had the courage to ban them from their streets, but there is strong opposition from those who see it as an attack on their personal freedom.	e) Their biggest advantage is that they can travel from door to door, and because they are always on the move they do not cause parking problems.
F **Bicycles** are an excellent way of getting around in cities, apart from the danger to their riders from cars, buses and lorries.	vi) In some countries they still are, and many systems have in fact been extended and modernised.	f) However, where systems are in place, and cities are prepared to continue with the necessary investment, this is certainly one of the best answers to the problem of urban transport.

SUGGESTED APPROACH FOR PART 3 OF THE READING PAPER

1 Read the text through once.
2 Look at the sentences A–I, cross out the one used in the example.
3 Read the paragraph that contains the first gap and look for clues:
  • Are there any reference words to help you?
  • Is there a linking word before or after the gap?
4 Look for a sentence that changes or continues the 'flow'.
5 When you've decided on the appropriate sentence, check that it fits grammatically and follows the sense of the text.
6 Remember, there is an extra sentence there – just to confuse you!

Exercise B5   Exam practice

You are going to read a magazine article about a woman who only eats certain foods. Eight sentences have been removed from the article. Choose from the sentences **A–I** the one which fits each gap (**1–7**). There is one extra sentence which you do not need to use. There is an example at the beginning (**0**).

What a Fruitarian Eats

In many countries, the number of vegetarians, people who cut out meat and fish from their diets, is growing. Susie Miller has gone a few stages further; she's a fruitarian – a diet not recommended for most people!

I have my breakfast at about eight o'clock. Yesterday this consisted of two apples, an orange and four tomatoes; I like a big breakfast. I don't drink anything during the day such as tea or water as I find I get all the fluid I need from my diet. After breakfast I take the children to school and then go to the gym until eleven. I work out every day. **0** **I**

I then went home and did some work. **1** The organisation provides information on the benefits of raw food for health.

I quite often take lunch upstairs with me to eat while I'm working. Yesterday I had about 12 tomatoes, half a lettuce and then a couple of apples and orange. Some people think I have an incredibly boring diet but this isn't the case. **2**

I make sure my children have freedom of choice about what they eat. **3** If they feel like cooked food, I'll prepare them a vegetarian meal.

I don't like to eat food too late, it doesn't seem to agree with me. **4**

I'm very unusual for a raw food eater as I do not eat the complex foods such as nuts, seeds etc. **5** I have been a fruitarian for about three and a half years and I don't miss anything. People think I have strong willpower. But it's not really anything to do with that. Generally speaking, I don't have to stop myself eating other things, I just don't want to.

In the winter I might have a bit of steamed vegetable once or twice a week and I usually eat more at that time of the year than in the summer. Occasionally I get longings – you know, a strong desire for something else. **6**

It's not that you can't eat certain things, you just find the diet to suit you. **7** And I've found a regime that I'm comfortable with. But it's my regime and I don't recommend it for anybody else.

A I usually have a final snack at about eight in the evening of a couple of apples, and that's it.

B Last winter, for example, I had a few baked potatoes but my body felt so strange after eating them I haven't wanted them since.

C Because I only eat raw food, this heightens my senses and so I find my diet wonderfully exciting.

D There are in fact no rules – everyone works out their own.

E I run an organisation called Fresh Network, which is a support and information network on the raw food lifestyle, and every three months we produce a newsletter.

F People often contact me about raw food diets and general health problems.

G I certainly don't force them to eat raw food but just teach them about the goodness of it.

H My body is extremely sensitive and I find I no longer need those things.

I After this morning's session I had a snack of a couple of apples and a small bunch of seedless grapes.

Paper 1 Part 4

INFORMATION

In Part 4 of the Reading paper, you have to read a number of short texts, all on the same topic, and answer 13–15 questions. The questions ask you to find specific pieces of information and to say which texts they come from.

- This part of the exam can look quite complicated (see Familiarisation exercise): you need to read the instructions very carefully.
- It is also important to understand the questions clearly, so that you know what you are looking for **before** you read the texts.
- Because you are reading to find specific information, you will not need to understand every detail of the texts – and time is short.

Familiarisation exercise

You are going to read some reviews of new CD singles. For Questions 1–6, choose from the CDs (**A–D**). Some of them may be used more than once. When more than one answer is required, these may be given in any order. There is an example at the beginning (0).

CDs

A Natalie Imbruglia: 'Torn'
B Mansun: 'Closed for Business'
C The Ganja Kru: 'Gone are the Days'
D U2: 'Please'

Which CD

uses a surprising instrument?	**0**	**B**
needs to be listened to carefully?	**1**	
is similar to another one?	**2**	
is not long enough?	**3**	
stays in your mind?	**4**	
disappointed the reviewer?	**5**	**6**

This week's NEW SINGLES *REVIEWED BY* Brix Smith

A NATALIE IMBRUGLIA: 'Torn'

Lovely voice, beautiful girl, good production. But not very exciting. She could afford to take a few more chances. Reminds me of Madonna's 'Like a Prayer'.

B MANSUN: 'Closed for Business'

Really, really good – really interesting. Love the harpsichord – people should use unusual instruments more. This one takes chances and is very different. A bit short – I could hear more.

C THE GANJA KRU: 'Gone are the Days'

Boring – heard it all before. I thought this track would be the best one but it was just drums and bass. Pity.

D U2: 'Please'

Heavy. Not advised for background music – sit and pay attention. I don't want to like U2 but I do. They don't hit you over the head with the melody, it just slowly goes into your mind and two hours later it's still with you.

The exercises in this unit give you practice in:
► finding specific information quickly in short texts
► doing the same, but in exam-length texts

Exercise B1

You are going to read six short texts based on interviews with different people about their 'first ambitions'.

What to do:

- Read Questions **1–6**.
- Underline the words in the **questions** which tell you what information you need to find.
- Read the short texts about first ambitions. Read quickly, looking only for the information that relates to the question.
- It may help you if you also underline the part of the text that gives you your answer. Sometimes more than one person's ambition is involved.

Whose first ambition:

was the <u>same</u> as their <u>mother's</u>?	1 C

It says: My mother was an outstanding concert pianist …
I developed quite an ambition to be a pianist …

is helpful in their present job?	2	3
was unfulfilled due to a physical characteristic?	4	
has been fulfilled, despite negative advice?	5	
was given up as soon as it was achieved?	6	

```
People
A  Jackie Collins      D  Max Clifford
B  Gloria Estefan      E  Rosemary Alexander
C  Lady Parkinson      F  Cherie Lunghi
```

FIRST ambitions

A Jackie Collins: To be a writer – from when I was 10 or 11. But everything was against me – I was expelled from school at 15, nobody in my family had written, everybody told me I had to go to college to be a writer and my teachers told me I couldn't do it, but I've proved them all wrong.

B Gloria Estefan: To be a psychologist. But by graduate school I had already been in a band a couple of years and singing had always been my first love so I chose that. But my psychology degree helps me a lot in my career. I constantly auto-analyse myself.

C Lady Parkinson: My mother was an outstanding concert pianist. She was playing in public at the age of 12. I developed quite an ambition to be a pianist, but when you live with someone who is extremely talented, you soon learn how untalented you are.

D Max Clifford: To win the boxing championship at school. I won, but I didn't box anymore after that because I didn't enjoy being hit back. I've never had any ambitions except sporting ones.

E Rosemary Alexander: As a child I saw the film The Red Shoes and thought it would be wonderful to be a ballet dancer. Unfortunately, by the time I decided I was 14 and rather fat.

F Cherie Lunghi: To be a ballet dancer. I went to see Margot Fonteyn and waited outside the stage door afterwards. She shook my hand and I was thrilled. I started dancing when I was five or six and kept on with it until I switched to drama at 12 or 13. Ballet taught me self-discipline, which I've found vital as an actor.

Exercise B2

Read Questions 1–6. This time the questions are in the form of statements made by the person. They are not exactly the same words that the person used but are a 'summary' of what they said. As in Exercise B1, underline the important word(s) in each statement before reading the texts. The people are all talking about their first time in trouble.

People

A Max Clifford
B Ralph Steadman
C Jackie Collins
D Ray Davies
E Michael Bogdanov
F Chris Eubank

Which person expressed the following?

I've always been lucky in my life. `1` ☐

It was the way the person looked at me that was terrible. `2` ☐ `3` ☐

I've learnt from the experience. `4` ☐

I wasn't bad, just full of youthful energy. `5` ☐

I had to put right what I'd done wrong. `6` ☐

FIRST time in trouble

A Max Clifford: Fighting. When I was 15, I was warned by the police. It was very much "Now listen here, son, you behave or we'll be round to see your parents." I was just high-spirited.

B Ralph Steadman: When I was seven, I stole a box of paints from a shop in town. I put them inside my coat and a lady came up and took them out – she didn't say anything, which made me feel worse, somehow. I never stole again.

C Jackie Collins: Forging my mother's signature on a note saying, "Jackie can't attend school. She's got a really bad cold." I did it several times until she caught me doing it one day and gave me the most awful look. I hated school.

D Ray Davies: Stealing apples from a farm. The farmer's son chased us on his motorbike and my mate Dave couldn't run as fast as me and got caught. He got the blame and I managed to get away. I guess that's the story of his life – and mine.

E Michael Bogdanov: My best friend John and I found some pots of brown paint. We decided the doors of our block of flats needed painting and we went round doing it. The caretaker caught us at it. I was forced to repaint over the brown bits as a punishment.

F Chris Eubank: When I lived with my grandmother in Jamaica, she was very strict. On this occasion she was angry because I was late for dinner. I'd been told to come inside to eat, but I was playing with my cousin who was pulling me along on a large banana leaf. Playing was more important, but the result was a lot of shouting and black looks. I was afraid of her anger and disapproval.

SUMMARY

⇑ You have:
• practised finding specific information quickly, from short texts

⇓ You are now going to:
• develop a system for tackling longer texts and more questions

SUGGESTED APPROACH FOR PART 4 OF THE READING PAPER

1 Read the instructions first, very carefully. Make sure you understand the task.

2 Look at the layout of the page: identify the questions with their numbers, and the letters that represent the different texts. Is there one set of questions or two (see Exercise B4)?

3 Read the questions, **one by one** and underline/highlight the key words that tell you what you must look for.

4 You may find it helps to fix the questions in your mind if you actually write down the key words at the side of the question paper.

5 As you are reading the questions, be aware of:
 – negatives (e.g. *doesn't*, *not enough*, *a lack of*, prefixes such as *un*, *dis* etc.)
 – similarities between questions (e.g. more than one question on the same subject).

6 Now read the texts quite quickly – don't worry about understanding every word. You'll probably find that as you're reading, you are already spotting and underlining bits in the texts that relate to certain questions. Note down the relevant question number by the appropriate bit of text.

7 When you've finished reading, go back to the questions. Fill in any answers that you've already found (having checked that they are a good 'match') and then, read through the texts again to find any missing bits of information.

8 You'll often find that the words used in the questions are not the same as in the texts. Be prepared for the way things are rephrased.

Exercises B3 and B4 are both in the format of the exam question.

Exercise B3

You're going to read five reviews of films. For Questions 1–13, choose from the films (**A–E**). The films may be chosen more than once.

Which film:

takes place in the middle of this century?	0	**B**	doesn't have much to say?	7
gives prominence to food?	1		is visually impressive?	8
is fast moving?	2		has uneven performances from actors?	9
is too long?	3		is well acted?	10 11
has characters who are foreigners?	4	5	brings back an old style of entertainment?	12
has good special effects?	6		is not going to be successful?	13

FILM REVIEWS

A CONTACT

Ellie Arroway (Jodie Foster) has devoted her scientific career to looking for signs of life from other planets. One day she s rewarded with a radio transmission from a distant galaxy and it s clear that the aliens have plans for us.

The best thing about this film is the special effects — some of which are most original. But the story is thin, the characters have nothing interesting to say and the acting is very up and down. It feels even longer than its 140 minutes.

B BIG NIGHT

New Jersey, the late 1950s: two Italian immigrants (brothers) are struggling to make a business of their restaurant, The Paradise. The elder brother is the master chef with belief in the traditional food of the old country; the younger brother wants changes.
This beautifully acted film is a big-hearted delight. It finds time to explore the brothers relationship but also to develop in some depth other characters. It has a simple story line, but always keeps to the point and is warmly human.

C BROKEN ENGLISH

Set in Auckland, New Zealand, the film is nicely shot, has some great acting but still proves a little disappointing. It tells the story of a Croatian immigrant woman who falls in love with Eddie, a good-looking fellow restaurant worker. Her father reacts strongly against the relationship, locking her in her room. Eddie goes back to his home town. The future does not look good. And the same is probably true for the future of this film.

D EVERYONE SAYS I LOVE YOU

This Woody Allen film revives the old musical and is tremendously well done. Set in springtime in New York it s a romantic, nostalgic film. The musical numbers are funny and imaginative and well sung. Enjoy yourself!

E WILLIAM SHAKESPEARE S ROMEO & JULIET

Wow! It takes about 20 minutes to catch up with this film. Everything happens so quickly. The director s version of this romantic tragedy is fresh, exciting and new. He has stayed with Shakespeare s original dialogue but the central element of this film is visual. The camera races wildly around or settles on luminous close-ups. The scenery, costumes, characters and above all the colours show the chaos between these two families of Verona. It is highly original, funny in places and energetic!

Exercise B4

You're going to read about five travel books. For Questions **1–5**, choose from the books (**A–E**) and for Questions **6–9**, choose from the authors (**A–E**). The books or authors may be chosen more than once.

A Walking to the Mountain	**A** Wendy Teasdill
B The Sea on our Left	**B** Richard and Shally Hunt
C Gobi: Tracking the Desert	**C** John Man
D A Grain of Sand	**D** Brendon Grimshaw
E Tarantulas, Marmosets and Other Stories	**E** Nick Gordon

Which book:

makes readers question their way of life?	0	B
deals especially with rare creatures?	1	
involves different forms of transport?	2	
tells about danger from unfriendly people?	3	
describes the author's diet?	4	
destroys a popular belief?	5	

Which author:

seems to be a very patient person?	6	
has an unfulfilled dream?	7	
made big changes in order to make this trip?	8	
went where many people had been before?	9	

BOOK *REVIEWS*

A
Walking to the Mountain

Not just any mountain but Mount Kailash. It's a special place for pilgrims of all religions and has been for thousands of years. Author Wendy Teasdill took the hard route, the 'Southern Road'. She hitch-hiked, rode trucks and walked the final 400 miles. She crossed flooded rivers and survived on biscuits, noodles and wild plants and lived to tell her story!

B
The Sea on our Left

At the age of 52 and at the height of their careers (he a dentist, she a physiotherapist) Richard and Shally Hunt gave up their steady middle-class lifestyle to spend a year walking the 4,300 miles around the British coast. This book tells their story and leaves you wondering why you haven't got the courage to do the same.

C
Gobi: Tracking the Desert

Until recently the Gobi Desert was seen as a wasteland of intense heat, polar cold and frightening sandstorms. But it also has the world's second largest national park, the world's only desert bear, the world's only surviving wild horses, snow leopards and is where the first dinosaur eggs were found. Writer and broadcaster, John Man, explored 1,000 miles of this remote area to research his book.

D
A Grain of Sand

Author Brendon Grimshaw is a modern day 'Robinson Crusoe'. For over 25 years he has lived alone on the tiny palm-covered tropical Seychelles Island of Moyenne. Over the years he has had many experiences which show that living alone on a desert island is not as romantic as it sounds. During this time, Grimshaw has also led a never-ending search for buried treasure, said to be worth £30m.

E
Tarantulas, Marmosets and Other Stories

Nick Gordon, the author, is one of those amazing wildlife cameramen that spend their lives waiting for the perfect shot. For the last ten years Gordon has lived in the Amazon basin filming jaguars stalking freshwater turtles, and giant eight-eyed tarantulas in their underground homes. This book is an account of his time. It's a lot more than just a wildlife book though, with Gordon telling stories of escaping from hostile tribes as well as eventually gaining acceptance among these rarely contacted inhabitants.

CHAPTER 1

READING

Exercise B5   Exam practice

You are going to read about an organised holiday in Malaysia. For Questions 1–13, choose from the options (**A–E**). Some of the options may be chosen more than once. When more than one answer is required, these may be given in any order. There is an example at the beginning (0).

To which days do the following refer?

The train will take you up to a wonderful view. | 0 | B |

You can camp if you want to. | 1 |

Start the day with some fruit. | 2 |

Home cooking is on offer. | 3 |

The walks are wonderful, but not easy. | 4 |

You can really appreciate the wildlife. | 5 |

Take an evening walk through traffic-free streets. | 6 |

You can escape from the heat. | 7 | 8 |

It's small enough for you to see it all in one day. | 9 |

Take your time to get used to the climate. | 10 |

You can learn something about the background of Malaysia. | 11 |

If you're short of time, just take a short walk. | 12 |

There's a view over the neighbouring country to enjoy. | 13 |

MALAYSIAN Experience

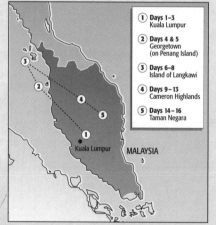

① Days 1–3
Kuala Lumpur

② Days 4 & 5
Georgetown
(on Penang Island)

③ Days 6–8
Island of Langkawi

④ Days 9–13
Cameron Highlands

⑤ Days 14–16
Taman Negara

Kuala Lumpur   MALAYSIA

A   DAYS 1–3

KUALA LUMPUR

If you're staying in Chinatown then getting around is easy – just walk. The National Museum is a good introduction to Malay history, art and culture.

Save some energy for a late night stroll around one of the busy night markets. Jalan Petaling is full of market traders who sell everything. The road is shut off to traffic at night and tables and chairs are set up outside the restaurants. This is the best place to people-watch and enjoy Chinese food and a cold drink.

B   DAYS 4 & 5

GEORGETOWN

Hire a trishaw (bicycle rickshaw) to get around – it's the best and cheapest way. Visit some of the Buddhist temples, particularly the Temple of the Reclining Buddha which is home to a 32-metre long Buddha. If you're looking for a shady spot at midday, the gardens at Fort Cornwallis offer an escape from the sun.

For great views of Georgetown, take the small funicular railway up to the Botanical Gardens at the top of Penang Hill. If you walk up, it will take around two and a half hours.

C   DAYS 6–8

ISLAND OF LANGKAWI

You will arrive by ferry and the Tourism office is nearby to help with accommodation, information etc. Breakfast offers you banana pancakes and fresh pineapple juice. After breakfast hire a motor-bike to explore the island. The roads are good and the island can easily be done in a day. The mountain of Gunung Raya is at the centre of the island. The drive up is through mountain jungle and once at the top you can see the whole island and beyond to Thailand.

There are some wonderful beaches to visit, as well as Telaga Tujuh. Here you'll find seven natural waterfalls which cascade 100 metres down the hillside. The views from here are beautiful and it's wonderful just to sit in one of the icy pools to cool off and enjoy the scenery.

D   DAYS 9–13

CAMERON HIGHLANDS

From the Tourist Information you can buy a map of walks in the area. Most of the walks are short and can be done without a guide. It's the jungle walks that the Highlands are famed for and they are indeed breathtaking. However, be prepared for hard work – balancing on narrow, muddy paths, fighting your way through exotic vegetation etc.

A 'must' is a visit to the Boh Tea Plantation – there are guided tours of the factory and the tea-making process, and you can even do some tasting in the tea-room.

Stay at the Holiday Chalets at Bala on the outskirts of the town. It's a quiet spot on a green hill where the owner prepares all the meals herself from produce bought at the local market.

E   DAYS 14–16

TAMAN NEGARA

The most basic type of accommodation here is a tent, which can be hired. However, you can also stay in a luxurious bungalow.

This area is very humid and you need to take it easy on the first day until you adjust. Then you're ready for the walks that everyone comes here for. Guides can be arranged at the Wildlife Department Office. Even if you don't have time for a long trek, just being in the rainforest and doing some of the shorter walks, listening to the buzz of insects and the call of birds is truly amazing.

Writing

The Writing chapter is in two sections.

Section A Ways of writing teaches general writing skills which you'll need for all parts of the exam.

Section B Writing exam answers applies these skills to the Paper 2 exam format. In this section you'll get help and practice in tackling the different writing tasks found in this paper.

SECTION A

Ways of writing

Unit 1 Writing about events
Unit 2 Describing
Unit 3 Writing about ideas
Unit 4 Writing personally
Unit 5 Language for letters

SECTION B

Writing exam answers

Unit 6 Transactional letters
Unit 7 Writing a story
Unit 8 Discursive writing: compositions and articles
Unit 9 Reports
Unit 10 Set books

EXAM OVERVIEW   **PAPER 2 WRITING (1 hour 30 minutes)**

Paper 2 has two parts:

PART 1	**Question 1** one compulsory letter writing task (120–180 words)
PART 2	**one** task to be chosen from Questions 2–5 (120–180 words) **Questions 2–4** • an article • a letter • a report • a discursive composition • a descriptive or narrative writing task **Question 5** tasks in any of the above forms, based on a set book

Each question carries equal marks.

UNIT 1 — *Writing about events*

Many of the questions in the Writing paper require you to write about 'what happened' as all or part of the question. This unit gives you practice in making your writing more interesting by:

- ▶ using a variety of verb tenses
- ▶ using linking words and phrases

Verb tense variety

Exercise A1

Look at the ten pictures below. They tell the story of Sarah's first business presentation.

Imagine you are Sarah and you are telling someone about your business presentation. Begin with:

I took a deep breath, opened the door and walked in, smiling.

Continue telling the story for each picture (don't write it, just talk it through).

Exercise A2

Read the sample story, and then answer the questions below it. The first one has been done for you.

The Business Presentation

I took a deep breath, opened the door and walked in, smiling. A sea of faces turned to look at me. I tried not to show my nervousness as I walked up to the platform and stood there in front of 200 people, including my boss who was sitting in the front row. This was the first time I had made a presentation to such a large number but I knew that if I did it well my company would offer me the chance of promotion.

Having organised my papers in front of me, I started. At the beginning my voice sounded a bit shaky, but gradually I began to relax and during the next half hour I even managed to make the audience laugh occasionally. I was in the middle of explaining my sales predictions when things started to go wrong. First, half the lights in the hall went off and then, worse still, my boss interrupted. As soon as he raised his hand, I knew he was going to ask a tricky question – and he did. So, by the time I reached the end of my presentation, my earlier confidence had left me. I sat down and, much to my surprise, the audience clapped – even my boss looked pleased. Perhaps my promotion was still possible after all.

1 What two things made the presentation an important event for her?

It was the first time she had made a presentation to such a large number of people. If she did well, she would be offered promotion.

2 Describe the changes in her feelings during the whole event.

3 What is the most frequently used verb tense?

4 What other tenses can you find examples of?

Stories will be more interesting to read if you can avoid using only the past simple tense, e.g. 'First we went to … and then we saw … and then I played …' Most stories use a variety of past tenses.

Read the following review of story-telling tenses.

Past simple

This is the 'normal' story-telling tense. Use it unless there is a special reason for using another past tense.

Paul picked up the keys and left the room.

Past continuous

This sets the scene for a story, describing an action in progress.

When I arrived home, Tina was sitting in the chair, happily watching TV.

This also describes a long, background action which is 'interrupted' by a shorter action in the past simple.

Everybody was waiting for me to start. I was feeling very nervous. Then, suddenly, there was a loud bang.

Past perfect

The 'double past' is a way of going back further when you're already using the past simple. It says clearly that something had already happened before the past event in the story.

Ben was surprised to find that everyone had already left.

Jane thought she had turned all the lights off but …

Past perfect continuous

This is used to describe actions or situations which had been continuing for a longer time, up to a certain moment in the past.

The ground was very wet because it had been raining for two days.
I had been working hard all day and I was tired.

Future in the past

This describes something that was in the future at the time of writing.

I knew he was going to ask a tricky question. She didn't stop to talk to me because she was meeting her boyfriend in five minutes.
I hoped the weather would improve before the weekend.

Exercise A3

Read the story 'A chance meeting' and choose the form of the verb that fits best.

A chance meeting

It happened a few weeks ago as I (1) *walked* / *was walking* home from work.

The rain (2) *poured* / *was pouring* down and I (3) *was feeling* / *had felt* miserable. I (4) *left* / *had left* my raincoat at home that morning because I thought it (5) *was going to be* / *will be* fine all day. I (6) *was really looking forward to* / *really looked forward to* lying in a lovely hot bath. Just then, somebody (7) *was bumping* / *bumped* into me quite roughly. I (8) *looked* / *was looking* at this stupid person and was just about to say something rude when I realised I (9) *knew* / *had known* him.

It was a guy I (10) *had last seen* / *had last been seeing* 20 years earlier when we were at primary school together. He (11) *didn't change* / *hadn't changed* very much! Apparently he (12) *was living* / *had been living* round the corner from me for the past ten years but this was the first time we (13) *had met* / *met* since our school days.

I invited him in for coffee and we started talking and remembering all the funny things that (14) *had happened* / *had been happening* to us in those days. It was great meeting Tony again like that. Since that day we have stayed in touch; in fact we're going on holiday together next month.

Exercise A4

Fill in the gaps with the most appropriate past form of the verbs in brackets.

Tom's strange experience

ONE EVENING last summer Tom (1) was driving (drive) along a narrow country road, (2) _____ (enjoy) a rather beautiful sunset. He (3) _____ (have) the car window open and the soft air (4) _____ (blow) on his face. He was on his way to visit a friend, Gillian, for the weekend. He (5) _____ (work) really hard for several weeks and (6) _____ (look) forward to a weekend of peace and quiet. Then, in the distance, he (7) _____ (see) a bright light. It (8) _____ (attract) his attention because it was a rather strange colour and so intense.

Tom (9) _____ (carry on) driving westwards and the light (10) _____ (stay) in the same position, directly ahead of him. He was curious to know what it was as he (11) _____ (never/see) anything like it before. He (12) _____ (get) closer and closer until he (13) _____ (actually/drive) through it. The car (14) _____ (surround) by a greenish light. Suddenly, it was no longer a pleasant summer's evening. Tom (15) _____ (close) the window

and at that same moment, the car engine (16) _____ (stop). He heard the sound of approaching footsteps, but could see nothing.

He (17) _____ (wake) up hours later in the back seat of the car. Gillian (18) _____ (bend) over him and (19) _____ (say) something. He couldn't remember anything that (20) _____ (happen); all he said was something about a green light. Nobody (21) _____ (believe) him – they all thought he (22) _____ (climb) into the back of the car for a quick sleep. But Tom knew something strange had happened that night.

Ways of linking ideas and actions

Another way to bring variety into your composition is to use different connecting words and phrases (linkers) like *although, when, however*.

Exercise A5

Look back to the sample story of Sarah's presentation on page 63 and find the different ways in which pairs of actions were written as one sentence. The first one has been done for you.

1 I tried not to show my nervousness. I walked up to the platform.
  I tried not to show my nervousness as I walked up to the platform.

2 I organised my papers in front of me. Then I started.

3 My voice sounded a bit shaky. Then I began to relax.

4 My talk continued for half an hour. I even managed to make the audience laugh occasionally.

5 I was explaining my sales predictions. Things started to go wrong.

6 Half the lights went off. My boss interrupted.

7 He raised his hand. I knew he was going to ask a tricky question.

8 I reached the end of my presentation. My earlier confidence had left me.

9 I sat down and the audience clapped. I was very surprised.

Study the following linking words and phrases.

Two actions in the same time period

As Zoe left the building she saw two men racing down the street.

I worked in a bar during my student days.

While Joe was living in France he learnt all about wine.

When Jane told me the news, I was standing in the kitchen.

Sequence of actions
(which action happened first?)

When Phil opened the door, he was shocked to see the mess.

Kate rang me as soon as she got the results.

After she'd told the police everything, Chris was left alone.

After leaving school, my brother started work as a newspaper reporter and then later, he moved to television.

By the time I realised what was happening, the man had gone – with my money.

We started walking at dawn and before long we were in the countryside.

We waited for three hours before he turned up.

It wasn't until Simon read the letter that he realised how much he missed her.

WRITING

Interrupted actions

Sarah was just about to start frying the onions when there was a power cut.

I was in the middle of telling a dreadful joke when Mr Taylor walked in.

Mike was having his breakfast when he remembered what Sue had said.

Change or introduction to change

Suddenly, I knew someone was behind me.

At first, Marilyn was unhappy but then/later/after a while she began to feel more at home.

At the beginning, Wally didn't understand anything but gradually/slowly he began to get the hang of it all.

All the decorating took a long time but eventually the house began to look much better.

Exercise A6

Read the following story about a pop concert. Look at the linking words and phrases below the text. Choose the best one to fill each gap. The first one has been done for you.

The concert

He was late, but that was no surprise. Twenty thousand people were cheering and clapping in the stadium that night; all of them, including me, were waiting for Jake Cocker to appear.

It was the first time that Cocker had appeared in our town and (1) _as soon as_ we heard he was coming we rushed out to get tickets. We had to queue for hours to get them, too. In fact we took it in turns, Jane stayed in the queue (2) _while_ I went to get something to eat, then I took over.

We'd been in the stadium for about an hour (3) _when_ the first singer, Annie Carter, came on the stage. (4) _____ she had a few problems getting the audience to appreciate her –

we all wanted to see Cocker – (5) _____. people started joining in and she left to loud applause and cheers.

(6) _____ the interval, people went to get drinks or ice cream or just carried on dancing. Then, (7) _____, there he was. Cocker! Live on stage! This was what we had been waiting for.

(8) _in the middle of_ doing some of his famous hits, he began to play some new stuff. It was different, much quieter and slower. He was (9) _____ singing 'Lazy Days' (10) _____ the sound system went. Disaster! We couldn't hear anything.

Some technicians came on and Cocker went off. Half an hour (11) _later_, he came back, apologised for the breakdown and said he would do an hour extra to make up for it. You can imagine the noise that greeted that announcement. We all went wild.

It was a fantastic evening; (12) _____ I got outside the stadium that I realised I had lost my voice. It must have been all that shouting and screaming.

| but gradually | suddenly | ~~as soon as~~ | while | | at first | in the middle of |
| before | during | it wasn't until | when suddenly | after | later |

Exercise A7

Look at the following story about Sue and her job. Write sentences using the given linking words. Sometimes you may need to put the second piece of information first or make some other changes. Look back to the example sentences on page 65 to remind yourself how to use the linkers.

Sue and her job

Sue came home. I was making dinner.

1 Join these sentences, first with *when* and then with *while*.

When Sue came home I was making dinner.

or Sue came home when I was making dinner.

2 Which of these linking words can **not** go before *Sue*?

She walked in the front door. The dog ran to greet her.

3 Use *as* or *when* to join the two sentences.
4 Which word, *as* or *when,* makes it sound as if the actions happened at almost the same time?

She told me she was leaving her job. We were eating our dinner at the time.

5 Use *while* to join these two sentences.
6 Join the two ideas with *during* to make one sentence.

I looked at her face. I knew she didn't really want to give up her work.

7 Use *when* or *as soon as* to join these two pieces of information.
8 Which of the two sounds more dramatic?

She admitted the real reason. But first, I had to ask her to tell me.

9 Use *before* at the beginning to link the information.

She told me about her boss. I then realised how unfair he was.

10 Use *it wasn't until* to link the information.
11 Express similar information by continuing this sentence:

I didn't realise how unfair her boss was …

She was telling me all the horrible details. The telephone rang.

12 Use *when* to join the sentences.
13 Add *in the middle of* to your new sentence.
14 Which sounds more dramatic?
15 Use a different phrase to express the idea that the telephone rang just before she started telling me.

It was her boss. He was trying to be nice to her. Then he changed and became quite aggressive.

16 Use a 'change or introduction to change' expression to join the last two sentences.

........................, she just put the phone down and came back into the dining room.

17 What word could you put at the beginning to show the action happened after a certain amount of time had passed?

UNIT 2 *Describing*

Many writing tasks in the exam include the need to give descriptions as part of what you write. The work in this unit gives you practice in:

- ▶ describing people
- ▶ describing objects
- ▶ describing places, buildings and how to get to them

Describing people

Exercise A1

Look at the table below, which shows some categories you can use when writing a physical description of a person. Think of a good friend of yours and add some vocabulary to the appropriate columns.

Age	Hair	Facial features	Body	Clothes
Jill's in her twenties.	Her hair is quite curly.	Her eyes are blue.	She's quite athletic.	She looks very fashionable.
Jack's an elderly man.	He's got short grey hair.	He's got a neat beard.	He's tall and well-built.	He always wears a tie.

Write answers to the following questions about your friend. Look at the example sentences to help you.

1 Which physical feature is the one that you notice first about your friend?
The thing you notice first about Jill is her eyes. Jill's most striking feature is her eyes.

2 What else can you say about this most noticeable feature?
They are very blue and when she looks at you, you feel she is looking straight through you.

3 Can you relate this feature to her/him as a person? (This is not always possible!)
Some people find her direct look a bit worrying, but in fact she is the kind of person who really concentrates when you have something to say. She's the most understanding person I know.

Exercise A2

Look at the following ways of beginning sentences. Think of different people that you know, and in each case finish the sentence with your own ideas.

1 (S)he is an easy-going person / the same age as me / quite small …

   (Martina) is very sporty.

2 He has (got) curly hair / a bad temper …

3 She always wears jeans and trainers / wonderful hats / black …

4 Her most striking feature is her voice …

5 The most striking thing about him is the way he walks / his height …

6 She (sometimes/always/hardly ever etc.) looks/seems bored with life / tired …

7 He (sometimes/usually etc.) looks/seems as if he doesn't care about anything / he is angry …

8 She gives (someone) the impression of always being too busy to talk / that she understands everything …

9 At first he can appear very confident …

   … but when you get to know him better you realise that deep down, he's quite a shy person …

10 She's the kind/sort of person you can always have a laugh with / who has a big influence on others …

11 The best/worst/most interesting thing about her is her sense of humour / the way she dresses …

12 What I like/appreciate (most) about her is the way she makes everyone around her feel special …

13 The reason why I/people like him is because he has always been very honest/never criticises others …

Exercise A3

In Exercise A2 you wrote single descriptive sentences. Now complete the following, and in each case add a further sentence to make your description more interesting. Write about either real or imaginary people.

1 The strangest thing about my grandfather is …

   his way of speaking. He sounds as if he's giving orders, but perhaps this is because he was in the army and had to shout at people.

2 My younger brother always wears …

3 What I find interesting about this character in the book is …

4 The President's most striking feature is …

5 The woman next door has got … which …

6 I often give people the impression …

7 When people first meet my boss they often think …

8 My mother is the sort of person who …

9 I've always enjoyed the company of my friend because …

Exercise A4

Read this sample paragraph describing the writer's favourite person.

My Grandmother

My grandmother has always been my favourite person. She is an elderly woman in her mid-seventies, with greying hair, who always wears clothes that she makes herself. She has a gentle, kind face, but the thing you notice first about her is her friendly smile. She gives the impression of being a very sympathetic person and it's true that if ever I had a problem when I was little, I used to go to her.

Use the model paragraph on page 69, and the 'skeleton' below, to help you write your own paragraph about a favourite person.

– who (s)he is
– physical description (age, size, hair, facial features, clothes)
– what you notice first
– the impression (s)he gives

Describing objects

Exercise A5

Read the following description of a favourite possession and then answer the questions.

My Favourite Possession

It's a watch and it's exactly right for me. It's quite traditional in appearance. The face is round and it's got all the numbers on it, which I like because it makes it easy to read. The strap is made of the same silvery metal as the watch and it's sort of elastic, so it's simple to put on in the morning. It feels good on my wrist. I was given it for my last birthday by a good friend, so that makes it a bit more special. It means a lot to me.

What does the writer tell you about this object? (Not everything is included.)

1 what is it?
2 size/shape?
3 weight?
4 appearance?
5 made of?
6 use/purpose?
7 where it came from?
8 owner's feelings?

Choose a favourite object of your own. Use the questions above to help you get some ideas of what to include. Then write the details into a paragraph. Follow the structure of the watch description where possible.

Describing places and buildings

Exercise A6

Position

The following phrases can be used to describe where a room, building or town is. Divide the phrases into these three groups. Some phrases can go in more than one group.

Room	Building	Town etc.
overlooks the main road	on the left hand side of the street	on the coast

~~on the left hand side of the street~~
~~overlooks the main road~~
~~on the coast~~
not far from the station
west of the capital
with a view of the mountains
about 2 km from the university
on the tenth floor
within walking distance of the centre
in Broad Street
on the outskirts of the town
on the site of an old church
in the basement
in a pedestrianised area
quite close to the town hall
surrounded by countryside
opposite the bathroom
in the city centre

Now write three sentences giving factual information about the position of the room, the building and the town you are in at the moment. Use the phrases above to help you.

1 My room …
2 The building I'm in …
3 This town …

Exercise A7

What kind of places could the sentences below describe?

Size

1 It holds 20,000 people. *stadium/ concert hall*

2 It's big enough for us.
3 It has a population of 20,000.
4 It's uncomfortably small.
5 There's enough room for 12 tables.
6 It's got at least 20 rooms.
7 It used to be much bigger.

Use

8 It's a place where people can meet friends.
9 People can get fit there.
10 It offers young people the opportunity to learn a new skill.
11 It has a wide range/variety of things to look at.
12 The programme changes regularly.
13 The place is quite expensive compared with the burger bar.
14 It used to be a church.
15 You have a choice between upstairs and downstairs.
16 The leisure facilities are fantastic.

Now, think of two different places you know and write a brief factual description of each. Describe the **position, size** and **use**. Use structures from Exercises A6 and A7.

Exercise A8

What's it like?

When you're writing a description of a place, you want not only to give physical detail, but also to tell the reader what the place is like – the atmosphere, or the impression the place gives. To do this you need a variety of adjectives and some useful phrases.

Look at the two lists of adjectives. Which three pairs of adjectives are 'opposites'?

'positive' adjectives	'negative' adjectives
lively	old-fashioned
well-organised	dull
picturesque	chaotic
welcoming	depressing
impressive	sleepy
cosy	dirty
spacious	unfriendly

Use one positive and one negative adjective (of your own or from the lists above) to describe each of these places.

Museum   Disco   Bedroom

Village   Restaurant

Exercise A9

Look at the following ways of describing the **impressions** that places give. Use these phrases, together with adjectives from Exercise A8 (and some of your own) to write sentences about places you know. Give the name of the place and begin 'I like … because …' or 'I don't like … because …'

I like the Sound Bite café because there is a lively atmosphere there on Friday nights, when local bands play.

It looks/seems/feels well-organised.
It looks etc. as if nobody has looked after it for years.
It gives (you) the impression of being well-used.
You get the impression/feeling that a lot of money has been spent on it recently.
It makes you feel as if you're in your own home.
You are made to feel very welcome.
The general effect is of an area that has been neglected.
In general, it's a very welcoming place.
There is a friendly/uncomfortable atmosphere there.

Exercise A10

Read the following paragraph describing the writer's favourite room in her house. Underline the ways in which the following are expressed:

what place it is; where it is; what size it is
what it's used for; special features
what feelings/impressions it gives
why it's her favourite place

Write a similar paragraph about one of the following:

– your favourite room in your apartment or house
– your least favourite building in your town
– the best street market you know

My Favourite Room

My favourite room is the attic at the top of the house. It used to be just a storage space but now it's my workroom. It's not very big – but big enough for me and my books. Up there I've got my computer and all the books, magazines and papers I need. It overlooks the garden so it's really peaceful. What I love about it is the amount of natural light in the room; it always feels cheerful and welcoming.

Exercise A11

How to get to places
Look at the map of Cambridge. Start at the railway station (X) and follow the arrows. Complete the paragraph, describing the route.

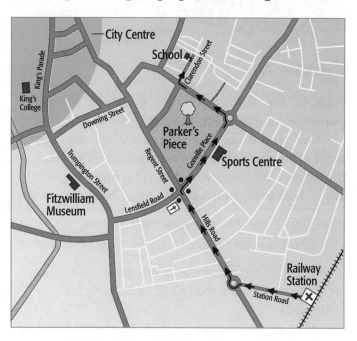

turn right into   until you come   into
carry on past   you'll see
at the lights   ~~along~~   towards   on the left
as far   next   take the second turning

Go straight (1) ___along___ Station Road,
(2) _____ to the roundabout at the end.
(3) _____ Hills Road, and carry on (4) _____
as the traffic lights – (5) _____ a big church on
your left. Turn right (6) _____, and
(7) _____ the sports centre to the (8) _____
roundabout. Turn left here (9) _____ the city
centre, and (10) _____ on the right,
(11) _____ Clarendon Street. The school is
about 50 metres down the street, (12) _____ .

Read the following directions (they don't refer to Cambridge). The writer has made some mistakes in the way (s)he uses the 'direction phrases'. Correct the underlined mistakes.

To get to my house from the city centre, you have to go down the High Street until you (13) arrive to the roundabout. (14) Turn round the roundabout and take the second exit. At the next traffic lights, go (15) straight for about 500 metres and then (16) on your left hand, you'll see a cinema. (17) Turn the left here – that's Finlay Road – and my house is (18) in the right side, (19) opposite to the park. OK?

Exercise A12

Use the phrases in Exercise A11 to help you write a short paragraph telling someone how to get from Cambridge station to King's College **or** how to get from the city centre of your own town to your house.

UNIT 3 *Writing about ideas*

The work in this unit focuses on:

▶ stating information or ideas
▶ putting your points in order
▶ adding and linking points
▶ introducing contrasting ideas

Stating information

An exam writing task may ask you to state facts before giving your personal views. Exercises A1 and A2 give you practice in this.

Exercise A1

Complete the sentences below with an idea which is a fact, not an opinion. In other words, say something that is 'real' not how you personally feel about it.

1 In most cities, traffic … *has increased enormously over the last few years.* ✓ *(This is a fact.)*
   Traffic in cities … *should be reduced.* ✗ *(This is an opinion.)*
2 Newspapers are …
3 Learning a foreign language can …
4 … electricity.
5 Families are …
6 Dreams are …
7 My home town …
8 … the environment.
9 Flying …
10 Mobile phones …

Exercise A2

Look at some ways of stating a fact or idea which is not necessarily your own.

> People say/believe that dreams are a way of sorting out the events of the day.
> It is said/believed that our weather is changing.
> According to experts/the newspaper/a recent report (means 'this is where you got your information from'), tigers will become extinct in the next 50 years.

Choose from the above phrases, and write three sentences about books and then three sentences about shopping.

Putting your points in order

If you've got more than one thing to say, you need to show this by putting your points in order. If you are writing notes, you will probably number the points 1, 2, 3 etc. If you are writing in full sentences, a simple sequence is:

> First of all, … *or* To begin with, …
> Secondly, …
> Another point/thing/argument/(dis)advantage is …
> Finally, … (introduces your last point)
> In conclusion, … (usually introduces a comment or opinion)

Exercise A3

Think of either four points **in support of**, or four points **against** keeping cats as pets. Write these ideas in sentences, introducing each one with one of the phrases from 'Putting your points in order'.

Adding and linking points

In Exercise A1 sentence 9, you wrote something about flying. Maybe you said something like:

Flying gets you to your destination quickly.   (positive point)
Flying is the safest form of transport.   (positive point)

Look at the ways in which a **second** piece of information can be introduced. The phrases below are used to introduce a second idea on the same subject when both ideas are positive.

Flying gets you to your destination quickly …

It is also the safest form of transport.
In addition (to this/that), it's (also) the safest form of transport.
What's more, it is the safest form of transport.
Moreover, it is the safest form of transport.

The same constructions can also be used to link two ideas which are negative in meaning.

Traffic in cities pollutes the atmosphere (negative point); moreover, it can cause damage to people's health. (negative point)

Exercise A4

Use the constructions above to add the second piece of information to the ideas below. The symbols (+) and (–) show whether the ideas are positive or negative.

1 Football is a good way for people to get some exercise.   (+)
   … (exciting game)   (+)
2 For young people, living in a village often means there is not much to do in the evenings.   (–)
   … (go to nearest town for work)   (–)
3 People say that computer games can become addictive.   (–)
   … (some are quite violent)   (–)
4 Cats are good pets because they don't cost very much to keep.   (+)
   … (don't need to be taken for walks)   (+)

There are other ways of linking similar ideas together.

Flying gets you to your destination quickly …

As well as this it is the safest form of transport.

Apart from getting you to your destination quickly, flying is the safest form of transport.

Apart from the fact that flying gets you to your destination quickly, it is the safest form of transport.

As well as getting you to your destination quickly, flying is the safest form of transport.

Besides getting you to your destination quickly, flying is the safest form of transport.

Exercise A5

Write three sentences joining each of the following pairs of ideas in three different ways. Use *as well as*, *apart from* and *besides*.

1 TV: entertaining/educational
2 Bicycles: dangerous to ride in cities/not good in the rain
3 Music: helps you to relax/gives you pleasure

Exercise A6

Read the following text about mobile phones. Look at the underlined phrases, which the writer has used to introduce and link the ideas.

Why I Hate Mobile Phones

<u>First of all</u>, very few people really need a mobile phone. If you need to speak to someone, there are plenty of public phone boxes around. A mobile phone is a status symbol. People like being seen with one – they think it makes them look important and successful. <u>It's also</u> very fashionable nowadays. People buy them, in the same way as they buy the latest trainers or jeans, and very often don't use them.

<u>In addition</u>, mobile phones are often used in public places like trains and restaurants and other people around have no choice but to listen to the conversation, which is very irritating. <u>As well as this</u>, it can actually be dangerous in some situations to use a mobile, <u>for example</u> when driving. <u>According to the police</u>, speaking on the phone while driving is a major cause of accidents.

Write a similar short text entitled 'Why I think mobile phones are a good thing'.

Get help from:
- the model text above, for its structure and use of linking phrases
- the linkers practised in Exercises A3–A5
- the notes on the right, if you don't have your own ideas

Notes
- public phones are very often not working or you don't have the right money for them
- you can use a mobile phone wherever you are e.g. for business
- they can be used if you break down in your car, or for other emergency situations
- useful for old people – they could carry them around with them and feel safer

CHAPTER 2

WRITING

Introducing contrasting ideas

Exercise A7

There are several words and phrases which you can use to introduce contrasting ideas. Look at the examples, then complete the sentences with your own ideas. The symbols (+) and (–) show whether the ideas are positive or negative. Look carefully at the punctuation, especially commas.

but
I'd love to come with you, but unfortunately I've got too much work to do. (+ –)

1 The government promised to introduce new laws to fight crime, but *so far they have done very little.* (+ –)

however
A lot of people find winter a depressing season; however, for me it's a good time because I love cold, frosty weather. (– +)

David thought he was going to get the job. However, he was wrong. They gave it to an older person. (+ –)

2 Flying is a quick way of getting to your destination. However, … (+ –)
3 The film we went to see last night wasn't very good; however, … (– +)

on the other hand
Travelling by coach is much cheaper than any other method of transport. On the other hand, it is a lot slower. (+ –)

Some people from northern countries tend to be rather reserved. Those from tropical countries, on the other hand, are often more open. (– +)

4 People say that living in a foreign country is difficult. On the other hand, it …
5 Personally, I don't need any breakfast. Dinner, on the other hand, …

whereas (quite a 'formal' word)
The USA is a republic, whereas Britain has a monarch.

Most people used to live in small houses in the countryside, whereas nowadays the majority live in apartments in the city.

6 In Japan, people drive on the left, whereas …
7 I prefer spending my free time in the open air, whereas …

although
A lot of tigers are killed every year (main piece of information), although they are protected by law.

Although it was raining hard, Nina went out for a walk (main piece of information).

8 Many restaurants put a 10% charge on the bill, although …
9 Although a few professional sports people can earn a lot of money, most …

in spite of/despite
A lot of tigers are killed every year in spite of/despite the fact that they are protected by law.

In spite of/Despite the fact that it was raining hard, Nina went out for a walk.

In spite of/Despite his decision to leave the team, he still tried hard to win.

10 The number of bicycles in cities has decreased despite the fact that they …
11 In spite of the fact that computers have come down in price recently, …
12 Their plan failed despite … (plus noun)

Exercise A8

Imagine that you have to travel 800 km. Look at the following positive and negative aspects of two different ways of travelling.

	Positive (+) points	Negative (–) points
	quick way to get there easy – you don't have to do anything	long transfer from airport to city expensive boring – nothing to do on journey not much leg-room in front of seat horrible food possible long delays – weather?
	no weather delays convenient – goes straight into city centre can look out at scenery plenty of space	have to carry own luggage relatively slow

Use some of the ideas above to complete the following sentences. You can use the same idea more than once.

1 The plane is quicker. However, if there are weather problems *you can be delayed for hours.*
2 Although the train is slower, …
3 The train is slower. On the other hand, you …
4 Flying is boring, whereas …
5 When you fly, everything is done for you, whereas …
6 You can save time by flying. However, …
7 Flying is comfortable, although sometimes …
8 I prefer flying in spite of …
9 I wouldn't choose the train, although …
10 Despite the fact that …, it's quite a comfortable way to travel.

Exercise A9

Now use the language from this unit in a piece of your own writing. What leisure facilities are there for young people in your town? Note down some that are available.

What are the good and bad points about some of the facilities you have noted?

The cinema doesn't show the latest films.
The sports centre has wonderful showers.

Which is the most popular of the ones you have chosen?

What facilities don't you have that you'd like?

Use some of these ideas and write two paragraphs on 'The good and bad points about the leisure facilities in my town'. Remember to use some of the linking words and phrases from the previous exercises.

You can begin with the following sentence, or choose your own beginning:

Although my town is quite large, the leisure facilities for young people are not very good. There is no sports centre in spite of the fact that …

CHAPTER 2

WRITING

UNIT 4 *Writing personally*

The work in this unit gives you practice in writing about what you think or feel by:

- ► expressing opinions and making suggestions
- ► extending your ideas (explaining, justifying, giving reasons etc.)
- ► making recommendations

Opinions, suggestions and reasons

If you express an opinion, you are saying what you think or feel about something.

I think everyone should be allowed to choose when they leave school.

If you make a suggestion, you are saying what could or should happen.

Why not let everybody do a minimum of ten years at school, and then leave it up to the individual?

It's often good to back up your ideas by giving an explanation or justification, and perhaps mentioning possible results.

They should be allowed to choose, because they will not learn if they are not interested.
By letting people choose, you would increase interest or motivation.

Exercise A1

Complete the following sentences in order to express an opinion, a reason or a suggestion.

1 I don't think smoking in public is ...
  acceptable. (opinion)
2 I think smoking in public should ...
  (opinion/suggestion)

3 The reason why a lot of people do not vote is that ... (reason)
4 In my view, reading is ... (opinion)
5 It would be a good idea if all restaurant owners ... (+ past tense)(opinion/suggestion)
6 Money is one reason why ... (reason)
7 Don't miss going to London. It is ... (reason)
8 I doubt whether most childhood friendships ... (opinion)
9 It seems to me that more young people ... (opinion)
10 Why don't shops ...? (suggestion)
11 What I like about music is the way ... (reason)
12 I suggest that English should ... (suggestion)

Look at a possible way of completing sentence 5.

It would be a good idea if all restaurant owners had to display their menus outside.

Why? What would be a possible result of this? Read the following ways of extending your ideas.

In this way, they could save their customers time and trouble.
This would mean that possible customers knew what to expect.
As a result (of this), customers would have a better idea of the prices.
If this happened, then customers would know what kind of food was on offer.
By doing this, they would help people decide whether they wanted to eat there or not.
(Make sure that the subjects of both sentences are the same – in this example, it is the restaurant owners.)

Exercise A2

What do you think about the programmes on the television channels in your own country, or a country that you know well? What suggestions have you got for the programme makers? What might be the results of your suggestions?

Personally, I think the news programmes are not worth watching because they are too short. (opinion and reason)
It would be better if they could give important subjects more time so they can be discussed. (suggestion)
In this way, people would have more chance of understanding what was happening in the world. (possible result)

Use the structures in Exercise A1 and above, and write a paragraph like the example, giving your idea about TV programming. Make sure you give an opinion (and reason), a suggestion and a possible result.

Exercise A3

Your college proposes to save money by closing the student social club. The student newspaper has asked for reactions to the plan. In each of the following three letters sent to the newspaper, <u>underline</u> the phrases which introduce personal opinions or feelings, reasons for these opinions, suggestions, and possible results

Some of these phrases were used in the previous exercises, and some are new.

Letter 1

opinion

Dear Editor,
I don't agree at all with the proposal to close the student club. My personal view is that this institution is an extremely valuable part of college life. What I like about it most is the cultural and sporting activity that it encourages, and I believe that all this would be lost if the club closed. To my mind, it would be a much better idea to sell the club to a private company who could run it on a commercial basis.

Letter 2

Dear Editor,
I am most disappointed about the college's proposals for saving money, and feel that they should reconsider their plan to close the social club. College life is not only about academic study, but also about relationships, and this is the reason why the club plays such a central part in student life. My suggestion for the future of the club is that a special fund should be established, and an appeal made to all former students for support.

Letter 3

Dear Editor,
It seems to me quite ridiculous that the college is planning to save money by closing our student social club. In my opinion more facilities are needed for students, not fewer, and this proposal appears to me to be very short-sighted. Why don't the college authorities allow a student committee to run the club for a certain period? In this way, they could see if it is possible to make a profit.

CHAPTER 2

WRITING

Exercise A4

Below are some ideas for another letter protesting about the closing of the student social club. Write the ideas into a complete letter using phrases which introduce opinions or feelings, reasons or explanations, suggestions, and possible results.

Dear Editor,
- closing the social club
- very bad for students
- club is an important part of college life
- gives students from different departments the opportunity to meet and relax
- save money by increasing parking charges for staff and students who park their cars on the campus

Making recommendations

A recommendation is a kind of suggestion, but stronger – *go to this place, don't eat there, buy it today* etc.

Exercise A5

First, underline the five phrases in the following article which make recommendations. In each case, say why the place or activity was recommended.

VISITING THE CITY

If you are only in the city for a day, don't miss a visit to the Royal Parade, where you will see some of the finest surviving architecture by Henry Wood, and you must go to the city museum, the largest in the country outside London. If you are staying overnight, I would certainly recommend the Kings Hotel for its friendly efficiency and reasonable prices. For evening entertainment it's well worth visiting the Multi-Media Centre for an hour or two: there is nothing quite like it anywhere in the world. Finally, make sure you don't leave the city without having coffee at Blake's. It's famous mainly because of the personality of its owner, but it serves excellent coffee, too!

Now, underline the four phrases this person uses to say that (s)he does not recommend certain things.

Activity weekend

Last month I decided to do something different. I went on an activity weekend, but it wasn't a good decision. I wouldn't really recommend the course; it was too hard for the average person. Don't bother trying rock climbing – you need to be Spiderman or Spiderwoman to enjoy that. And as for the white water canoeing, definitely not recommended for anyone!

My conclusion? It was not worth spending all that time and money just to get wet and frightened.

Exercise A6

Imagine you have written a report, an article or a letter about a particular film, car, book, café, museum and place for a holiday. Write the **final sentence** for each of your pieces, recommending or not recommending it, and supporting your recommendation with a reason if possible.

I would certainly recommend 'Trainspotting'. Although it's a bit depressing, the acting is excellent and it's concerned with an important subject.

Exercise A7

Write sentences which express opinions, suggestions, reasons, results or recommendations in answer to the following questions. Write more than one sentence in each case.

1 What do you think of the new shopping centre?
2 Where can you find the best burgers in your town?
3 Why are you against the new motorway?
4 Are you in favour of changing your national flag?
5 What kind of clothes should I pack for Los Angeles?
6 Why should people give money to charity?
7 How can I stop myself from being seasick?
8 Which is the best English grammar book?

UNIT 5 *Language for letters*

The work in this unit gives you practice in the language you need for letters. When writing letters you need to pay attention to:

► openings and general style
► contents, or main body of the letter
► endings

Openings and style

Exercise A1

Fill in the gaps with names or other forms of address to show you are writing to:
  – a friend
  – a person in business whose name you know
  – a company, or a person whose name and gender you don't know

1 Dear ....
2 Dear ....
3 Dear ....
  Only **one** of the greetings below is an acceptable form of address. Which one is it?

4 Dear my friend   Dear Manager   Dear Mrs
  Dear all   Dear Sales Department
  Dear Lady and Gentleman

Writing to a friend is a bit like speaking to him or her, so you can:

  – use contractions: *doesn't, she'll*
  – miss out some words: *(It was) Good to get your letter yesterday.*
  – write shorter sentences: *So that was that.*
  – start with an imperative: *Tell me when he's coming.*
  – occasionally use a dash (–) for punctuation: *He gave me a present – a beautiful watch.*
  – use exclamation marks: *What a day!*
  – ask direct questions: *What do you think?*
  – use phrases like: *anyway, well*

Exercise A2

Below are some opening sentences from different letters. Decide which ones you would use when writing to a friend (informal), which ones are fairly neutral, and which ones are more business-like (formal). Show your answer by using left, vertical or right arrows.

If you think a phrase is informal, mark (←).
If you think a phrase is neutral, mark (↓).
If you think the phrase is more business-like, mark (→).

1 Great to hear from you again! ←
2 Thank you for your letter. ↓
3 I don't know if you remember me but I ... ←
4 Thanks for the information about ... ↙
5 I am writing to inquire about ... →
6 Sorry to hear that you've had some problems. ↙
7 It's ages since I heard from you. ←
8 With reference to my recent holiday ... →
9 I have seen your advertisement in ... ↓
10 Have you heard the latest? ←
11 Well, here I am in ... ←
12 Further to your recent inquiry, ... →

Contents (the 'body' of the letter)

Exercise A3

Below are some sentences taken from different letters. Use this material as a reference bank when you write your own letters. The sentences are 'graded' from informal down to more business-like (the first one in each group is the most informal). Answer the question that follows each group.

Asking for information

Let me know how much it costs, could you?
Can/Could you tell me how many people will be in the group?
Would it be possible to add another name to the list of participants?
I would like to know whether/if we can hire the rooms for the whole weekend.
I would/should be grateful if you could send me details of the courses you offer.

1 Who do you think might have written the first sentence, to whom and what about?

Responding to requests for information

You asked me to let you know how many rooms we wanted.
You wanted to know whether/if we were going to meet before April.
As requested, I am sending you all the relevant information.

2 Which two words in the last sentence show its 'formal' tone?

Giving information

Here are the details: Price £200 per week.
You'll be happy to know that we can easily change the arrangements.
I would like to add that the service we received was excellent.
I'm afraid I have some bad news for you about your booking.
As stated in our brochure, you will be met at the airport and taken to the villa.

3 Which sentence could come from a letter written by a holidaymaker?

Explaining why

So you see, it's just not possible.

The reason (why) we want to go in March is it won't be so hot.
We can't come with you because Robin will be in Tunisia at that time.
This is why it is not possible for us to come.
The reason for this is that I will be attending a conference in Madrid.

4 Which two sentences refer to a reason that's already been given?

Making suggestions – and asking for a response

Why don't we go later?
What do you think about my suggestion?
I don't think we should change our plans.
Let me know what you think.
I think it would be a good idea if we wrote to them.
The best thing would be to tell him directly.
I would be interested to know your reaction.

5 Which three sentences do not directly ask for a response (even though one would probably be given)?

Making complaints and asking for action

I'm really not happy about the situation.
What are you going to do about it?
First of all, it was really noisy as it was on a main road.
I am writing to tell you about the problems we had with the tickets you arranged.
I am sorry to say that your company let us down.
In view of all the problems we had, I feel your company should refund our money.
We should/would be interested to know what you intend to do about this

6 What possible problems do you think the writer of the sixth sentence ('In view of ...') might have had?

Expectation and reality

About the cost of the flight: it wasn't £300, as you said, it was £350.

It wasn't what we were expecting at all.

The advertisement said the rooms were small but to our surprise they were quite spacious.

We expected to be met at the airport but unfortunately nobody turned up.

According to your brochure, the hotel had a sauna and jacuzzi. But in fact, it had neither.

Your advertisement clearly stated that everything was included in the price but we discovered that excursions were extra.

7 Which sentence doesn't say whether the reality was worse or better than the expectation?

Expressing feelings

I understand how you feel. I'd feel the same.

You must be feeling very pleased about the results.

I'm sorry I didn't manage to speak to you at last night's meeting.

I can't tell you how disappointed I am about our experience.

I was really surprised to hear your news about the job.

I am writing to apologise for not sending you all the information you requested.

8 Which four sentences do you think are answers to a letter that the writer has already received?

Exercise A4

Look back to the examples of openings in Exercise A1 on page 81 and to the sentences in Exercise A2 on the same page. Write the **first two sentences** for the following letters. Before you start, think about who you are writing to and how formal you need to be.

1 Write to your friend, Anna, who has just lost her job.
2 As a result of an advertisement in a student magazine, write to Adtrak International asking for information about their new sports shoes.
3 Reply to a letter from Steve, who wants to know details of your proposed holiday to Japan.

4 Write to Carefree Villas, cancelling your booking for a two-week holiday, explaining why you have to cancel.
5 You are on holiday in Florida. Write to your friend, Sarah, telling her why it's disappointingly different from what you expected.
6 On your return home, write to the holiday company who arranged your holiday in (5) to complain.

Endings

Exercise A5

Answer the following questions.

1 Which of these ways of closing a letter would you describe as: **a** friendly, **b** neutral and **c** most business-like?

Looking forward to seeing you in March.
I look forward to hearing from you soon.
I'm looking forward to meeting you next week.

2 In what two ways can this be expressed more informally?

I hope to hear from you soon.

3 What's wrong with these two sentences? Rewrite them.

Drop me a line soon if you require any further information.
Please do not hesitate to contact me if there's anything else you want to know.

4 Which of the endings below are possible with these three different styles of opening address?

Dear Hilary   Dear Mr Kinnock
Dear Sir or Madam

Yours sincerely   With best wishes   Yours truly
With love   Yours faithfully   Kind regards
Yours

Exercise A6

Look back to Exercise A4. Choose one or two of the letters that you started, and complete them. Write approximately 120 words.

Paper 2 Part 1

INFORMATION

Part 1 of the Writing paper is a compulsory letter-writing task. You are given some material to read – for example an advertisement, part of a letter, a postcard, a diagram or some notes. Using this information, you have to write a letter of 120–180 words. You do not write the address.

In your letter you must:

- select the relevant information from the question
- use appropriate language for the reader
- make sure you include all the points you're asked to cover

Unit 5 (Language for letters) should be referred to when working through this unit.

Understanding the task

Exercise B1

Read the sample question below. (Do **not** write the letter at this stage.)

Sample Question 1
You are interested in a walking holiday this summer but need more information. Read this advertisement and the notes you've made. Then use the information to write a letter to the Himalayan Expedition Company. You may add any other relevant points of your own.

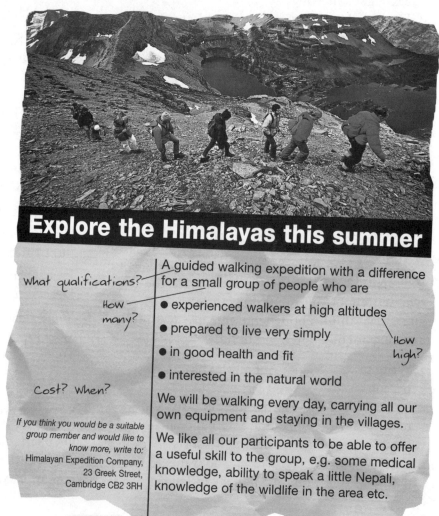

Explore the Himalayas this summer

what qualifications?

How many?

A guided walking expedition with a difference for a small group of people who are

- experienced walkers at high altitudes
- prepared to live very simply
- in good health and fit
- interested in the natural world

How high?

Cost? When?

If you think you would be a suitable group member and would like to know more, write to:
Himalayan Expedition Company,
23 Greek Street,
Cambridge CB2 3RH

We will be walking every day, carrying all our own equipment and staying in the villages.

We like all our participants to be able to offer a useful skill to the group, e.g. some medical knowledge, ability to speak a little Nepali, knowledge of the wildlife in the area etc.

Answer the following questions referring to the sample question on page 84.

1 Who are you writing to?
2 How did you learn about the holiday?

3 Why are you writing? (two reasons)
4 What style should you write in: friendly or business-like?

Exercise B2

It is essential to select the right information to put in your letter. You should:

- include all the relevant points
- not fill the letter with unimportant information
- keep to the facts

Read the whole of the sample question in Exercise B1 again. Which of the following questions would you ask in your letter? Answer *yes*, *no* or *maybe*.

1 dates?
2 medical knowledge necessary?
3 how many people in the group?
4 details about the guide?
5 what clothes to take?
6 how high you will be going?
7 whether a backpack is necessary?
8 cost?

Which of the following pieces of information would you include in your letter? Answer *yes*, *no* or *maybe*.

9 personal information (such as your age)
10 details of a friend's experience on a similar trip
11 your ability to paint and draw
12 the fact that you are a smoker
13 your experience of climbing over 4,000 m
14 last year's camping holiday by the sea in France
15 your experience of long-distance walking

Exercise B3

First, read all the information in the sample question below. (Do not write the letter at this stage.)

Sample Question 2
You are interested in this advertisement for diving lessons, which you saw in a student magazine. You wrote down some questions to ask the company, Underwater Exploration. Read the advertisement and the questions carefully. Write a letter to the company asking for the information you need.

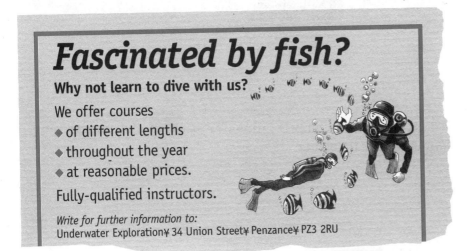

Fascinated by fish?

Why not learn to dive with us?

We offer courses
◆ of different lengths
◆ throughout the year
◆ at reasonable prices.

Fully-qualified instructors.

Write for further information to:
Underwater Exploration¥ 34 Union Street¥ Penzance¥ PZ3 2RU

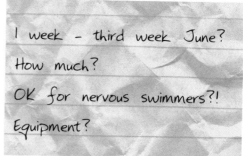

1 week – third week June?

How much?

OK for nervous swimmers?!

Equipment?

CHAPTER 2

WRITING

Now look at the two sample answers below. Which one answers the question better? (There are no grammatical errors in either letter.) Check the following points in each letter:

- **the content:**
  all required points included?
  any irrelevant points? if so, what?
- **the style:**
  any examples of language that is too informal or too formal for the task?
- **the effect on the reader:**
  would the person who read your letter feel 'positive' about it?

Sample answer 1

Dear Sir or Madam

I saw your advertisement in a student magazine and I am interested to know more about your diving courses.

First of all, I should explain that although I can swim I am not very confident in the water. But you mentioned in your advertisement that your instructors were fully qualified, so I assume they will be able to teach someone like me to dive.

I have one week's holiday in the third week of June and would like to know if there is a course running at that time. How much does a week's course cost?

Finally, if I decide to go ahead, is there any special equipment I need to buy or is everything provided by your company?

I look forward to hearing from you.

Yours faithfully

Sample answer 2

Dear Sir or Madam

I am a 22-year-old student studying Sociology at university and I am very interested in learning to dive. While I was in the doctor's waiting room recently reading "Shoot" magazine, I saw your advertisement and I decided to find out more about your courses.

I learnt to swim when I was a teenager. Most of my friends learnt when they were much younger. I was always a bit afraid of the water. Anyway, as I was saying, I can swim but not very well. Do you think this will prevent me from learning to dive?

You said that your courses are of different lengths and run throughout the year. I can only come the third week of June because I have exams before that and afterwards I will be working in my father's office. I hope that there is a course running at that time. If there is, why don't you drop me a line and tell me how much it costs.

Sorry about all these questions!

Yours faithfully

Exercise B4

Sometimes the information you are given contains abbreviations or uses special punctuation. Check that you understand how to interpret the following.

Abbreviations

e.g.   means 'for example'

i.e.   means 'that is': it explains or clarifies what has just been written

N.B.   means 'pay attention': it introduces an important bit of information

etc.   means 'and so on': it indicates there is more to add

p.a.   means 'per annum' (each year) and is often linked to a salary, e.g. £20,000 p.a.

per   means 'each', as in 'per week'

Special punctuation

Look at these notes about the possibility of hiring a club for a private birthday party. Answer the questions about the use of the punctuation.

> 1) Cost?
> 2) Music? <u>not</u> Europop
> 3) 100 (150?) people
> 4) Bar!
> 5) Only till midnight????

1 What's the question going to be?

2 Why is *not* underlined?

3 What's the question going to be?

4 Why is there an exclamation mark?

5 Why are there four question marks?

Rephrasing and expanding

When you have identified the key points to include in your letter, you should then decide if any of them can be rephrased or expanded a little. It will make your letter more interesting if you avoid using exactly the same words as you were given in the question.

Exercise B5

Read the following sample question. (Do not write the letter at this stage.)

Sample Question 3

Your friend is interested in working as an instructor at an international sports camp this summer. You did a similar job last year. She has sent you the advertisement and asked you for your comments. Look at the advertisement and the notes you've made. Using this information, write a letter to your friend and encourage her to apply for the job. You may add other relevant points of your own.

Fighting Fit International

Fighting Fit International

needs instructors for 24 summer sports camps in Europe

You will be working with 12–16 year olds

Qualification in your sport necessary   *Yes!*

Ability to speak a foreign language desirable   *Thank goodness for my Spanish*

▼ **on site accommodation for staff**   *camping!*

▼ **good rates of pay**   *?*

▼ **free time to explore**   *1 day free per week & some evenings*

▼ **friendly working environment**   *Yes!!! Other people great!*

For application form: write to

CHAPTER 2

WRITING

Rephrase the following key points, and **expand** them a little either by adding information contained in the notes at the side of the advertisement, or by adding something relevant from your own imagination. Look at how this has been done for the first key point.

1 qualification in your sport necessary

Try to **rephrase** this so that the content stays the same but the structure is different.

> *You need to be qualified in your sport to get a job with the company.*

Now think about **expanding** this a little, without going away from the point. It's not necessary or possible to do this for every point you mention, but it shows that you are making good use of the material.

> *You need to be qualified in your sport to get a job with the company. They're really strict about this but it won't be a problem for you as I know you passed all your swimming exams.*

2 ability to speak a foreign language desirable
3 on site accommodation for staff
4 good rates of pay
5 free time to explore
6 friendly working environment

Style

Exercise B6

The language you use in a letter depends on who you are writing to. If you're writing to a friend, you can write as if you are talking to him or her; whereas if you're writing to a company, your language needs to be more business-like.

Read the following letter in answer to Sample Question 3 in Exercise B5.

Dear Jenny

With reference to the advertisement you sent me, I would like to comment as follows:

First of all, you do need to be qualified in your sport. The organisation is very strict about this. However, you informed me of your success on the swimming course which resulted in a teaching diploma, so I am confident you will have a satisfactory qualification.

In addition to a sports qualification, I found that being able to speak Spanish – as I know you do too – was a great benefit. As mentioned in my previous correspondence, a lot of the teenagers who come to the camp are from South America.

With regard to accommodation, tents are provided for the employees. I, personally, enjoyed camping – the weather was good and the other people working there were such good company. We each had one day a week when we did not have to work, in addition to some evenings. Time was spent exploring the beautiful countryside around.

On the other hand, the pay we received was not very satisfactory. Despite this negative point, I found the whole experience very worthwhile and I urge you to apply for the job. I feel sure you will enjoy it too.

Love Barbara

This letter contains all the necessary information but is not written in an appropriate style. Barbara and Jenny are friends, but Barbara's language is too formal. It would be more appropriate to write:

> *Thanks for the advert you sent me. The organisation is the same one that I worked for last year, so I can tell you quite a bit about it.*

Continue the letter making it sound as if Barbara is talking to Jenny, not writing a composition!

Organisation

A letter should be structured as follows:

Greeting: Dear Mr Turner etc.
Introduction: reason for writing / purpose of the letter
Main body: information, details, questions etc. (may be more than one paragraph)
Conclusion: action to be taken / what happens next
Ending: Yours sincerely etc.

Exercise B7

Below are some notes for a letter of application for a job as a guide to overseas tourists in your country. The notes (A–G) are not in the logical order. Decide the best order (there may be more than one possibility) and put the correct letter in the boxes provided.

A you will see from enclosed cv / have experience of this kind of work

B speak French, English, Italian / am studying Spanish

C have seen your advertisement / wish to apply for job

D hope to hear from you soon / look forward to meeting you at interview

E worked for past three years as tour guide in Switzerland / enjoyed very much

F am available for work from April 1st / when current contract finishes

G have a cheerful personality / am used to long hours and hard work

Introduction: 1 ☐
Main body: 2 ☐   3 ☐
                4 ☐   5 ☐
                6 ☐
Conclusion: 7 ☐

SUGGESTED APPROACH FOR PART 1 OF THE WRITING PAPER

1 Read the whole question carefully.
2 Check that you understand the task, and underline the key points in the instructions.
3 Read the information you are given, i.e. the advert, article, notes etc. and underline the key points that you will need to bring into your answer.
4 Make your plan. Remember you can add an idea or some information of your own in order to show off your English.
5 Write your letter.
6 Check you have:
  • used the right form of greeting and ending
  • divided it into paragraphs
  • used appropriate language for the task
  • included all the relevant points

Exercise B8 Exam practice

You have just returned home after a month's stay at the Falcon School of Languages. You were not very happy with what the school provided. Read the advertisement for the school and the diary notes you made while you were there. Then write a letter to the director of the school to complain and to ask for some of your money back.

Learn English in California!

The Falcon School offers:
● small classes, average 12
● mixed nationality groups
● 16-place language laboratory open from 08.00–18.00
● varied social programme
● bed & breakfast accommodation in our own hostel

Falcon School of Languages, Marine Drive, Bradley, California, USA

The Falcon School

Diary

Day 2   Hostel really nice, but no breakfast provided. Everyone goes to café next door.

Day 3   No chance to use English much – 20 students in class

Day 4   Everybody seems to speak Spanish, not English. Lang. lab. out of order

Day 10 Another visit to city bars with social organiser! and another game of volleyball!

Day 12 Volleyball again!!! – why not tennis, or swimming?

Day 20 They've listened to my complaints! Now in smaller class, much better.

Write a letter of between 120 and 180 words in an appropriate style. Do not write any addresses.

For further practice

Go back to the 'Explore the Himalayas' question in Exercise B1 and write a letter of between 120 and 180 words. (There is a model answer on page 204.)

UNIT 7 *Writing a story*

Paper 2 Part 2

> **INFORMATION**
>
> In Part 2 of the Writing paper, there may be a question which asks you to write about an event or tell a story. The question might ask for this in the form of a short story, a description of an event, or it could be based on your reading of one of the set books (see Unit 10).
>
> **Examples:**
>
> 1 A student magazine has asked readers to send in short stories with the title 'The best thing that's ever happened to me'.
> 2 Your local newspaper wants readers to send in short descriptions of a memorable visit to a concert or sports event. Write your account of your visit.
> 3 Based on your reading of one of the set books, describe an event of significance in the book.
>
> When writing about something that happened you should:
>
> • have a plan of what you want to say
> • use a variety of verb tenses
> • include some interesting vocabulary and idioms

Understanding the task

Exercise B1

Look at Example Question 1 in the Information Box. Check you have understood what to do by answering the following questions.

1 Who has set the task? *A student magazine*
2 Who's going to read it?
3 What style of writing is needed?
4 Is it in the form of a story or a letter?

5 Is it based on my own experience or someone else's?
6 Have I been given the title or a line to include?
7 What must I write about?
8 Are there any dangers?

For further practice on understanding the task, look at the second example question in the Information Box above and answer the same eight questions.

Style

In the case of the sample question in Exercise B1, an informal and relaxed writing style is appropriate. This particular question asks the writer to narrate a personal experience so it's appropriate to use:

- contractions: *I'm, there's etc.*
- direct speech occasionally: *…and she shouted, 'Get out!'*
- idiomatic language: *I couldn't believe my eyes; he turned up completely out of the blue.*

In general, short stories require informal or neutral language – the important thing is to have a story that keeps the reader interested.

Getting some ideas

What is 'the best thing that's ever happened to me' that I can write about?
Passing my driving test.
(It doesn't really matter what you choose. It may be easier if you can write from personal experience, but if you have a good imagination, use it!) You can get some ideas by asking yourself:

Who?   What?
When?   Where?
Why?   How? How long/much/often etc.?

Look at how these questions might apply to the idea of passing your driving test.

Who?   *me, the examiner, my girlfriend*
What?   *passing my driving test*
When?   *hot, sunny day last summer*
Where?   *in city centre, in rush hour*
Why?   *now I can go and see my girlfriend, who has moved to another town*
How?   *with difficulty – I was nervous; had a bad start*
How long?   *half an hour, but seemed like longer*

Exercise B2

Using the questions you have just studied, note down your ideas for an answer to Question 2 (the memorable visit to a concert or sports event) in the Information Box on page 91.

Organisation

When organising your ideas, think in terms of blocks or paragraphs:

Beginning: set the scene, confirm the title
Middle: describe the event(s) – what happened, why, how you felt etc.
End: the end of the event/day/meal etc.; refer to the title again?

Exercise B3

The following sentences are taken from a possible answer to the Example Question 1 in the Information Box on page 91, but the sentences are not in the right order. Read them through, paying particular attention to the linking phrases and time references. Re-arrange the order of the sentences to make a logical story. The first one is in the right place.

The best thing that's ever happened to me

1 Passing my driving test – that's the best thing that's happened to me. I'd been learning to drive for a few months, but wasn't particularly good at it.

☐ Then ... the car hit the pavement while I was reversing round a corner, and I thought "That's it. I've failed." The rest of the test seemed to take ages.

☐ I couldn't wait to tell Carmen the good news!

☐ So six weeks later I was sitting beside my examiner, Mr Street. After answering a few questions, I drove away down the busy main road.

☐ In fact, I was just about to ask when I could do the test again when he said "You've passed".

☐ Then one day my girlfriend, Carmen, told me that she and her family were moving to a town 200km away. Suddenly, passing my driving test became my number one priority.

☐ At first, my hands were shaking, but gradually I became more confident.

☐ Eventually, we drove back to the test centre. I stopped the car and waited. Mr Street started talking about what I'd done wrong. Then he closed his notebook.

☐ By this time, I was convinced I'd failed.

Now look at the complete story in Exercise B4 below. It's possible that you decided on a different order for the sentences. If so, does yours make sense? Do phrases like *by this time* and *in fact* link to the previous point? Are the verb tenses logical?

Exercise B4

Here is the complete story about the driving test with the sentences in the correct order. The text is not divided into paragraphs. Suggest where paragraph breaks could be put in. Remember to think of what goes into the beginning, the middle (maybe more than one paragraph) and the end. There is more than one possible answer.

The best thing that's ever happened to me

Passing my driving test – that's the best thing that's happened to me. I'd been learning to drive for a few months, but wasn't particularly good at it. Then one day my girlfriend, Carmen, told me that she and her family were moving to a town 200km away. Suddenly, passing my driving test became my number one priority. So six weeks later I was sitting beside my examiner, Mr Street. After answering a few questions, I drove away down the busy main road. At first, my hands were shaking, but gradually I became more confident. Then ... the car hit the pavement while I was reversing round a corner, and I thought "That's it. I've failed." The rest of the test seemed to take ages. Eventually, we drove back to the test centre. I stopped the car and waited. Mr Street started talking about what I'd done wrong. Then he closed his notebook. By this time, I was convinced I'd failed. In fact, I was just about to ask when I could do the test again when he said "You've passed". I couldn't wait to tell Carmen the good news!

Range of structure and vocabulary

Exercise B5

Look back at Unit 1 (pages 63–64) to remind yourself of the **variety** of verb tenses you can aim for in this type of writing.

1 Underline examples of the various structures in the sample answer in Exercise B4.

I'd been learning …

You should also try to include some interesting **vocabulary** and **idioms** in your writing. A limit of 120–180 words doesn't give you much opportunity, but aim to put at least one item in that you're proud of!

2 What idioms or items of vocabulary do you think the writer in Exercise B4 was proud of?

Exercise B6

Look at the following sentences. Decide how you could make them more interesting by using more colourful alternatives to the word *nice*. Write one sentence that more or less follows the original, and a second sentence which is more creative.

1 Yesterday was a nice day so Jenny decided to go for a nice swim.

   a) *Yesterday was a beautiful sunny day so Jenny decided to go for a relaxing swim.*

   b) *The weather was warm yesterday and Jenny thought how refreshing it would be to have a swim.*

2 She telephoned her nice friend, Sam, and asked her to come too.

3 They met at the nice lake nearby.

4 Sam was wearing a nice swimsuit.

5 The water was nice and warm.

6 Afterwards, they had a really nice picnic.

7 They decided they'd had such a nice time together that they'd do the same again the following week – if the weather was nice!

Exercise B7

Don't forget adverbs! The use of an appropriate adverb can make a sentence more alive. Adverbs can express:

– **how** something happens or is done (*well, patiently* etc.)

– **how often** something happens (*hardly ever, occasionally* etc.)

– **how completely** something happens (*totally, almost* etc.)

– **how sure** we are of something (*definitely, probably* etc.)

Complete the following sentences using different adverbs of your own choice.

1 She brushed her hair ____*slowly*____ .

2 After four hours shopping, I was ____completely____ exhausted.

3 I don't remember him ____well____ .

4 He will _____ be the next president.

5 She asked me to come to her office ____quickly____ .

6 The concert was ____well____ organised.

7 They talked _____ on the phone for hours.

8 The restaurant is normally very busy but today it's _____ quiet.

9 She walked home _____ . Immediately she opened the front door, she knew something was _____ wrong.

10 I _____ go to discos as I'm not very keen on dancing.

Checking for accuracy

When you've finished writing, it's important to give yourself about five minutes to check through your work.

Have you divided your work into paragraphs? If you've made any corrections, are they readable?

Have you checked your spelling?

Have you checked your punctuation?
– full stops (.) at end of sentences
– capital letters after full stops
– question marks (?)
– exclamation marks (!)
– speech marks ('…' or "…")
– commas (,)

Have you checked your grammar? What about careless mistakes like the ones below?

– no 's' on third person singular (She sing well.)
– plural subject and singular verb (The men goes tomorrow.)

– singular subject and plural verb (The rice are boiling.)
– wrong word order (I like very much coffee.)
– missing articles (It was beautiful day.)
– too many articles (She gave me an interesting information.)
– wrong verb forms (He has seen it yesterday.)

Your most common mistakes will depend on you and your first language. Some time before the exam, find out from your teacher what your most common mistakes are when writing. Keep a record of these and look particularly for these mistakes when you are checking through your work.

Exercise B8

The story below contains 21 errors (including the example). Read it carefully and make the necessary corrections. Look out for verb forms, structures, articles, wrong choice of word, word order, punctuation and spelling. The number of errors in each paragraph is shown.

.He

five errors

One day last winter, Pete Daniels left his office earlier than usual; he had a appointment, but he didn't want that anybody know about it. In fact, he would go to an interview with another company which had offered him a better work.

six errors

But while he was at his interview, his manager was looking for him back at an office. One of Pete most important customer from Brazil had come to see him and everybody was trying desperately to find Pete. Anybody could find him. I'm sorry, Mr Cavalho,' said the manager, 'Pete seems to be disappeared.'

Mr Cavalho was absolutely disappointed. He must fly back to Rio the following day and he particuly wanted to see Pete.

three errors

The following day, Pete went into the work as usually he was feeling very pleased because his interview had been sucessful. While he sat down at his desk, his phone rang. It was his manager, who he wanted to see him immediately in his office. Pete had no idea what was it about, but he wasn't worried – until he opened the door and saw the look on his boss's face.

seven errors

SUGGESTED APPROACH FOR WRITING A STORY IN PART 2 OF THE WRITING PAPER

1 Read the question carefully.
2 Check that you understand the task. It may not immediately be clear from the question that you are being asked to write a story.
   e.g. Write a report of an accident (i.e. tell the story).
   e.g. Describe what happened (i.e. tell the story).
3 Organise your ideas into a beginning, a middle and an end.
4 Check your work carefully after you've finished writing.

Exercise B9   Exam practice

A student magazine is organising a short story competition. Entrants must write a short **story** about a day when something surprising happened. The story must begin like this: 'Sonya put the letter on the table and left the room.' Write your **story** in 120–180 words. (There is a model answer on page 204.)

UNIT 8 Discursive writing: compositions and articles

Paper 2 Part 2

> **INFORMATION**
>
> In Part 2 of the Writing paper, there may be a question which asks you to discuss the good and bad points of something or to express your views on a particular subject. These tasks may also include giving reasons, making suggestions or recommendations (see Units 3 and 4).
>
> **Examples:**
>
> 1 An international students' magazine is asking for contributions for a series entitled 'The future is exciting'. Write a short **article** for the magazine on this topic, giving your views.
>
> 2 You have been invited to write a short **article** for your college magazine on a teacher who has been important in your life. Write the article. Include details of the teacher's character and say why the person is/was important.
>
> 3 Your local newspaper is asking readers to write and say what they think should happen to some empty ground in the centre of town. The choice is between making it into a park or building an exhibition and conference centre. Write a **letter** to the newspaper saying which you prefer and why, and give suggestions about what could be included.
>
> 4 As part of a media project, your teacher has asked you to write a composition on the advantages and disadvantages of having a nationwide television-free day every week (there would be no broadcasting for 24 hours). Write your **composition**.
>
> • The format of this type of question (e.g. article, letter, composition) may vary.
> • The style of an article will be lighter and more lively than a discursive composition.

Understanding the task

Exercise B1

Look at the four examples in the Information Box and, for each one, answer the questions below. Example 1 ('The future is exciting') has been done for you.

1 What kind of task is it? *an article*
2 Who has set the task? *an international students' magazine*
3 Who is going to read it? *students from different countries*
4 Has it got a title? If not, write one. *yes: 'The future is exciting'*
5 What different 'parts' are there to answer in the question? *two: discussion on the title and personal views*
6 Should it express personal views, or is it more impersonal? *could include general ideas and personal views*
7 Any possible problems? *danger of over-personalisation (too much 'My future' as opposed to 'The future')*

Getting started

The way you plan your answer will depend on the kind of task you have been given. Example 1 ('The future is exciting') is a very 'open' question with not much help as to how to start or what to include. With tasks like this the following procedure may be helpful.

1 What's my personal reaction to the question?

Do I agree? Disagree? Agree, but feel that there are dangers?

What aspects of the future do I feel strongly about – technological? medical? social? personal opportunities?

2 Use questions to help you get some more ideas. (You may not always find answers to every question.)

Who? *my own future, the next generation's?*

Where? *developing countries, richer countries, other planets?*

What? *technology? communications? jobs?*

When? *near future, long-term future?*

Why? *it's unknown – anything might happen*

How? *(no answer)*

But? *environmental problems? growing world population?*

3 Write down some ideas that you feel you can say something about or develop in some way.

– *advances in information technology (I.T.), e.g. people will get lots of information through the Internet*

– *medical progress, e.g. cures for illnesses, people will live longer*

– *personal opportunities, e.g. travel, work*

– *environmental problems, e.g. global warming or pollution*

Exercise B2

Use the procedure above to make notes for an answer to the following.

Your teacher has asked your group to write compositions giving opinions and suggestions in answer to the question: Do you think old people should be looked after by their families when they can no longer manage by themselves?

Exercise B3

Read Example 2 in the Information Box on page 96 again (an article about an important teacher) and answer the questions below.

1 Who are you going to choose?
2 Where/when is or was this person important in your life?
3 Character details? (think of some adjectives)

4 Why important?
5 Situation today?
6 Give one example to illustrate any of the above points.

Exercise B4

Read Example 3 in the Information Box on page 96 again (a letter about what to do with an empty space in your town) and answer the questions below.

1 Which plan do you want to support?
2 Why?
3 What's wrong with the other one?
4 Any disadvantages to the plan you've chosen?
5 Give examples of features that could be included in the plan you prefer.

Exercise B5

Read Example 4 in the Information Box on page 96 again (advantages and disadvantages of a TV-free day) and complete the tasks below.

1 Give three advantages.
2 Give three disadvantages.
3 What's your personal opinion?

Organisation

You have only 120–180 words in which to write your answer, so it's unlikely you will need more than four paragraphs:

– an introduction which sets the scene
– two paragraphs in which you give your ideas
– a conclusion which in some way 'summarises' what you've said or restates your main feeling, opinion etc.

Exercise B6

Read the following sample answer and mark where you would put paragraph breaks.

The Future is Exciting

I think people have always found the future exciting and certainly fascinating. Just think of all the science fiction books that have been written on the subject. The 21st century will bring wonderful advances in the world of information technology. Already we can see through the Internet the amazing possibilities for communication and learning. Another exciting area is medical progress. It would be good to think of a world where cancer, for example, is no longer a frightening word. I'm sure medical research will soon find a cure for this disease and many others too. Apart from these technical developments, the future is exciting on a more personal level too. Most young people think of their future with hope and optimism. Who knows what the future will bring in the way of jobs, opportunity to travel, marriage. The fact that we don't know, makes it exciting. So yes, the future is exciting, but maybe a bit frightening sometimes, too. It's rather like going to the cinema to watch a thriller – you don't know what's coming next.

First and last paragraphs

First and last paragraphs are important. The first paragraph should give a good first impression (or even a surprising one) and make the reader want to go on. The last paragraph should leave the reader with a clear idea of what your conclusions are. It should feel as if you have tied all the ends together neatly, not just stopped because you've written enough.

Exercise B7

Imagine you've been asked to write the following two articles. You've made some notes about what you want to include, but what can you write in the first paragraph?

Article 1: What would you like to 'un-invent' and why?
Article 2: The good things about TV.

Read the **two** alternative **first** paragraphs for Articles 1 and 2, and decide which one is better in each case. Use the following checklist to help you.

- Is it an introduction or is it the first point?
- Does it use the same words as the question?
- Does it refer to the question in any way?
- Does it make you want to read on?
- Do you feel you know what the next paragraph will be about?
- Is it a reasonable length? Does it say something without using up too many of the 120–180 words?

Article 1

a
> The plane, because I think it has done a lot of damage to environments all over the world. There are airports everywhere which move people in and out without a thought for the effect it's all having on the environment around.

b
> If it was possible ever to un-invent something, then I'd choose the plane. Most people probably think of a plane as an exciting and quick way of travelling but for me it has brought more harm than good.

Article 2

a
> Many people nowadays criticise the programmes on TV; too much violence, too many cartoons, too much sport. It's easy to forget that there are some good points too.

b
> You get up-to-date information from the TV. Nowadays, people know what is happening all over the world almost at the time it is happening. This is the best thing about TV.

Now write a first paragraph for an article entitled 'How well do schools prepare students for their future?'. If you're working in a group, exchange paragraphs with someone else and compare.

Exercise B8

Read the **three** alternative **last** paragraphs for Articles 1 and 2 in Exercise B7 (the invention and the TV), and decide which one is best, and why. Remember, a good last paragraph should do some, if not all, of the following:

- use a word or phrase at the beginning to tell the reader this is the end
- summarise the main points
- relate back to the original question

Article 1

a
> For all the above reasons, I would like to un-invent the plane.

b
> To sum up, I believe that even though our lives would be more limited in many ways, I would be happier if the plane had never been invented.

c
> And my final point is that the plane is a military weapon and has killed millions of people. It carries bombs which can destroy our world.

Article 2

a

> So television has a lot to offer its viewers. It can educate, entertain and join people together. These, in my opinion, are the good things.

b

> In conclusion, we can see that there are good and bad things about television. It is important, however, that we do not become too concerned about the negative points – it's there to be enjoyed.

c

> I don't know why people criticise TV. I think it's great! I'd be bored without it.

Now write a last paragraph for the article 'How well do schools prepare students for their future?'

Putting it all together

Exercise B9

An international magazine is investigating the question: 'Can the ordinary person do anything to prevent a crime happening?' Write a short **article** for this magazine.

Look at the sample text which follows and answer the questions on page 101.

Style

If you are writing an article which asks for your ideas, then the style you use will be fairly neutral – neither too informal nor too formal. In general, this means:

– don't use conversational language, e.g. direct speech
– use connecting words and phrases to link your ideas (see Units 3 and 4)

The two most important things are:

– remember who you are writing for – fellow students, international students, the local tourist board, your teacher, the local newspaper, readers of a certain magazine, a friend. Your 'audience' is important, and should help you to write in an appropriate way
– be consistent, e.g. don't suddenly introduce a 'chatty' phrase into a serious discussion

---

<u>Can the ordinary person do anything to prevent a crime happening?</u>

It is true that crime generally is on the increase; it is also true that the ordinary person doesn't always make life difficult for the criminal.

The first point concerns our houses. We could do more to make it hard for a burglar to steal from us. Even if we don't want to have burglar alarms, we should make sure that all the doors and windows are locked properly when we go out. As well as good locks, a dog is excellent protection for your property – burglars are not keen on dogs, for obvious reasons. In addition, some street crime could be prevented. If we were more sensible about where we walked, and at what time, then maybe we would be safer.

On the other hand, there is not much the ordinary person can do against a serious, professional criminal. It doesn't seem to matter how careful you are, or how sensible; if you're faced with someone carrying a gun or a knife you would be stupid to try and do anything.

So yes, by being more aware the ordinary person can do something sometimes, but, in my opinion, not very much. In the end, it is the legal system not the individual that has to fight crime.

1 Does the introduction give you a clue about what's coming next?

2 What are the two main 'positive' points, i.e. that people **can** do something about crime?

3 And the main 'negative' point?

4 What examples are given to support these points?

5 Does the conclusion summarise/relate to the question?

6 Does the article answer the question satisfactorily?

7 Is there a reasonable variety of vocabulary and structure? Underline examples of this.

SUGGESTED APPROACH FOR WRITING ARTICLES ETC. IN PART 2 OF THE WRITING PAPER

1 Give yourself about five minutes' planning time.

2 Make sure you understand the task. Underline the parts of the question that are important.

3 Make a decision about your opinion, your choice etc.

4 Write down some ideas.

5 Think of illustrations or examples to support your points.

6 Begin, paying attention to the first paragraph.

7 Write your ideas in paragraphs. Remember to think carefully about how you link one idea to the next.

8 Make sure your last paragraph ties everything together.

9 Give yourself five minutes to check through your work for accuracy (see Unit 7, page 94).

Exercise B10   Exam practice

Look back to Examples 1–4 in the Information Box on page 96 and write your answers to some or all of the questions. Each answer should be 120–180 words. (There is a model answer for Question 2 on page 205.)

UNIT 9 *Reports*

Paper 2 Part 2

> **INFORMATION**
>
> In Part 2 of the Writing paper you may be asked to write a report. This usually involves giving factual information and making a personal comment like an opinion, a suggestion or a recommendation.
>
> **Examples:**
>
> 1 You are just about to finish a course at college and have been asked to write a report for students starting on the next course about the best local place where you can hear live music. Write your **report** describing the place, the music it offers, and comment on its good and bad points.
>
> 2 Your college is starting a video library. You have been asked to report on a film you've seen recently with a view to including the video in the library. Write your **report**: give a brief description of the film, comment on the level of language difficulty, and say who the film might appeal to.
>
> 3 You work for the local tourist office and your boss has asked you to join an organised tour of a local factory and to report on it. Write your **report** giving information about the tour, its good and bad points and whether a similar tour would be suitable for international visitors to your town.
>
> 4 As a member of a local health and fitness club you recently went on a weekend training course for members interested in helping elderly people to keep fit. Write a **report** for your club newsletter giving details of the course and commenting on its usefulness.
>
> • The tense you use in a report will depend on the task: some may require present tenses (Examples 1 and 2 above), others past tenses or a mixture of both.
> • Organisation, and clarity of presentation, are important.

Understanding the task

The instructions you are given tell you everything you need to know. You are told who you are, who the report is for and what it must include. Your main task is to make sure you use all the information you're given.

Exercise B1

Look at the four example tasks in the Information Box above and, for each one, answer the questions which follow. Example 1 (the best place for live music) has been done for you.

1 What's your role? *an old student*
2 Who are you writing the report for? *new students who don't know the area*
3 Why are you writing it? *to give them information*
4 What information does the reader want? *to know all about the best place to go for live music*
5 What title could you give the report? *the name of the place*
6 What tense will you write in? *present tense*

Organisation

If you were writing a report in real life, for example at work, you would set it out clearly showing the subject of your report. You would probably also use headings to help the reader get the information quickly and clearly. You can do the same in the exam. Your report on Example Question 1 might be organised under these headings:

Subject / Report on *The Zodiac Club*
The place
The music
Comments

You could use numbered or lettered points to help you organise your report.

Exercise B2

Write possible headings, like those above, for Example Questions 2–4 in the Information Box on page 102.

Style

If you're writing a report for a student magazine, it's appropriate to use informal language. You are, after all, writing for people of a similar age group or status. If, on the other hand, you are writing a report for your boss, it would be better to use more business-like language and not to write in contracted form (*it's, won't* etc.).

Content

A report needs facts first, followed by a conclusion in the form of a comment, recommendation or summary. The facts will depend on the subject of the report, but could include:

location   type of entertainment   decoration   opening times   who it appeals to   atmosphere subject matter or theme   characters   length   facilities   organisation   what activities it includes size   what it's about   cost

Exercise B3

Choose from the list above what facts you might include in your report on the Zodiac Club (Example Question 1 in the Information Box on page 102). Under each fact write **one** piece of information. If you prefer, use a real club in your town instead of the Zodiac.

Location: *in a basement room, next to the bank in the High Street*

A report should only include relevant information. For example, in the report on the Zodiac Club it would **not** be relevant to include a detailed description of your visits there, or information about a particular event there, or a comparison with another club.

Exercise B4

Read the following three alternative paragraphs from reports on the Zodiac Club. Which one do you think is best? Why? What makes the other two weaker?

Version 1

The place: The club is situated in the city centre. It's open every evening, except Monday. Drinks are expensive, for example, a Coke costs £3. The decor in the club is good - lots of black and silver - and it makes for a lively atmosphere. Saturday is the best night to go.

Version 2

The place: It's situated in the city centre, next to Barklands Bank. It's open every evening except Monday from 9 o'clock until midnight, two o'clock on Saturdays. Cost of admission is £5 and the drinks are a bit more expensive than in an ordinary bar. From the outside it doesn't look very big but when you go down the stairs from the street you'll be surprised at the space - there's lots of room to dance or just sit and listen to the music.

Version 3

The place: The club is in the city centre and is a great place to hear live music. It's quite a big place and it has a good atmosphere. Some people think it gets too crowded but I enjoy dancing with lots of others. The drinks are a bit expensive but most people expect to pay more when they go to a club. In any case, you can always make one drink last all night.

Now read the following complete sample answer on the Zodiac Club. Note how the final comments are written. The question asked for comments on the club's good and bad points. However, your report is based on your choice of the best local place to hear live music, so there should not be too many negative comments.

Subject: <u>The Zodiac Club</u>

The place: It's situated in the city centre, next to Barklands Bank. Its open every evening except Monday from nine o'clock until midnight, two o'clock on Saturdays. Cost of admission is £5 and the drinks are a bit more expensive than in an ordinary bar. From the outside it doesn't look very big, but when you go down the stairs from the street you'll be surprised at the space — there's lots of room to dance or just sit and listen to the music.

The music: Most of the bands that play there are local groups except on Saturday nights when there is often someone more well-known. The kind of music varies, for example Tuesdays and Thursdays are jazz evenings, Wednesday is folk night and Fridays and Saturdays offer dance-type music.

Comments: It's a great place — in my opinion, the best in town. It's well run; the atmosphere there is friendly and the music is exciting. My only criticism of the place is that it closes too early during the week.

Exercise B5

Read the following question and then look at the answer on the right.

You've been asked to contribute to a leaflet for business visitors to your town. You are going to report on three places where business people can go to eat in the evening. Write your **report**, describing the places, what they offer and what you consider to be the best feature of each one.

There are lots of great places in the town where you can eat without spending too much – I should know, because I'm always short of cash! There are also some places where it costs a lot, so don't forget to read the menu before going in.

The first place I want to tell you about is Gino's. It's an Italian restaurant serving the usual things like pizzas and spaghetti. It's really cheap and very friendly. In fact, the waiters are the best thing about the place.

Then there's Black's Bistro. This is a café which is open all day and you can eat anything there from toast, sandwiches, salads, burgers to full meals. Again it's not expensive and is very popular with young people – I really like it!

And finally, how about Peppers? Go there if you want some really nourishing Mexican food. Mexican food can be a bit hot – all that chilli – but you can choose dishes which are milder too. The best thing about Peppers, apart from the food, is the music. There's live guitar music every evening.

Do you think this was a good report that answered the question well? Answer the questions in the checklist below to help you decide. (There are no language mistakes in this answer.)

1 three places mentioned?
2 details of where, when etc.?
3 food described in each?
4 best feature for each?

5 in the form of a report?
6 style?
7 makes a good impression on reader?
8 task achieved?

Accuracy and relevance

Exercise B6

Look back to Example Question 4 in the Information Box on page 102. Read the following two answers, which both contain mistakes of various kinds.

Candidate A

<u>Helping the elderly to stay fit</u>
The course:
    It was being held at the National Sports Centre over the weekend of July 27th. The cost,
inclusive accomodation for two nights and all our meals, was £250 per person.
    Altogether there were about 30 persons on the course with 3 qualified teachers.
    Day 1 was spent to learn about our bodies and what we could and couldn't expect elderly people to make.
    Day 2 gave us lots of practical suggestion for exercises and activities, although we were only able to practise these
with each other.
Comments:
    I learn a lot and I think it was good worth for money. The teachers were excellent. They gave us a lot of informations and
at the same time allowed us to ask questions etc. However, it would have be better if we'd been able to try the exercises
on some elderly people instead of our younger selves. I'm looking forward to visit our local old people's home to see if they
work. I would recommend other members of the club going on the next course. (180)

Candidate B

The aim of the 2-day course I went on was to training people to help elderly to keep fit. It was organised by Care for the Aged and held in their headquarters. I learnt a lot from the excellent teachers and also met some people very friendly there.

We were taught a lots of activities we could do, for example arm exercises while sitting down, and some gentle stretching exercises too. To be honest, I'm not too keen on the theory part on the first day – you know, which muscles get used in which exercise, but I'm suppose is necessary to know all that.

All in all, I'd say it was a good weekend. We learnt a lot what I'll be able to use in the future and had a good laugh at the same time.

Now read the comments that the examiner made on each candidate's performance. Which set of comments belongs to which candidate?

Examiner's comments on Candidate ☐   Examiner's comments on Candidate ☐

Some errors, but showed good range of structure and vocabulary. Covered the main points required but not much detail, except for one part which was excellent. Lacked organisation and a clear picture of how the course was organised. Sometimes a bit chatty, danger of missing the purpose of the report.

Generally accurate although some tense errors and gerund/infinitive problems. Good coverage of points with good detail. Easy to read because organisation was clear. Good linking devices. Style appropriate for the task.

Go back to the two answers. Correct the language mistakes and find examples to illustrate the examiner's other comments.

SUGGESTED APPROACH FOR WRITING A REPORT IN PART 2 OF THE WRITING PAPER

1 Give yourself about five minutes' planning time.
2 Underline the important parts of the question.
3 Decide the main heading, i.e. the subject of the report.
4 Decide how to organise your report under further headings.
5 Remember who/what you are writing for.
6 Give facts. Make sure you include everything you're asked for.
7 Make sure you include a final comment or recommendation.
8 Give yourself five minutes to check through your work.

Exercise B7   Exam practice

Look back to Example Questions 2–4 in the Information Box on page 102 and write your answers to some or all of the questions. Your answers should be 120–180 words. (There is an example answer for Question 2 on page 205.)

UNIT 10 *Set books*

Paper 2 Part 2 Question 5

Why read a set book?

If you're thinking about reading a set book, consider the following questions:

- Do you enjoy reading in your own language?
- What kind of books do you prefer?
- Will you choose what to read or will someone choose for you?

Ideally, reading a book should give you **enjoyment**. Reading for the exam has two other benefits: it will help you to broaden your vocabulary and it will give you a bigger choice of questions to answer in Part 2 of Paper 2.

Exercise B1

Look at the statements below about reading set books and preparing for questions about them. In each case tick the box to show whether you agree or disagree with the statement. Can you explain the reasons for your choices?

	Agree	Disagree
1 Reading a book isn't a useful way to improve your English.	☐	☐
2 A bilingual dictionary will be useful to help with your first reading.	☐	☐
3 Only people who have studied literature should decide to prepare for the set book question.	☐	☐
4 You should read all the suggested books.	☐	☐
5 Preparing for the set book question will take quite a long time.	☐	☐
6 Candidates who have not read a book have only three choices of question in Part 2.	☐	☐
7 It's a good idea to write notes about the book after each page that you read.	☐	☐
8 You will benefit from an extra reading of the book a week or so before the exam.	☐	☐
9 You will need to be organised and methodical in your preparation.	☐	☐
10 The effort of reading a book is not worth the possible result.	☐	☐
11 If you read a book, you will have five possible questions to choose from in Part 2.	☐	☐

Suggested procedure for preparation

Most of the statements you thought about in Exercise B1 are included in the following step-by-step procedure:

1 If you have a choice of which book to read, get advice from someone who knows the book(s) – which one(s) do they recommend?

2 If possible, get your own copy of the book you have chosen, so that you will feel free to underline, highlight and make notes on the page.

3 Read the book once right through, using a bilingual dictionary to help with difficult words. This is a really good way of extending your vocabulary.

4 As you read, make notes under the kind of headings suggested on page 109.

5 By the end of your first reading, you should have a good overview of the book – you could summarise the story if a friend asked you what it was about.

6 Think about the kind of questions that could be asked and write some practice compositions (see Exercise B2 on page 110).

7 Read through the whole book again after you have completed your preparation – preferably about a week before the exam.

8 If you've enjoyed reading your first set book, and if you have the time, you may decide to read another one. This will give you more flexibility of choice in the exam.

Getting to know the book

Taking systematic notes about the set book is probably the most important part of your preparation. You can make notes as you read or at longer intervals – whichever you find most helpful. The important thing is that they should be well organised and easy to refer to. The headings under which you group your notes may vary a little for different books, but those suggested here should be suitable for most.

Possible headings

	Facts	Opinions (your own, or in the story)
Characters/People	age, appearance rich, poor job, interests, hobbies past life family, friends	likeable reminds me of …
Places	city, town, village house, flat, room size, description countryside, seaside office, school, club	pretty, ugly dull, sinister similar to … old-fashioned unpleasant
Events	what happened turning-points in story deaths, weddings	frightening unexpected amusing
Objects	cars, personal possessions things found/stolen	things I'd like unusual things
Relationships	who loves/hates whom friendships, families changes during story	like real life? moving
Book/Film/Play	been on TV/stage?	part I'd like to play
Beginning/End	content and style of first and last few paragraphs	successful

Thinking about exam questions

The tasks in Question 5 are 'multi-purpose' – that is, they are not specific to one book, but can be answered with reference to any of the set texts. Here are some points to remember:

- Make clear which book you are writing about by writing the title, as well as the number of the question that you are answering, in your question booklet.

- Give enough detail to show that you really have studied the book, and to make what you write understandable to someone who has **not** read it.
- Write what the question asks you to write. It is no use giving a summary of the story, or writing something which you have prepared beforehand.
- You are always told whether to write an article, a report, a letter or a composition.

CHAPTER 2

WRITING

Exercise B2

Below are some possible exam questions, arranged under different headings. Read through one group at a time, and familiarise yourself with the variety of questions that could be asked. Choose one question from each group and note down what you might include in your answer, with reference to the set book you've read.

People/Characters

- Describe your favourite character in the book, and say why you find her or him attractive.
- Describe a character in the book whom you disliked, and give an account of some of this person's actions.
- Say how one or more of the minor characters in the book play an important part in the story.
- Think of a person in the story who reminds you of someone you know, and illustrate some of the similarities.
- Did you find any of the characters particularly difficult to believe in as people? Give some examples to illustrate your answer.
- Imagine that you spent a day as one of the characters in the book. Describe some of the things that happened to you.

Places/Settings

- Write a composition describing a place which is important in the story, and make clear why it is significant.
- In what way is the setting of the book connected with the people and what happens to them?

Objects

- Choose three things in the book which you found particularly unusual, and explain why.
- Which thing or things in the book would you most like to see (or have) in real life? Give your reasons.
- Describe a particular possession, or piece of clothing, belonging to one of the characters, and say what it tells us about this person's character.

Events/Situations/Moments

- Describe a situation or event in the book which you found amusing, moving or frightening.

- Can you imagine any of the events in the book happening in your own life? Give examples to illustrate your answer.
- Describe an important moment in the book, when something happens which affects everything that follows.

Time

- Do you think people will still enjoy the book in 20 years' time? Give some examples of aspects of the story that may seem out of date by then.
- In what ways is the period in which the book is set significant for the story?

Media

- If the book were made into a film, which would be the most difficult parts of it to adapt?
- In a film version of the book, which role would you least like to play, and why?
- Would the book be suitable for adaptation to a TV series? Which parts would be most effective on the small screen?

Summarising

- To improve your English, you are corresponding by e-mail with a friend in an English-speaking country; your friend suggests that after reading a book, you should describe it briefly. Write your e-mail, saying what the book is about, who the main characters are, and why you did or did not enjoy it.

Relationships

- Describe the relationship between two or more of the people in the book, and say why it is important in the story.
- Imagine that you could meet one of the book's characters: say who you would choose, and what kind of relationship you think you would have.

Beginning/End

- Describe the beginning of the book, and say whether you think it is successful or unsuccessful in getting the reader's attention and interest.
- Could there have been any other ending to the book? Say why it had to end as it did, or else suggest your own alternative ending.

Visual

- Choose a situation or character from the story that you think should be pictured on the outside cover of the book. Why do you think that this captures the essence of the book?

- Do you think it would be helpful or not for the book to have illustrations of people or scenes? Give your reasons.

The reading experience

- What did you gain from reading the book? Describe your process of preparation, and give details, with reference to the book, of some things that you learned.
- Write a letter recommending the book to a friend, and saying why you think she or he would like it.

Exercise B3

Read the sample question below and the answer that follows it.

Sample Question 1
What are the three most interesting things in the book? Give reasons for your choices.

The Hound of the Baskervilles

For me, the three most interesting things in the book are the moor where most of the action takes place, the character of Sherlock Holmes and the hound.

Dartmoor is described in the book as a really wild and mysterious place. Very few people live in the area so you get the impression that lots of horrible things could happen without anyone finding out about them. There's also a prison on the moor which makes it an even more frightening place. And of course there's Grimpen Mire where people disappear.

I was interested in Sherlock Holmes himself because I wanted to know what this famous character was like. In fact, I was disappointed because he seemed a very cold and unemotional man and not really someone I would want to meet. He doesn't seem very friendly towards his assistant, Watson. It seems more of a master/servant relationship.

And the hound was great! Right up until the end I didn't know if there really was a dog or not. If there was, I wanted to know how a dog could kill people without leaving a mark on them. So those are my three things.

Do you think this is a good answer? Answer the questions in this checklist to help you decide.

1 Does the answer include the title of the book?
2 Does the answer cover all the required points?
3 Is the answer the right length?
4 Do you think the writer shows a good knowledge of the book?

5 Is the organisation clear, with:
  – good paragraphs?
  – different ways of linking?
  – a good ending?
6 Is there a range of structure and vocabulary?
7 Would a reader have a positive feeling about the book?

Now do the same with a different sample question. Read the question below carefully and then answer the checklist questions above.

Sample Question 2

Imagine that you could meet one of the book's characters: say who you would choose, why, and what kind of relationship you would probably have.

The story was very exciting and I enjoyed reading it but I didn't like any of the characters very much. However, if I could choose, I'd like to meet Laura Lyons, the woman who loved Mr Stapleton. She seems to have been very badly treated by the men in her life. First of all, by her husband who left her, although he still has some legal powers over her. And then there was Stapleton who didn't tell her he was married so he could use her to help him get what he wanted. I would like to become friends with Laura and talk to her about why she thought these men were so horrible to her. She sounds to be someone who doesn't have much self-confidence, and falls in love too easily. Maybe she needs good women friends to talk to. She certainly needs someone to help her ask the right questions before she starts a relationship. She might, of course, not want to hear my friendly advice. Perhaps she feels that any man is better than no man.

Exercise B4   Exam practice

Look back to the bank of questions on pages 110 and 111. Answer one of the questions based on your reading of a set book. Write the title of the book (and the title of the composition). Your answer should contain enough detail to make it clear to someone who may not have read the book.

Some final advice about all the questions in the Writing paper

1 You must write for the 'audience' you have been given in the question.
2 Keep to the word limit (120–180 words).
3 Write your answers in pen. Make sure your handwriting is readable.
4 In Part 2 you only write one answer from a choice of three (a choice of five if you have prepared a set book).

5 If Part 2 has a 'letter' question, it will require a different style from the letter in Part 1 (i.e. formal – informal or vice versa).
6 Your answer in Part 2 will probably be livelier if you choose a subject of which you have personal experience or knowledge.
7 Leave time at the end to check what you've written.

CHAPTER 3

Use of English

The organisation of the Use of English chapter follows the format of Paper 3 in the exam. The work covers areas of structure and usage which are commonly tested in this paper, and suggests techniques for tackling particular kinds of questions.

Unit 1	Multiple choice cloze
Unit 2	Open cloze
Unit 3	Key word transformation
Unit 4	Error correction
Unit 5	Word formation

EXAM OVERVIEW PAPER 3 USE OF ENGLISH (1 hour 15 minutes)

Paper 3 has five parts:

PART 1	Multiple choice cloze 15 questions	1 mark per question
PART 2	Open cloze 15 questions	1 mark per question
PART 3	Key word transformation 10 questions	2 marks per question
PART 4	Error correction 15 questions	1 mark per question
PART 5	Word formation 10 questions	1 mark per question
Total:	65 questions	

UNIT 1 *Multiple choice cloze*

Paper 3 Part 1

> ### INFORMATION
> In Part 1 of the Use of English paper, you must fill a gap in a text by choosing one word or phrase from a set of four (A, B, C and D). There are 15 gaps. The emphasis is on vocabulary.
>
> **What's being tested:**
> - single words that have something in common, or have a similar meaning:
>   *frontier, border, boundary, limit*
>   *say, tell, talk, speak*
> - linking words: *because, since, as, for*
> - word + preposition: *comparison between*
> - preposition + word: *by heart*
> - phrasal verbs: *to go through, pull through, see through*
> - collocations: *a high standard of living, to do research*

Familiarisation exercise

For Questions 1–3, read the text below and decide which answer **A, B, C** or **D** best fits each space. There is an example at the beginning (0).

DESERT CACTUS

The Arizona desert is hot and extremely dry, but row (0) ..B.. row of giant cacti, up to 18 m tall, grow there, all well-supplied with water. How do these plants survive in a land that hardly ever sees rain?

Nature has (1) .... cactus plants with a special design which enables them to collect and keep rain in desert conditions. (2) .... ordinary plants, whose roots go deep underground for moisture, cacti have very shallow roots that grow a long way round the plant. These take in water very quickly. On a large cactus, the roots can (3) .... an area 100 m from the plant itself.

0 **A** by	**B** after	**C** with	**D** for
1 **A** given	**B** allowed	**C** provided	**D** granted
2 **A** Because	**B** But	**C** Although	**D** Unlike
3 **A** radiate	**B** spread	**C** include	**D** cover

Understanding the task

Exercise 1

Identifying the kind of language that is tested in Part 1 can help you to anticipate problems. It may be helpful to think of three categories:

Category 1 single words that don't depend on anything else in the sentence except the meaning
Category 2 linking words that must fit the meaning and structure
Category 3 phrasal vocabulary – the word being tested depends on other words in the sentence to make a complete phrase

Look at the following sentences and decide, with the help of the examples, what category is being tested and which answer A, B, C or D best fits each space.

1 At the age of 65, Geoff retired and lived off his .... *D* ....
   A allowance   **B** salary   **C** grant   **D** pension
   Category 1: single words all connected with money. The right word must describe the money you live off when you've retired from work. The other words refer to money in different situations.

2 I was allowed to leave early .... *C* .... I did the work the following day.
   A in case   **B** even if   **C** providing   **D** otherwise
   Category 2: the sentence is saying that the person would only get permission to leave early if he did the work the following day. The linking word or phrase must fit this meaning.

3 David has never been .... *D* .... in football. He prefers rugby.
   A keen   **B** eager   **C** fond   **D** interested
   Category 3: these words have similar meanings, but the correct choice depends on the preposition 'in'.

4 Please confirm your reservation in ....
   A letter   **B** writing   **C** words   **D** paper

5 Can you lend me some money? I've .... my wallet at home.
   A let   **B** forgotten   **C** left   **D** taken

6 The accident investigators are looking .... the cause of the crash very thoroughly.
   A for   **B** into   **C** out   **D** after

7 .... the lights went out, I was having a maths test.
   A During   **B** While   **C** As soon as   **D** When

8 Everybody knew Harry had .... a crime but nobody wanted to tell the police.
   A done   **B** made   **C** performed   **D** committed

9 Everyone knows that it was wrong to .... Meg for the accident.
   A accuse   **B** blame   **C** charge   **D** connect

10 Cathy's only been here a week. I think you should .... that into consideration before you complain about her.
   A take   **B** put   **C** bring   **D** carry

11 I've never .... that strange building before, have you?
   A realised   **B** remarked   **C** noticed   **D** recognised

12 Alex went for a long walk .... he was feeling very tired.
   A although   **B** because   **C** however   **D** despite

Understanding the task

'Single word' vocabulary

Exercise 2

Below are two extracts from a woman's personal diary, in which there are some single word gaps. Read the first extract. Then look at the three choices given. They are all **wrong**. Write a **correct** fourth choice.

DIARY ENTRY FOR JUNE 2nd

My (1) *journey* .... to work today took twice as long as usual because the train broke down on the way. By the time I (2) .... the office I was cold and fed up. I (3) .... everything is back to normal by this evening. Perhaps I'd better (4) .... the situation before I leave the office. It's quite likely that something else will go wrong tonight. I feel it's going to be one of those days!

	A	B	C	D
1	A travel	B trip	C drive	D *journey*
2	A arrived	B got	C came	D
3	A think	B wish	C believe	D
4	A control	B test	C prove	D

Now do the same with the second extract.

LATER THE SAME DAY ...

I was right! Going home was just as bad! First of all, when I left the office the rain was (5) .... down, and (6) .... where I had left my umbrella – at home, of course. I ran to the station in order to (7) .... getting too wet. I wasn't really looking where I was going and I didn't (8) .... a small child standing outside the station entrance and I knocked her over. She wasn't (9) ...., thank goodness, but her father wasn't at all (10) .... when he saw that she'd fallen into a large (11) .... and was completely soaked. I kept apologising and helped to pick her up. Eventually, I left them and ran for my train. The one I usually catch had gone so I (12) .... an hour waiting for the next one. I've decided to take the car to work tomorrow.

	A	B	C	D
5	A falling	B spilling	C dropping	D
6	A remember	B think	C say	D
7	A prevent	B resist	C stop	D
8	A remark	B recognise	C look	D
9	A wounded	B damaged	C broken	D
10	A contented	B delighted	C satisfied	D
11	A pool	B pond	C water	D
12	A lost	B passed	C saved	D

Exercise 3

Look at the following gapped sentences and the correct missing word given below each one. Imagine you are the examiner. What words would you put for the two **wrong** choices? Think of words which have some similarities to the given word, but which are definitely wrong. Don't worry if you can't think of two alternatives.

1 Listen to the .... about the gate number for Flight BA264.
  A *warning*   **B** announcement   C *advertisement*

2 We had a delicious dinner but the waiter took ages to bring our .... , and then it was wrong!
  A ....   B ....   C bill

3 There was a(n) .... between the two halves of the play, so Joe was able to leave the theatre and get some fresh air.
  A ....   **B** interval   C ....

4 The .... from the top of the mountain was unbelievable – we could see for miles.
  A view   B ....   C ....

5 My parents want to .... our kitchen so that all eight of us can eat comfortably together.
  A extend   B ....   C ....

6 What's your .... of modern art?
  A ....   B ....   C opinion

7 Do you think professional sportspeople should .... such high salaries?
  A ....   **B** earn   C ....

Linking words and phrases

Exercise 4

Read the job application letter below and decide which linking phrase best fits each space.

Dear Sir or Madam

I am writing to inquire whether there is any possibility of my working for your company
(1) like / with regard to / according to / as ~~as~~ a translator.

(2) Because / Since / As / For you will see from the enclosed CV, I studied English at college for three years (3) but / and / as well as / besides

spent six months in England at a language school (4) in order / so as to / so that / for improve my spoken English.

(5) When / As soon as / Since / After I finished there, I have been working for a travel agency in my country, organising tours and excursions for tourists from all over the world.

CHAPTER 3

USE OF ENGLISH

(6)
However
Despite
In spite of
Although
I enjoy this work, I feel I would like to become more involved with translation work,

(7)
including
regarding
particularly
moreover
in the field of tourism.

Please do not hesitate to contact me (8)
in case
even if
provided
if
you would like any further information.

I look forward to hearing from you.
Yours faithfully

Exercise 5

Look at the following three short texts. Choose the linking word or phrase that fits in each space. In the exam, there is only one possible correct answer, but in this exercise there may be **more than one** in some cases. Check carefully that the answers you choose are correct in both **structure** and **meaning**.

REALLY COLD PLACES

(1) ..A & D.. we may complain about bad weather from time to time, most of us live in reasonable comfort (2) ..A.. climate is concerned. But in the Arctic region, the temperature may drop to –57°C and (3) .... in summer the temperature doesn't often rise above 7°C. And as for Antarctica, no human beings, (4) .... research scientists, live there.

1	**A** Although	**B** However	**C** Despite	**D** Even though
2	**A** as long as	**B** as regards	**C** as well as	**D** as far as
3	**A** yet	**B** even	**C** still	**D** also
4	**A** apart from	**B** except for	**C** especially	**D** particularly

WHAT CAUSES COLDS

The common cold is the illness we most love to hate, but (1) .... this fact we are not much closer to finding a cure for this annoying illness than doctors were a century ago. The first laboratory to concentrate on the common cold was set up in 1946. (2) .... that time, groups of volunteers have been given colds in the interests of medical science. (3) .... the efforts of these volunteers, we now know that a cold is not caused by a single cold virus (4) .... can be caused by many different ones. (5) ...., finding the cause, or causes, is only the beginning.

1	**A** in spite	**B** however	**C** despite	**D** nevertheless
2	**A** From	**B** Since	**C** For	**D** After
3	**A** According to	**B** Thanks to	**C** Owing to	**D** Due to
4	**A** however	**B** but	**C** and	**D** which
5	**A** However	**B** Although	**C** Nevertheless	**D** Despite

THE POWER OF TORNADOES

(1) .... the fact that tornadoes cause terrible damage, the area that they devastate at any one time is actually quite small. The path of greatest destruction is often not more than 100 m wide. (2) .... a tornado can demolish a house on one side of a street, (3) .... a house opposite escapes undamaged. At the centre of a tornado the speed of the wind is incredible. In fact, it is difficult to measure (4) .... monitoring equipment rarely survives.

1 **A** In spite of   **B** Despite   **C** Besides   **D** As well as
2 **A** But   **B** As a result   **C** So   **D** In addition
3 **A** while   **B** but   **C** when   **D** then
4 **A** and   **B** since   **C** unless   **D** because

Word + preposition / Preposition + word

Exercise 6

The correct choice in all these sentences depends on matching the right preposition with a particular word. Think about the meaning of the sentence as well as the word and preposition combination. There is only **one** correct answer. (Look at Appendices 1 and 2 to help you.)

1 Skiing doesn't .... *C* .... to me at all. I don't like snow.
   A interest   **B** attract   **C** appeal   **D** like

2 I don't think Jim will ever .... in finding peace of mind.
   A manage   **B** succeed   **C** arrive   **D** achieve

3 The National Bank was closed today .... of a robbery during the night.
   A in view   **B** in spite   **C** in case   **D** as a result

4 Ruth can't go to Mike's wedding because she'll be away .... business.
   A for   **B** on   **C** at   **D** with

5 Lucy was forced to stay at home .... of whether she wanted to.
   A regardless **B** on account   **C** because   **D** despite

6 It was a very popular film .... by the amount of money it took.
   A referring   **B** judging   **C** regarding   **D** estimating

7 Plastic .... flexibility with great strength.
   A joins   **B** connects   **C** combines   **D** involves

8 Stuart arrived .... good time to catch the 7.15 train.
   A with   **B** on   **C** at   **D** in

9 .... to office gossip, Neil Turner is going to lose his job.
   A Referring   **B** According   **C** Regarding   **D** Attending

10 A large number of seabirds are now at .... as a result of an oil tanker disaster.
   A danger   **B** threat   **C** difficulty   **D** risk

11 There's not much new about this car. It's very similar .... last year's model.
   A as   **B** to   **C** with   **D** like

12 The new hospital is to be built .... to the old one.
   A nearby   **B** beside   **C** next   **D** alongside

Phrasal vocabulary

Exercise 7

Decide which answer A, B C or D best fits each space. This exercise concentrates on phrasal vocabulary, that is collocations, phrasal verbs and prepositional phrases. In Part 1 of the Use of English paper there will be a number of questions which test your knowledge of this aspect of English vocabulary. Good luck!

EARLY NEWSPAPERS

Did you know that Julius Caesar introduced the earliest known official written news as far (1) ..B.. as 59 BC? The *Acta Diurna* (Daily News) was a handwritten sheet, posted daily in the Forum of Rome. Its contents would not have been out of (2) .... in a modern newspaper. Accounts of battles, military appointments, and political events were written about in (3) .... detail. Citizens in distant (4) .... of the Roman Empire sent men to Rome to copy the news and send it back (5) .... letter. In this way they were able to keep in touch with what was (6) .... on at the centre.

After the death of this early form of newspaper, it was left to travellers to spread the (7) ..... Until the invention of the printing press in the 1450s, information was carried from place to place by (8) .... of mouth.

1 **A** ago   (**B**)back   **C** before   **D** away
2 **A** order   **B** time   **C** line   **D** place
3 **A** large   **B** huge   **C** great   **D** big
4 **A** parts   **B** pieces   **C** places   **D** portions
5 **A** in   **B** with   **C** by   **D** through
6 **A** coming   **B** being   **C** keeping   **D** going
7 **A** issues   **B** news   **C** affairs   **D** communications
8 **A** way   **B** means   **C** speech   **D** word

SUGGESTED APPROACH FOR PART 1 OF THE USE OF ENGLISH PAPER

1 Look at the title of the text. It is a kind of summary of what you're going to read, and can help your understanding.
2 Read through the whole text at least once to get the general meaning. Don't look at the A, B, C, D choices while you are reading.
3 Look at the words surrounding the spaces before you look at the choices. In the case of a missing linking word, remember to check that it fits with the meaning of the whole sentence.
4 Make your choice – don't leave any blanks. Even if you have no idea, it's still worth having a guess.
5 Read the completed text through.

Exercise 8   Exam practice

For Questions 1–15, read the text below and decide which answer **A, B, C** or **D** best fits each space. There is an example at the beginning (**0**).

WINDMILLS AND WATERMILLS

For 1,000 years, windmills and watermills were the largest and most complex machines in our world. (**0**) ....C.. the development of steam in the 18th century, their (**1**) .... declined, but many remain as (**2**) .... of an age of silent power.

The earliest type of mill, used for (**3**) .... corn, was a handmill which was (**4**) .... up of two circular stones – one fixed and the other rotating. This was the forerunner of the method used in all later mills.

Watermills were (**5**) .... to the Greeks during the 1st century BC and are thought to have been introduced into Britain by the Romans. (**6**) .... it was the Saxons, 500 years after the Romans had left, who developed the use of watermills on a large (**7**) .... .

Records show that the Arabs invented windmills as (**8**) .... as the 7th century. They were used where water power was unavailable or unsuitable. They were usually built on high (**9**) .... to catch the winds, and could be seen for miles (**10**) .....

Nowadays there are very few (**11**) .... mills of either sort left in Britain, although in (**12**) .... years there has been a movement to (**13**) .... some of the others to their former glory. This is good news because mills are not only attractive to look (**14**) .... but also environmentally friendly in that they get their energy from (**15**) .... resources.

0	**A** With regard to	**B** According to	**C** Because of	**D** As a result
1	**A** strength	**B** usage	**C** employment	**D** importance
2	**A** mementoes	**B** souvenirs	**C** remnants	**D** reminders
3	**A** cracking	**B** grinding	**C** pressing	**D** breaking
4	**A** made	**B** done	**C** consisted	**D** comprised
5	**A** used	**B** invented	**C** known	**D** designed
6	**A** Although	**B** But	**C** Then	**D** Therefore
7	**A** way	**B** size	**C** scale	**D** measure
8	**A** early	**B** soon	**C** long	**D** far
9	**A** place	**B** hill	**C** earth	**D** ground
10	**A** away	**B** around	**C** afar	**D** apart
11	**A** manufacturing	**B** living	**C** working	**D** running
12	**A** present	**B** many	**C** recent	**D** later
13	**A** restore	**B** build	**C** renew	**D** make
14	**A** at	**B** for	**C** after	**D** into
15	**A** normal	**B** natural	**C** primitive	**D** common

UNIT 2 *Open cloze*

Paper 3 Part 2

> ### INFORMATION
>
> In Part 2 of the Use of English paper, you are given a text which has 15 gaps in it. **One** word is needed to fill each gap. The emphasis in this question is on structural accuracy, although some phrasal vocabulary is also tested.
>
> **What's being tested:**
> - grammar:
>   adverbs, articles, auxiliary and modal verbs,
>   conjunctions, prepositions, pronouns
> - 'balance' structures:
>   *more ... than; as ... as; the same ... as; at first ... but later;*
>   *so/such ... that; the more ... the -er*
> - some vocabulary:
>   phrasal vocabulary, preposition phrases
>
> The word you choose for each gap must be grammatically correct and also have a logical meaning in the sentence and the complete text.

Familiarisation exercise

For Questions 1–4, read the text below and think of the word which bests fits each space. Use only **one** word in each space. There is an example at the beginning (0).

DO FISH SLEEP?

(0) ....*Although*.... fish have no eyelids and so cannot shut their eyes, (1) .... still need to rest and sleep. Some sleep under the sand, while (2) .... look for a small space in the rocks. The little clownfish, (3) .... is found in tropical seas, hides among the poisonous tentacles of the sea anemone and depends on these (4) .... protection.

Exercise 1

Read the sentences below and think of the word which best fits each space. Use only **one** word in each space.

In order to find a suitable word you need to decide what **function** the missing word has in the sentence. The kind of thoughts that should go through your mind are shown in this exercise, to help you reach the right decision.

1 David was .... fed up with working in the same boring job.
   The sentence is complete in meaning so the missing word must be a way of describing 'fed up'. So an adverb is needed, e.g. 'totally' or 'completely'.

2 Nadia sat at her desk to .... a letter from her sister.
   Needs a verb. But 'from' is important. What can you do with a letter <u>from</u> someone?

3 .... I have never actually met him, I have seen him often on TV.

Needs a linking word to introduce a contrast.

4 Gordon works every morning and then spends .... the afternoon playing golf.

Sentence is complete already, so must be something that tells us how much of the afternoon he spends playing golf.

5 .... main reason for his success was his ability to communicate effectively.

Must be an article, and 'main' gives the clue.

6 Is my explanation clear .... , or would you like me to repeat it?

Sentence is complete already; must be a word that qualifies 'clear' so it's an adverb of some sort – and one that comes after the adjective.

7 For centuries, New York has .... regarded as the gateway to a new life for countless immigrants.

Between two verb parts, so it's going to be a auxiliary verb, part of a passive construction.

8 There aren't many countries .... you can ski in the morning and go swimming in the warm sea in the afternoon.

What relative pronoun can relate to 'country'?

9 .... needs somewhere to live and work, and most people seem to manage quite well, even in the most difficult circumstances.

The gap is the subject of the sentence, 'people' would be a good answer – but the verb is singular.

10 According to fitness experts, skipping .... burn up more calories than jogging, is .... damaging to the legs and is an excellent exercise for the heart.

The sentence is about the positive aspects of skipping. The first gap must be a modal verb ('skipping' is subject, 'burn up' is main verb). Second gap: how damaging is it compared with jogging?

Exercise 2

In each of the following sentences the gap has been filled with an incorrect word. Most of these 'mistakes' have occurred because the person who filled in the gaps didn't read the whole sentence carefully enough. Say what is wrong with each answer, and then write the correct word.

1 The next train ...*will*... arrive at platform four is the 20.10 for Manchester.

'The next train will arrive ...' looks fine, until you read to the end of the sentence. 'Will' doesn't fit with 'is the 20.10'. Correct word: 'to'.

2 There was hardly ...*no*... work to do in the factory.

3 Shakespeare wrote 37 plays, of ...*them*... the most famous is Romeo and Juliet.

4 There is more than ...*an*... answer to the traffic problem.

5 We all ...*arrived*... to the meeting with plenty of time to spare.

6 The film would ...*had*... been better if the ending had been different.

7 Richard Blair worked ...*like*... a bank clerk for many years before becoming an actor.

8 The result of the vote was ...*more*... closer than anyone had believed possible.

9 There has been an increase ...*of*... the number of people out of work.

10 James was an excellent tennis player ...*and*... was not very good at squash.

11 The woman who opened the door said ...*hello*... at first, but just stood there and stared at us.

12 Petra knew she had done badly in her exam. There was too ...*much*... time to answer all the questions properly.

123

> **SUMMARY**
>
> ⇑ You have:
> • thought about the function and meaning of the missing word
> ⇓ You are now going to:
> • focus on a number of commonly tested items. If you have difficulty with any of these constructions, refer to your grammar book

Exercise 3

Fill each gap using one of the following **relative pronouns**. One pronoun is used more than once.

who   which   where   when   whose   what

CARL VOGEL

Carl Vogel, **(1)** ..*who*.. was born in Vienna in 1920, died at the weekend. The country **(2)** .... he was most famous was not his native Austria, but America. Vogel moved to the USA in 1950 **(3)** .... he was invited to become a professor at Lincoln University. He stayed there until 1970 by **(4)** .... time he was beginning to be known in the psychology world. **(5)** .... really made him a household name in the States was his radical theory on dream interpretation. Towards the end of his life he was awarded the European Science Prize of **(6)** .... he was very proud. His colleagues described him as a man **(7)** .... whole life was dedicated to dreams.

Exercise 4

Fill each gap using one of the following **auxiliary verbs**. They may be used in more than one place.

were   will   has   been   was   would

INVENTIONS: THE INTERNET

It began in 1969 when some scientists in the US military thought it **(1)** ..*would*.. be handy to link together a few of their computers which **(2)** .... situated in different places. Two years later, 23 computers had **(3)** .... connected up. Today, the Internet serves over 40 million people worldwide. And as more people connect up, the potential for the system **(4)** .... become even more exciting in the future.

INVENTIONS: ANTIBIOTICS

This key breakthrough in medical history **(5)** .... probably never have happened if Alexander Fleming had **(6)** .... more careful about keeping his laboratory clean! He left a glass plate coated with bacteria lying around and a passing mould spore landed on it and performed its amazing bacterium-killing act. That was in 1918, but it took another 11 years before the mould's magic killer ingredient, penicillin, **(7)** .... found. This first antibiotic **(8)** .... since saved millions of lives and is perhaps the single most important discovery known to medical science.

Exercise 5

Fill each gap using one of the following words **once** only. They focus on '**balance**'.

however   other   despite   another   either   in

A COLONY ON MARS

It is one thing to land scientific instruments on Mars; **(1)** *however*, it is quite **(2)** .... to establish a base for humans to explore the planet. Daytime temperatures can rise above freezing, but, because of the extremely thin atmosphere, the sun's heat radiates back into space. Even at the equator, the temperature drops to –50°C at night. **(3)** .... fact, there is no ozone layer to keep out ultraviolet radiation, and hardly any oxygen for **(4)** .... breathing or burning conventional fuels. But **(5)** .... all these problems, scientists are currently working on transport and clothing for Mars and an artificial environment in which colonists could live. However, the potential cost makes the idea of human life on Mars nothing **(6)** .... than a fantastic dream.

Exercise 6

Fill each gap using one of the following **pronouns once** only.

them   these   they   our   another   it   themselves   their

CHATTING WITH CHIMPS

Naturalists have long known that the apes, **(1)** *our* nearest relatives in the animal kingdom, communicate with one **(2)** .... through gestures, sounds and facial expressions. But **(3)** .... was always thought that only human beings could use words and sentences. In the 1960s, however, researchers set **(4)** .... the task of teaching chimpanzees to communicate with humans.

At first the scientists tried to make **(5)** .... speak. But no chimp ever managed to acquire a vocabulary of more than four words and even **(6)** .... were spoken with great difficulty. The breakthrough came when two scientists from the University of Nevada decided to try American Sign Language, a system of gestures used by deaf people. After four years, **(7)** .... had taught their first chimps to use 132 signs correctly to communicate **(8)** .... wants and needs.

Exercise 7

Fill each gap in Sentences 1–4 using one of the following words. One of them is used in more than one place.

anywhere   somebody   nobody   something   everywhere

1 The organisers cancelled the conference because by the closing date __*nobody*__ had enrolled.
2 This town is really boring. There isn't _____ to go in the evenings. _____ should build a disco or a sports hall or _____ – they'd make a lot of money.

3 During the first few weeks, the new president was greeted by large cheering crowds _____ he went.
4 Datawork Inc. is looking for _____ who can manage a team of 12 computer programmers. If you think you are that person, write to us at Datawork Inc.

Fill each gap in Sentences 5–10 using one of the following words **once** only.

little   few   any   some   none   many

5 While Jenny was jogging this morning she slipped and fell. After a few minutes she picked herself up and carried on running. She didn't feel .... pain in her ankle until she got home.

6 .... of Jack's colleagues shared his pessimistic view. He was the only one who forecast a decrease in profits.

7 It's common for people who win large sums of money to spend a lot, but usually they do manage to invest .... of it.

8 There are very .... people who can honestly say they have never told a lie.

9 The game was so bad that not .... people stayed until the end.

10 Unfortunately, there is very .... chance of finding any more survivors of the earthquake.

SUMMARY

⇑ You have:
• practised filling blanks with some commonly tested words
⇓ You are now going to:
• use the suggestions and clues to help you make the right choice

---

Exercise 8

Read the following text and choose which of the two suggested answers fits in each gap.

'SAD' SYNDROME

Seasonal Affective Disorder (SAD) is a depressive condition **(1)** *which* affects one in every 20 people during the winter months. In the northern hemisphere, January to March are the months **(2)** .... sufferers feel the worst. However, for **(3)** .... badly affected, problems can start **(4)** .... early as August and last right through till spring. The condition is believed to be the **(5)** .... of a lack of sunlight. SAD sufferers feel increasingly tired and depressed and want to sleep and eat more.

Light travels **(6)** .... the part of the brain which controls moods and appetite, and **(7)** .... not enough light is received, then the chemical reactions in your body slow down. The condition was first recognised in 1987 but so **(8)** .... medical science has not come up with a cure for it. **(9)** .... is a treatment called 'light therapy' which involves sitting in front of a light box for **(10)** .... up to two hours a day. SAD sufferers can also help relieve their symptoms by wearing **(11)** .... special visor around the head which acts like a portable light box.

which/it

which/when
those/these   as/so

cause/result

from/to
so/if
long/far
There/It

anything/something
a/the

Exercise 9

Read the following text about Albert Schweitzer and then fill each gap with **one** suitable word. At the side of the text there are notes to help you make your decision.

ALBERT SCHWEITZER 1875–1965

Albert Schweitzer was a man of many talents, but perhaps he is

most famous (1) .... *for* his medical work in Africa.   (*preposition after 'famous'?*)

He went to Gabon in 1913 (2) .... *as* a doctor, together with his   (*'with' a doctor? 'as' a doctor?*)

wife. He wanted to help, in a practical (3) .... *way*, people who were   (*must be a noun because of 'a'*)

not as fortunate (4) .... *as* himself. When he began his medical   (*what completes 'as fortunate ...'?*)

studies (5) .... *at* the age of 30 he already (6) .... *had* three doctorates –   (*preposition/complete phrase – 'with', 'in', 'at'?*)
(*verb – what tense?*)

in music, theology and philosophy. Music was a passion

throughout (7) .... *his* life, and his talent for playing the piano and   (*pronoun – who are we talking about?*)

organ (8) .... *helped* him to raise money for the Schweitzer hospital,   (*verb, tense? followed by infinitive*)

(9) .... *which* was built in Gabon. Today's modern hospital, built   (*relates back to hospital*)

(10) .... *next* to the original one, looks (11) .... *after* patients with a wide   (*preposition of place, but followed by 'to'?*)
(*'looks like', 'looks for', 'looks after'?*)

variety of diseases. (12) .... *Although* Schweitzer died in 1965, his work   (*is there a negative/positive contrast?*)

continues, as does his belief (13) .... *in* 'reverence for life', which is   (*preposition after 'belief'?*)

still the guiding principle at the hospital in Gabon.

Now do the same with this text.

TRAIN JOURNEY TO WORK

The morning train seemed more crowded (1) .... passengers   (*preposition after 'crowded'?*)

than usual. As Emma pushed her way through she realised that

she (2) .... probably have to stand up all the way. This was   (*part of verb, modal?*)

(3) .... *not* how she wanted to start her day. Just at (4) .... *that* moment,   (*positive or negative?*)
(*which moment?*)

she spotted (5) .... *an* empty seat in the corner of the carriage.   (*this is the first mention of 'seat'*)

Strangely, (6) .... *none* of the other passengers seemed to   (*how many passengers saw it?*)

(7) .... *have* noticed it, so with a feeling of triumph she went   (*part of verb, auxiliary?*)

(8) .... sat down. Opposite her (9) .... *there* was a young boy playing   (*joins two verbs*)
(*subject of verb – 'it', 'he', 'there'?*)

with something which he was (10) .... to run over his hands and   (*verb, past cont.– followed by 'to ...'*)

arms. At (11) .... *first* Emma didn't pay much attention, but then a   (*when? contrast with ... 'but then'*)

sudden movement caught her eye. A large, hairy spider was

running up the boy's arm! So that's why (12) .... had taken the   (*who? positive/negative?*)

seat before her.

SUGGESTED APPROACH FOR PART 2 OF THE USE OF ENGLISH PAPER

1 Look at the title of the text. It is a kind of summary of what you're going to read, and can help your understanding.
2 Read through the whole text, **without** filling in any gaps, in order to get the general meaning.
3 Go back and start filling in; look at the words surrounding each gap to help you decide the grammatical form **and** the meaning of the missing word. Remember to think about 'positive/negative', 'singular/plural' and 'balance' structures.
4 Read the whole thing again. Make sure you've only written one word for each gap.

Exercise 10   Exam practice

For Questions 1–15, read the text below and think of the word which best fits each space. Use only **one** word in each space. There is an example at the beginning (0).

THE TRUTH ABOUT AMERICAN INDIAN SMOKE SIGNALS

Many adults, after watching Western films **(0)** .... children, grew up believing that American Indians could communicate with smoke signals almost as easily **(1)** .... people nowadays talk on **(2)** .... telephone. Sadly, the idea that the individual puffs of smoke represent complex messages is typical **(3)** .... the kind of exaggeration that Hollywood loves.

Smoke signals were indeed used, but their content **(4)** .... limited to a few simple messages **(5)** .... meanings had been agreed in advance. Returning Piman fighters in Arizona, for example, might signal the end of a successful battle **(6)** .... sending up a column of smoke, and the village **(7)** .... reply with two columns of smoke. One or two unbroken columns of smoke were **(8)** .... that was needed to send a message. **(9)** .... was the place that the signal came from – whether the fire was on a hill **(10)** .... in a valley – that was important.

When Apaches out hunting spotted another group of Indians **(11)** .... the distance, they lit a fire well to the right of their **(12)** .... group, which meant, 'Who are you?' The others, in order to **(13)** .... the Apaches know that they were friends, would then use a prearranged reply. Smoke signals were most **(14)** .... used to broadcast news of victory in battle, or to warn of dangers, **(15)** .... as approaching enemies.

UNIT 3 *Key word transformation*

Paper 3 Part 3

Familiarisation exercise

For Questions 1–3, complete the second sentence so that it has a similar meaning to the first sentence, using the word given. **Do not change the word given.** You must use between two and five words, including the word given. There is an example at the beginning (0).

0 I've never seen such a bad film as that one.
   ever
   That's the *worst film I've ever* seen.

1 I didn't find the lecture interesting.
   interested
   I .... the lecture.

2 Frank asked if I could look after his cat for him.
   take
   Frank asked me to .... for him.

3 Steve has such big feet it's almost impossible to get shoes for him.
   are
   Steve's feet .... it's almost impossible to get shoes for him.

Exercise 1

Rewrite each of the following sentences to say the same thing in another way. There may be several different ways of doing this, but you should only write one. No key words are given for this exercise, and there is no limit to the number of words you can use.

1 Ben took no notice of what I was saying.
   Ben didn't listen to what I was saying.
   Ben didn't pay attention to what I was saying.
   Ben ignored what I was saying.

2 What's your opinion of his work?
3 Do you know her reasons for leaving the company?
4 No smoking in here.
5 I'd rather not tell you the answer.
6 In my opinion, there's no chance of anybody failing the exam.
7 Who does this book belong to?
8 Let's go swimming this afternoon.
9 I've got no interest in art.
10 Anne spoke without looking at her notes.
11 Greg is very good at playing tennis.
12 It's not worth asking Jim the answer.
13 The students were bored by the lesson.

CHAPTER 3

USE OF ENGLISH

14 They paid a lot of money for their new car.

15 I spend two hours travelling to work every day.

16 It'd be a good idea if you went to the doctor.

17 I know everyone in the village except my neighbour.

18 Ella has hardly any money left.

19 I decided to stay at home because I thought Jo might ring.

20 As well as playing the piano, Penny also plays the guitar.

Exercise 2

Now look at the key words for each sentence in Exercise 1. You may find that you've already used some of them in your own sentences. If not, write the sentences using the key word.

2 think
   What do you __think__ of his work?

3 why

4 allowed

5 want

6 everybody

7 is

8 why

9 not

10 didn't

11 plays

12 point

13 found

14 cost

15 me

16 better

17 only

18 almost

19 case

20 addition

Structural transformations

In the following pages you will find notes and practice exercises on the kind of structures which are commonly tested in this part of the exam. You should work through this section over a period of time, focusing on one or two structures each time. Don't do too much, otherwise your brain will be overloaded!

▶ Active / Passive — page 130
▶ Passive with impersonal 'it' — page 132
▶ Passive with 'have / get something done' — page 132
▶ Make / Let / Allow — page 133
▶ Modals — page 133
▶ Reported speech — page 134
▶ Conditionals — page 136
▶ If only / I wish / I regret — page 137
▶ Past simple / Present perfect — page 137

▶ Preferences — page 139
▶ Opposite structures, similar meanings — page 139
  so / such / too / not … enough
  not as … as … / more than
  quite near / not far / a long way
  any/no/every
▶ Different forms of the same word — page 141
▶ Phrasal verbs — page 143

Active / Passive

Look at this example.

> They make excellent wine in Italy.
> **is**
> Excellent wine is made in Italy.

Now look at the process for changing a sentence from active to passive.

1 object of first sentence becomes new subject: *Excellent wine*
2 tense of first sentence: *simple present*
3 same tense (simple present) of 'to be': *is*
4 past participle of 'to make': *made*
5 new, passive sentence: *Excellent wine is made in Italy.*
6 words needed to fill the gap: *wine is made*

Exercise 3

Complete the second sentence, with between two and five words, including the word given, so that it has a similar meaning to the first sentence.

1 The Japanese export a lot of different goods.
by
A lot of different goods .... the Japanese.

2 Since I last went to Pam's house, she has painted her study pink.
been
Since I last went to her house, Pam's .... pink.

3 Donald's sister is teaching him chess.
taught
Donald .... his sister.

4 I sensed that someone was following me.
I
I had the feeling that .... followed.

5 They're going to set the hostages free at midday.
freed
The hostages .... at midday.

Look at how the process works with words like *must* and the infinitive.

> You must follow the captain's instructions at all times.
> **obeyed**
> The captain's instructions must be obeyed at all times.

1 new subject: *The captain's instructions*
2 'tense' of first sentence: *'must' + infinitive*
3 same form ('must' + infinitive) of 'to be':   *must be*
4 past participle – the key word: *obeyed*
5 new, passive sentence: *The captain's instructions must be obeyed at all times.*
6 words needed to fill the gap: *must be obeyed*

Exercise 4

Complete the second sentence, with between two and five words, including the word given, so that it has a similar meaning to the first sentence.

1 I want you to finish all this work before lunchtime.
should
All this work .... before lunchtime.

2 Why didn't you add your name to the list before leaving the building?
ought
Your name .... added to the list before you left the building.

3 Could you wake me up at 8 o'clock, please?
be
I'd like .... up at 8 o'clock, please.

131

Passive with impersonal 'it'

Constructions with *believe, say, think, consider, report, claim, suppose, find, know, acknowledge, understand*

Look at these examples.

> It is reported that he is the only survivor of the disaster.
> He is reported to be the only survivor.
> In ancient times, it was believed that the earth was flat.
> In ancient times, the earth was believed to be flat.

Exercise 5

Complete the second sentence, with between two and five words, including the word given, so that it has a similar meaning to the first sentence.

1 People believe that the President has a huge private fortune.
   to
   The President .... a huge private fortune.

2 Many scientists think that the world's climate is changing.
   believed
   The world's climate .... many scientists to be changing.

3 Some people say that apes can understand human speech.
   able
   Apes are said .... understand human speech.

4 It was thought by local people that the palace was haunted.
   by
   The palace .... local people to be haunted.

5 Everybody says that Florence is a very beautiful city.
   considered
   Florence .... a very beautiful city.

Passive with 'have / get something done'

This means that you don't do something yourself, but somebody else does it for you. Look at the example.

> Richard: Your hair looks nice, Jenny.
> Jenny: Thanks, I've just had it cut.
>   (by my hairdresser)

How to form the structure:

1 'have' (in the correct tense)
2 the object (e.g. 'my hair')
3 past participle (e.g. 'cut')
4 the agent if necessary (e.g. 'my hairdresser')

Exercise 6

Complete the second sentence, with between two and five words, including the word given, so that it has a similar meaning to the first sentence.

1 They are going to X-ray my knee on Friday.
   have
   I'm .... knee X-rayed on Friday.

2 The garage think they should service my car soon.
   serviced
   The garage think I ought to .... soon.

3 I can't tell you the time, because my watch is being repaired.
   my
   I don't know the time because I'm .... at the moment.

Make / Let / Allow

Look at these examples.

His boss made him cancel the reservation.
(active)
She was made to apologise. (passive)
Jane let me borrow her car. (active)
I was allowed to borrow Jane's car. (passive)
My parents didn't/wouldn't let me go to discos.
(active)
My parents wouldn't allow me to go to discos.
(active)
I wasn't allowed to go to discos. (passive)

Exercise 7

Using the information in the sentence below,
complete sentences 1–5 using the words given.
There is no word limit in this exercise. Use the
examples above to help you.

The police officer told Oscar that he couldn't
leave the room.

1 Oscar … (allowed)   4 The … (made)
2 The … (allow)   5 Oscar … (made)
3 The … (let)

Exercise 8

Complete the second sentence with between two
and five words, including the word given, so that
it has a similar meaning to the first sentence.

1 Because of our dog, the postman couldn't
deliver the letters.
let
Our dog would _____ deliver the
letters.

2 The border guards didn't give us permission to
enter the country.
not
We _____ to enter the country by the
border guards.

3 What was the reason he wouldn't allow you to
have the day off?
let
Why _____ have the day off?

4 My mother insisted that I kept my own room tidy.
made
My mother _____ my own room tidy.

5 As a child, I had no choice but to look after my
baby sister.
was
When I was younger I _____ look
after my baby sister.

Modals

Look at the following examples and the
explanations (in brackets) of what is in the mind
of the speaker.

Present situations

Terry may arrive late, of course. (It's possible,
because he has another appointment.)
You must be feeling fed up. (Everything has
gone wrong for you.)
Val ought to/should be in school. (*either* I think
that's where she is because that's her normal
routine. *or* She's not in school but it would be
good if she were.)
You can't be tired. (You've only just woken up.)
You have to/must go now. (It's late, so please go.)
Does Judy need to be told? (Is it necessary for
her to know?)
We don't have to do our homework. (Great! It's
not compulsory, I can choose.)

Past situations

Stella might not have got the message. (It's
possible that nobody told her.)
You must have been very angry. (It was a
situation that would make anyone angry.)
Really Lena shouldn't have come to work today.
(It wasn't a good idea at all.)
They can't have failed. (It's almost impossible
to believe it!)
Why did you have to tell him? (Why did you
feel it necessary to tell him?)
We didn't need to take any books. (It wasn't
necessary – maybe there were some there
already.)
You needn't have given me a present. (You did
give me one, but really it wasn't necessary.)

133

Exercise 9

Complete the second sentence with between two and five words, including the word given, so that it has a similar meaning to the first sentence.

1 You are not allowed to park your car here.
  must
  Cars .... here.

2 Yesterday was a national holiday, so there was no need to go to college.
  need
  Because yesterday was a national holiday, we .... to college.

3 It was a bad idea of ours to buy such a large dog.
  bought
  We really .... such a large dog.

4 Is it necessary for the garage to repair the car this week?
  have
  Does .... repaired this week?

5 I expect you were delighted to see her again after such a long time.
  must
  You .... to see her again after such a long time.

6 Linda was really lucky that she wasn't injured in the fall.
  could
  Linda .... in the fall.

7 It's not true that Frank is living in America – I saw him in the city centre yesterday.
  can't
  I saw Frank in the city centre yesterday, so he .... in America.

8 You're supposed to be working not watching TV.
  ought
  You .... , not watching TV.

Reported speech

Look at this example of how direct speech can be changed into reported speech.

'Did you find the answer?' asked Ian.
I
Ian asked me whether I had found the answer.

The following are the most important points to remember:

- **Verb tense changes – one step 'backwards'**
  'I'll see you later,' said Anne.
  she
  Anne said she would see me later.

- **Commands – use the infinitive**
  'Don't make so much noise!' said Debbie to her class.
  to
  Debbie told her class not to make so much noise.

- **Temporal changes**
  'I'll see you tomorrow, at 10 o'clock,' said Ray.
  the
  Ray arranged to meet me the following day at 10 o'clock.

- **Pronoun changes**
  'I'll give you a hand as soon as I can,' said Lesley.
  me
  Lesley told me she would give me a hand as soon as she could.

- **Position of verb in questions – no inversion**
  'How long have you been married?' Rosy asked her mother.
  she
  Rosy asked her mother how long she had been married.

- **Inclusion of *if* or *whether* when there is no question-word**
  'Would you prefer smoking or non-smoking?' asked the steward.
  enquired
  The steward enquired whether we would prefer smoking or non-smoking.

- **'Hidden' indirect questions**
  'Do you know what time it is?' asked Dave.
  I
  Dave asked if I knew what time it was.
- **Reporting verbs – see also below**
  'Why don't you go out for a walk, Sam?' said her father.
  she
  Sam's father suggested she should go out for a walk.

Words like *suggest* are very useful for reporting what a speaker said, because they give a kind of summary; they can also make the report more interesting.

Other reporting verbs

warn, tell, order, advise, invite, encourage, remind, persuade (plus pronoun plus infinitive with *to*)
  'I think you should stay at the Highland Hotel,' said Mr McPhee.
  us
  Mr McPhee advised us to stay at the Highland Hotel.

admit, deny, apologise for, accuse someone of … (plus *-ing*)
  'You took my money, Kevin!' said Angela.
  Kevin
  Angela accused Kevin of taking her money.

suggest (plus pronoun plus *should* plus infinitive without *to*)
  'I think you'd better stay in bed a little longer,' said the nurse.
  I
  The nurse suggested I should stay in bed a little longer.

suggest (plus *-ing*)
  'Why don't we go to the theatre for a change?' said Fiona.
  to
  Fiona suggested going to the theatre for a change.

offer, refuse, promise (plus infinitive)
  'You can't come in, I'm afraid,' the manager said to Pete.
  to
  The manager refused to let Pete come in.

Exercise 10

Complete the second sentence with between two and five words, including the word given, so that it has a similar meaning to the first sentence. (The sentences practise different aspects of reported speech.)

1 'I'm sorry I caused you a problem,' Paula said.
   for
   Paula _____ me a problem.
2 'I'll carry your case for you,' Lois told Clive.
   Clive's
   Lois _____ case for him.
3 'I didn't break the plate,' said Mandy.
   denied
   Mandy _____ the plate.
4 'You have beautiful hair,' said Don to Meg.
   she
   Don told _____ beautiful hair.
5 'I wouldn't do that if I were you,' Jan told me.
   advised
   Jan _____ that.
6 'Would you like to see my room?' Zoe asked Jo.
   felt
   Zoe asked Jo _____ seeing her room.
7 'Don't play with matches, they're dangerous,' Helen told her son.
   warned
   Helen _____ to play with matches.
8 'Can you tell me the way to the football stadium?' I asked Daniel.
   knew
   I asked Daniel _____ the way to the football stadium.
9 'Shall I make you a cup of tea, dear?' Mrs Honeybone asked Paul.
   to
   Mrs Honeybone _____ Paul a cup of tea.
10 'It'd be better if you flew on a weekday,' the travel agent told us.
   to
   The travel agent _____ fly on a weekday.

135

Conditionals

A 'conditional' idea can be connected to now, the past or the future and can be expressed using a variety of words including *if*. Look at the following examples, in particular:

– the verb tenses
– whether a 'positive' or 'negative' idea is being expressed

If the unemployment situation doesn't improve, many young people may find it difficult to get the kind of jobs they want.
Unless James arrives soon, I'm going without him.
Put your glasses on or/otherwise you'll damage your eyes.
If I were you, I'd go to Canada.
Anne wouldn't live in the city centre if she didn't have to.
My father said he would lend me $500 provided/as long as I paid it back within a year.
I would have a better job today if I'd gone to university.
Without/But for your help, I wouldn't have got the job.

Exercise 11

Complete the following sentences, which practise some of the basic conditional structures, so that they have the same meaning as the first sentence.

1 Say 'please', or I won't give it to you.
  If you don't …
  If you …
  Unless you …
2 I hope it stops raining soon, then I can go for a walk.
  If it doesn't …
  If it …
3 I'll tell you provided you promise to keep it a secret.
  If you …
  Unless …
4 Debbie is very tall, that's why she can't be a ballet dancer.
  If Debbie was/were …
  If Debbie wasn't/weren't …

5 I haven't got enough time to start again, unfortunately.
  If I …
6 They didn't understand the film because they missed the beginning.
  They would …
7 Sam forgot to set his alarm clock so he overslept this morning.
  If Sam …
8 You're cold because you forgot to bring a sweater with you.
  You wouldn't …
  If you hadn't …

Exercise 12

Complete the second sentence with between two and five words, including the word given, so that it has a similar meaning to the first sentence.

1 We couldn't have won the competition without your support.
  we
  If _____ your support, we couldn't have won the competition.
2 I really think you should ring Chris today.
  were
  If I _____ ring Chris today.
3 You'll understand him if you listen to him carefully.
  won't
  You _____ you listen to him carefully.
4 But for her map of the town, Maria would have got lost.
  she
  Maria would have got lost _____ a map of the town.
5 It's a good thing you brought some sandwiches, otherwise we'd be hungry.
  brought
  We'd be hungry _____ some sandwiches.

136

6 Ian isn't working here now because he didn't listen to Clare's advice.
he
If Ian had listened to Clare's advice,
.... here now.

7 Polly doesn't understand because nobody explained the situation to her.
somebody
Polly .... explained the situation to her.

If only / I wish / I regret

Look at these examples of structures which express a regret about something either in the past or the present.

I wish/If only I had some money. (but I haven't unfortunately)
I wish/If only I could swim. (but I can't)
David wishes he had worked harder. (but he didn't)
If only she had never met him. (but she did)
I wish/If only he would make less noise. (but he won't and I can't make him)
I regret telling her my telephone number.
Do you regret not marrying him?
Paula regretted her decision

Exercise 13

Complete the sentences to practise the verb tenses that go with these constructions. There is no word limit for this exercise.

1 John would love a car.
John wishes …
2 I should have gone to the party last night. I'm sorry I didn't.
I regret …
3 Zoe would like to live in a hot country.
Zoe wishes …
4 I'm really sorry I told them the truth.
If only I …
5 I really regret coming to work today.
I wish …

6 That phone has been ringing for ages. Why doesn't someone answer it?
I wish someone …

Exercise 14

Complete the second sentence with between two and five words, including the word given, so that it has a similar meaning to the first sentence.

1 Helen regrets not going to bed early last night.
wishes
Helen .... to bed early last night.

2 David was really sorry he hadn't managed to have a holiday.
able
David wished .... to have a holiday.

3 I don't see him anymore, which is a pity.
still
I wish .... him.

4 I'd love to be rich!
I
I .... rich!

5 Jill wished she hadn't resigned from her job.
regretted
Jill .... from her job.

Past simple / Present perfect

for/since/ago
Look at these examples, and do the exercise which follows.

It's five years since I last smoked.
for
I haven't smoked for five years.

I stopped smoking five years ago.
since
It's five years since I last smoked.

Henry lives in France – he moved there ten years ago.
living
Henry has been living in France for ten years.

Exercise 15

Complete the second sentence with between two and five words, including the word given, so that it has a similar meaning to the first sentence.

1 Brian started work here two and a half years ago.
worked
Brian .... two and a half years.

2 I haven't seen my cousin for ages.
saw
It's .... my cousin.

3 Clare has been a politician for 20 years.
politician
Clare .... 20 years ago.

4 I last saw Margaret in 1984.
seen
I .... 1984.

still/yet

Look at these examples, and do the exercise which follows.

> George began writing his book five years ago, and he's still writing it.
> When Dorothy arrived to take Richard out, he was still getting ready.
> Is my room free, or is it still being cleaned?
> Have you done your homework yet?
> You can't go in there, the maid hasn't cleaned it yet.

Exercise 16

Complete the second sentence with between two and five words, including the word given, so that it has a similar meaning to the first sentence.

1 We haven't received Ms Craig's application form yet.
still
Ms Craig .... sent in her application form.

2 The house is still unsold, I'm afraid.
yet
The house .... , I'm afraid.

3 The kidnapper is still in the house.
left
The kidnapper .... yet.

4 I don't think Bob has finished his meal yet.
is
I think Bob .... his meal.

the first time etc.

Look at these examples, and do the exercise which follows.

> I've never met her before.
> This is the first time I've met her.
> That was the best party I've ever had.
> I've never had a better party.

Exercise 17

Complete the second sentence with between two and five words, including the word given, so that it has a similar meaning to the first sentence.

1 I've never seen a better example of Dali's work, I'm quite sure.
seen
This is the best example of Dali's work ...., I'm quite sure.

2 Have you been to Tibet before?
first
Is this the .... visited Tibet?

3 That was the fastest Howard has ever run!
faster
Howard .... than that!

Preferences

Look at these ways of saying which of two things or activities you prefer.

> I prefer the theatre to the cinema.
> I prefer walking to running.
> I'd (would) rather work than sleep.

Look at these ways of saying what you want (or don't want) to do.

> 'Come up and have some coffee.' 'I'd rather go home, actually.'
> 'Shall we go?' 'I'd prefer to have another coffee.'
> 'How old are you?' 'I'd rather not tell you.'
> 'Let's go out.' 'I'd prefer not to.'

Look at these ways of saying what you want (or don't want) someone **else** to do.

> I'd rather you came early tonight, I don't want to be up late.
> Please say if you'd rather I didn't come at all.
> I'd prefer you to be honest, not just to say things that please me.
> Mummy would prefer you not to throw your food, children.

Exercise 18

Complete the second sentence with between two and five words, including the word given, so that it has a similar meaning to the first sentence.

1 Emily said she would rather listen than talk to people.
preferred
Emily said she _____ talking to people.

2 'I prefer listening to the radio to watching TV,' said John.
rather
John claimed _____ to the radio than watch TV.

3 Marilyn prefers Scotch whisky to Irish whiskey.
drink
Marilyn _____ Scotch whisky than Irish whiskey.

4 I'd rather you didn't talk to me like that!
not
I _____ to talk to me like that!

5 Sonja doesn't want to talk about it just now.
rather
Sonja _____ talk about it just now.

6 Please don't throw all that food away.
didn't
I _____ throw all that food away.

7 Mel told Fred that she'd rather he stayed away from her.
prefer
Mel told Fred that _____ stay away from her.

Opposite structures, similar meanings

so / such / too / not ... enough
Look at this example.

> The table was very heavy. Ewan could not lift it. He was not strong.

The table was too heavy for Ewan to lift.
Ewan was not strong enough to lift the table.
The table was so heavy that Ewan couldn't lift it.
It was such a heavy table that Ewan couldn't lift it.

Exercise 19

Using the four constructions above, link the following information in four different ways.

> The door handle was very high. Pam could not reach it. She was not very tall.

Exercise 20

Complete the second sentence with between two and five words, including the word given, so that it has a similar meaning to the first sentence.

1 The news was so terrible that nobody believed it.
such
It .... that nobody believed it.

2 Martin was such a slow walker that he got left behind.
so
Martin .... that he got left behind.

3 There were so many people in the room that I couldn't see anything.
was
The room .... that I couldn't see anything.

4 The weather was too cold for anybody to go out.
such
It was .... went out.

5 Wendy is too young to vote in the elections.
old
Wendy .... to vote in the elections.

not as ... as ... / more than
Look at these examples.

Gary is easier to understand than William.
William is not as easy to understand as Gary.
Sarah cooks better than I do.
I don't cook as well as Sarah (does).
People are much less friendly than they used to be.
People are not as friendly as they were.

Exercise 21

Complete the second sentence with between two and five words, including the word given, so that it has a similar meaning to the first sentence.

1 This computer isn't working as well as it used to.
work
This computer .... it does now.

2 People used to have more children than they do nowadays.
as
People don't .... they used to.

3 Geoff is not nearly as bad at chemistry as I am.
than
I'm .... at chemistry.

4 More money is spent on defence than on education.
as
Not .... on education as on defence.

quite near / not far / a long way
Look at these examples.

It's not far to the city centre from here.
The city centre is quite near here.
It's a long way from my home to the office.

Exercise 22

Complete the second sentence with between two and five words, including the word given, so that it has a similar meaning to the first sentence.

1 My office is not very far from my home.
quite
I live .... my office.

2 It's only a short distance from London to Oxford.
not
Oxford .... London.

3 Is Paris far from the Channel Tunnel?
long
Is Paris .... the Channel Tunnel?

any/no/every
Look at these examples.

There wasn't anybody/anyone in the room.
There was nobody/no one in the room.
Nothing will stop me going.
There isn't anything that will stop me going.
Everybody/Everyone left early.
Nobody/No one stayed late.

Exercise 23

Complete the second sentence with between two and five words, including the word given, so that it has a similar meaning to the first sentence.

1 Nothing is too much trouble for him.
   isn't
   There _____ too much trouble for him.

2 There isn't anywhere in the world that I haven't visited.
   nowhere
   There _____ that I haven't visited.

3 Because everybody remembered to bring a present, the party was a success.
   forgot
   The party was successful because _____ to bring a present.

4 People ate all the food on the table.
   left
   There _____ on the table.

Different forms of the same word

A sentence can be rewritten using one of the words in a different part of speech. This means moving between nouns, verbs, adjectives and adverbs. Sometimes this produces constructions with prepositions (see Appendices 1 and 2) or other phrasal vocabulary.

Exercise 24

Complete the following sentences. Write alternative ways of saying the same thing using the words given. Sometimes you will have to change the form of the given verb to make it fit. There is no word limit for this exercise. The sentences follow the order of the words given.

1 **rare (adj)   rarely (adv)**
   I don't go to the cinema very often nowadays.
   My visits *to the cinema are rare nowadays.*
   I *rarely go the cinema.*

2 **difficult (adj)   difficulty in (noun)**
   It was hard for David to make the decision.
   It was a …
   David had …

3 **by accident (noun)   accidentally (adv)
   an accident (noun)**
   I didn't mean to break your porcelain dish.
   I broke …
   I …
   Breaking …

4 **child (noun)   childhood (noun)**
   When I was young I lived in India.
   When …
   During …

5 **intend (verb)   intention of (noun)**
   Anne didn't mean to say that.
   Anne …
   Anne had …

6 **explain (verb)   explanation for (noun)**
   It's difficult to find a reason why the accident happened.
   It's difficult to …
   It's difficult to find …

7 **succeed in (verb)   success (in) (noun)
   successful (adj)**
   I've never managed to beat Tom at tennis.
   I've never …
   I've had …
   I've never been …

8 **apparently (adv)   appear (verb)**
   It seems that Nick refused to leave.
   Nick …
   It …

9 choose (verb)   choice (noun)
Joe hasn't decided whether to study history or politics.
Joe hasn't …
Joe hasn't made …

10 agree (verb)   agreement (noun)
The committee decided what to do by the end of the meeting.
The committee …
The committee reached …

11 apology (noun)   apologise for (verb)
The Prime Minister said he was sorry about the financial scandal.
The PM made …
The PM …

12 plan (verb)   plans (noun)
What are you going to do for Bernard's birthday?
What are you …?
What are …?

13 complain (verb)   complaint (noun)
Walter said he didn't like the way he was spoken to.
Walter …
Walter made …

14 possible (adj)   possibly (adv)
Do you think you could lend me some money?
Would it be …?
Could you …?

15 kiss (verb)   kiss (noun)
The princess quickly placed her lips on the frog's nose.
The princess …
The princess gave …

16 apply (verb)   application (noun)
Sam filled in a form in order to get a visa.
Sam …
Sam wrote/made …

17 blame (verb)   blame (noun)
Why do you always think it's my fault?
Why do you always …?
Why do you always put …?

18 responsible (adj)   responsibility (noun)
What you do is up to you.
You must be …
You have to take …

19 similar (adj)   similar (adj)   similarity (noun)
There's not much difference between Colin and Jill.
Colin and Jill …
Colin is …
There's a lot …

20 surprising (adj)   surprise (noun)
Kevin was surprised to see all his friends in the restaurant.
Kevin found …
To Kevin's …

Exercise 25

In Exercise 24 you practised moving between different parts of speech. Now do the same, but this time complete the second sentence with between two and five words, including the word given, so that it has a similar meaning to the first sentence.

1 We are in complete agreement with the majority.
totally
We *totally agree with* the majority.

2 The danger is that the boat will sink.
of
The boat ⸏ sinking.

3 I was surprised to see her appear so suddenly.
me
Her sudden ⸏ by surprise.

4 I think you must be mistaken.
must
I think ⸏ mistake.

5 Your anxiety is hard to control when your children are late home.
not
It's difficult ⸏ when your children are late home.

6 We have no time to discuss that problem now.
for
There is ⸏ of that problem now.

7 Barry washed his face quickly.
gave
Barry .... wash.

8 Why don't you call Tony and tell him the news?
a
I suggest you .... and tell him the news.

9 They were married 20 years ago.
took
Their .... 20 years ago.

10 It's important that we consider everyone's opinions before deciding.
into
Everyone's opinions must .... before deciding.

Phrasal verbs

It is possible to have your knowledge of phrasal verbs tested through sentence transformation. As with all kinds of phrasal vocabulary, you need to build up your knowledge slowly. However, in this part of the exam, you'll probably only have one question on a phrasal verb (and maybe not even one) – so don't worry too much.

Exercise 26

Complete the second sentence with between two and five words, including the word given, so that it has a similar meaning to the first sentence.

1 I don't see why I should tolerate the way you speak to me.
put
Why should ___I put up with___ the way you speak to me?

2 Alex and I enjoy each other's company a lot.
get
Alex and I .... together.

3 Barry spoke angrily to me because I'd damaged his bike.
off
Barry .... damaging his bike.

4 It's ages since anyone has thought of an idea.
come
No one has .... for a long time.

5 I used to enjoy watching horror movies but I don't now.
gone
I .... horror movies.

6 You can't change your decision now, I'm afraid.
to
You must .... what you've already decided, I'm afraid.

7 The publicity for the film was so awful I decided not to see it.
put
I .... the film by the publicity.

8 We waved goodbye to Jim at the airport.
off
We .... at the airport.

9 It's impossible for me to make sense of what she said.
work
I .... she meant.

10 The younger generation used to show respect for the older generation.
up
The older generation used .... by the younger generation.

SUGGESTED APPROACH FOR PART 3 OF THE USE OF ENGLISH PAPER

1 Read the whole sentence.
2 Look at the key word.
3 Think about what is being tested – passive, indirect speech, opposites, same word but different part of speech etc.
4 Write your sentence and remember:
   – you must not change the key word
   – you must use between two and five words to fill the gap

Exercise 27   Exam practice

For Questions 1–10, complete the second sentence so that it has a similar meaning to the first sentence, using the word given. **Do not change the word given.** You must use between two and five words, including the word given. There is an example at the beginning (0).

Example:

0 I've never seen such a bad film as that one.
   ever
   That's the .... seen.
   The gap can be filled by the words 'worst film I have ever' so you write:
   worst film I have ever

1 I didn't realise that the train station was so far from the city centre.
   way
   I didn't realise that the train station was .... from the city centre.

2 Amy regrets not telling her brother the truth.
   wishes
   Amy .... her brother the truth.

3 You can't compare the two tax systems.
   make
   It's not possible .... the two tax systems.

4 'I wouldn't sail too close to the rocks if I were you,' Lisa said to Roger.
   warned
   Lisa .... sail too close to the rocks.

5 Why don't you give David your answer?
   had
   I think .... David your answer.

6 I'm sure Jack left his job for a good reason.
   must
   Jack .... a good reason for leaving his job.

7 It was because Carol was so generous that the club managed to survive.
   to
   It was .... that the club managed to survive.

8 I'm very pleased to announce the opening of Connell's new supermarket.
   great
   It is .... I announce the opening of Connell's new supermarket.

9 The weather stopped the concert from going ahead.
   impossible
   The weather .... the concert to go ahead.

10 'You'll have to replace your printer soon,' said the salesman.
   have
   The salesman told me that my printer .... soon.

UNIT 4 *Error correction*

Paper 3 Part 4

Familiarisation exercise

For Questions **1–6**, read the text below and look carefully at each line. Some of the lines are correct, and some have a word which should not be there. If a line is correct, put a tick (✓) at the end of the line. If the line has a word which should not be there, write the incorrect word at the end of the line. There are two examples at the beginning (**0** and **00**).

FOREIGN TRAVEL

0	My first visit to another country was when I went	✓
00	with a school group to a seaside town in the Belgium.	*the*
1	I can't to remember much about it, but I know I found	
2	it very exciting being abroad and hearing different	
3	languages which being spoken around me. Nowadays,	
4	of course, people also travel abroad all the time, but	
5	in those days it was still considered quite unusual	
6	to go to another country for your own holidays.	

Checklist of errors that are often tested in Part 4.

Prepositions:	*about, at, by, for, from, in, of, through, to, up* etc.
Articles:	*a, an, the, some*
Pronouns:	*she, he, it, they, me, my, our, their* etc.
Auxiliary/modal verbs:	*be, been, being, do, has, had, must, was, will* etc.
Reflexives:	*myself, ourselves, itself* etc.
Miscellaneous:	*all, also, as, already, away, because, even, ever, how, just, more, much, one, no, only, out, own, quite, rather, so, such, since, still, than, that, those, very, when, which, while, who*

For Exercises 1–6 read each text and put a tick (✓) at the end of a line where the given word is used correctly, and a cross (✗) where it is used wrongly. These practice exercises allow you to concentrate on one or two words at a time, so the texts are not in exam format and the 'balance' of wrong and right lines is not the same as in the exam. They should not be done all together. Select one or two at different times, depending on where you feel you need the practice.

Exercise 1

to (three correct uses, five incorrect)
1 When we reached to our hotel that night, our ✗
2 hearts sank. There were no lights, and it seemed to ✓
3 us to be completely empty. But we rang the bell,
4 and soon we heard to the footsteps of someone
5 approaching to the door. When it opened, there
6 was Mrs Llewellyn, smiling and inviting to Ken
7 and me to come in and make ourselves at home.
8 We entered, and she gave to us a nice cup of tea.

for (two correct uses, four incorrect)
1 Traffic on the M25 motorway was worse than for
2 ever last night! It took me for more than four hours
3 to get for about five miles, and at one point we
4 didn't move for at least an hour – people got
5 out of their cars and walked around for to
6 relieve the boredom of sitting there for so long!

of (four correct uses, four incorrect)
1 We are very often not aware of dreaming. In fact,
2 many of people say they never dream at all. But
3 everyone does dream, even if they don't realise of
4 it. Several scientists think of dreams as being one
5 of the ways in which our brain sorts out all the events,
6 pictures and impressions of the past day – rather in
7 the way of a computer sorts all the new work
8 of which it has just done.

about (four correct uses, four incorrect)
1 I wish to complain about the bus service from York
2 to Hull. You recently promised us about more
3 buses, and we were happy about this, since we have
4 often said there were too few at about busy times.
5 However, yesterday we learnt about that you now
6 plan to *reduce* the number! When I heard about
7 this I was very angry about it, and I am now
8 considering about going to work by car in future.

Exercise 2

the (four correct uses, three incorrect)
1 Tresco, with a population of about a hundred, is the ✓
2 second largest of the six inhabited islands which ✓
3 make up the Isles of Scilly. This is a small group ✗
4 of the islands, lying about thirty miles or so ✗
5 south-west of the Land's End. Tresco is a private ✗
6 island, and it was the first place in England to ✓
7 make the education compulsory.

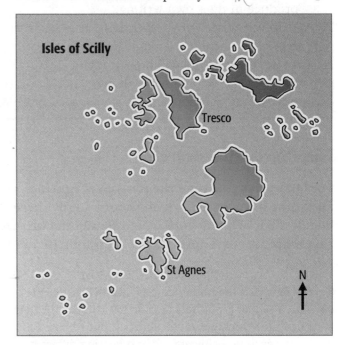

Isles of Scilly

Tresco

St Agnes

N

a (five correct uses, five incorrect)
1 Another of the islands is St Agnes, which has a ✗
2 quiet and gentle scenery. There are a few
3 guest houses, a couple of small tea-rooms, and
4 a very friendly pub by the water's edge where
5 they serve a wonderful food. The sea around the
6 island can be difficult when there is a strong
7 northerly wind, but in a good weather, boats will
8 take visitors out to the western rocks where a
9 lots of ships have been wrecked. The sea is a
10 very dangerous unless you are a good sailor.

Exercise 3

it (three correct uses, three incorrect)
1 My home town it is small, but a lot of things
2 happen there and it is actually a very nice place
3 to live. Sometimes I wish it that there was more for
4 people to do in the evening, and that it was a bit
5 nearer to the capital, but otherwise I like it the
6 feeling that it is my home, and I know most people
   I meet.

Exercise 4

will (four correct uses, two incorrect)
1 If you will really want to become a top athlete,
2 you will have to give up a lot of things.
3 Whenever you will go out for a meal with friends,
4 for instance, you will always have to explain
5 to them what kind of food will harm your training
6 programme, and what you will be able to eat.

be (three correct uses, two incorrect)
1 One problem with TV is that you can't always be
2 sure whether what you are going to be see when
3 you switch on will be fact or fiction – a picture of
4 people with guns could be part of the news, or it
5 might be come from a war film.

been (three correct uses, three incorrect)
1 Strange things have been happening in China,
2 where a car mechanic was recently been arrested by
3 the police: he had been started landslides above a
4 road, and the stones had been damaged cars which
5 had then been taken to his garage to be repaired.
6 The scheme had been quite successful for a while.

Exercise 5

much (three correct uses, five incorrect)
1 Some cities are much nicer to live in than others,
2 and it is not always much easy to say why. It doesn't
3 necessarily have much to do with size – New York ✗
4 and London are much desirable places to live,
5 despite their much greater size than other cities. ✗
6 It's difficult to say why Kyoto is so much attractive:
7 perhaps it's because the much hilly land around ✗
8 the city can be seen, giving a feeling much of space.

all (four correct uses, three incorrect)
1 You shouldn't always believe all what you read or
2 hear in advertisements. After all, you know that
3 all advertisers want is to sell you things you didn't
4 know you all needed. What adverts do is
5 tell you part of all the truth, the bit which they want
6 you to believe. They conveniently forget all about
7 all the negative aspects of their products.

one(s) (four correct uses, four incorrect)
1 Why do some ones of us have fears which we can't
2 explain, including ones which we know are illogical,
3 or even stupid? Perhaps there is a one part of our
4 mind where fears live, one which we can't reach
5 through logic or discussion. Whether it is one fear
6 of spiders, a fear of being on one's own, or any
7 oone other of a number of similar phobias, the fear
8 is very real to the unfortunate one who suffers.

so (two correct uses, three incorrect)
1 I don't think so that most young people today think
2 of 'industry' in terms of factories or of air so
3 dirty that people living nearby suffer so bad health.
4 Industry has changed so much in the last 50 years
5 so that our grandparents would hardly recognise it.

Exercise 6

In the following short texts, you are still concentrating on seeing how commonly tested items can be used correctly and incorrectly. This time the texts contain two or three different words to work on. Read each text and mark ✓ or ✗ as appropriate at the end of the line.

Find **one** correct and **one** incorrect use of each of the words below.

quite   then   more
1 On a flight from Rome quite recently, a passenger
2 then fell ill, so the steward asked whether there
3 were any more doctors aboard. There were 16 of
4 them! However, he then found that they were all
5 Doctors of Philosophy, who knew more about
6 maths than medicine, which was quite a pity.

Find **one** correct and **one** incorrect use of each of the words below.

had   being

1 I remember when I had first tried to play
2 golf. I was being on holiday in Spain with
3 friends who had played for years. But while
4 the rules were still being explained to me I
   was hit by a golf ball and knocked out!

Find **two** correct and **two** incorrect uses of each of the words below.

rather   own

1 'Shall we go out, or would you rather prefer us to
2 stay at home on our own tonight?' asked Sam.
3 'There's rather a good film on TV,' said Ben,
4 'and my own headache is still there, so really my
5 own preference is to stay in for a quiet evening.
6 But I'd rather not cook if you don't mind.'
7 'Fine,' said Sam. 'I'll get pizzas. I'd rather better
8 go before they get busy. I'll get my own coat.'

Find **two** correct and **two** incorrect uses of each of the words below.

it   itself

1 'The Great Fire of London' is the name which it
2 is given to an event which in 1666 it destroyed
3 houses, churches, and half the city centre itself.
4 The fire started itself in a bakery's bread oven
5 and it spread quickly in the strong wind.
6 Although it burnt for three days, not many people
7 died. There was itself plenty of warning and most
8 escaped and waited until the fire burnt itself out.

Find **two** correct and **two** incorrect uses of each of the words below.

even   also   always

1 The Finnish sauna (steam bath) is even very
2 important in the life and also the culture of this
3 country, where winters are always dark but
4 where the midsummer sun also never sets.
5 The sauna has stayed the same even for
6 years. It has always been central to people's lives
7 and once was even where babies were born! Today
8 the sauna is always as popular as ever, not only
9 in Finland, but also abroad – wherever Finns go
10 they expect a sauna, even if they have to build it
11 themselves. There are a million saunas also in
12 a country of five million people. There is always
   a sauna in the Parliament building.

Exercise 7

Look at the checklist on page 145 to remind yourself of the kinds of words which are tested in this part of the examination. Then read the text below. Twelve of the 18 lines contain a word which should not be there. If a line is correct put a tick, and if a line has an incorrect word write it at the end of the line, as in the example.

AIR TRAVEL

1 The first advantage of air travel it is that it's   *it*
2 quick. You can fly from Europe to Asia in a   ✓
3 few hours, and now with even faster planes, it   ✗
4 is getting quicker. It is very much easy travelling   ✗
5 by plane; your luggage is looked after and all what   ✗
6 you have to do is enjoy of a meal. Your   ✗
7 comfortable seat is reserved and there is a good   ✓
8 service from the staff. Another point in favour is so
9 that it is quite cheap also for long-distance flights.
10 On the other hand, flying has some disadvantages.   ✓
11 Perhaps the first is that you are fly directly
12 to your destination and you have no feeling of
13 travelling yourself from one country to another.
14 Another point is that because air travel is so
15 quick, people suffer from the tiredness; so they
16 save time travelling, but waste it for recovering.
17 One other problem is that fog can already delay
18 you and then all the advantage of speed is lost.

148

SUGGESTED APPROACH FOR PART 4 OF THE USE OF ENGLISH PAPER

1 Read the title of the text – it'll help you to know what's coming next.

2 Read the text through once quickly.

3 Read through sentence by sentence; remember the extra words must be wrong, not just extra.

4 Show your answer either by a ✓ or by writing the extra word itself. There must be something for every line.

Exercise 8   Exam practice

For Questions 1–15, read the text below and look carefully at each line. Some of the lines are correct, and some have a word which should not be there. If a line is correct, put a tick (✓) at the end of the line. If a line has a word which should **not** be there, write the word at the end of the line. There are two examples at the beginning (0 and 00).

APPLICATION FOR A JOB

Dear Sir or Madam,

0	I refer to your advertisement which I have seen in	✓
00	today's 'Gazette', and should wish to apply for the post of	should
1	Tour Leader. You will see from my enclosed CV that I have	
2	already had some experience of this kind of a work.	
3	Last summer I have worked with Korean visitors to York,	
4	showing to them the most famous attractions and at the same	
5	time explaining them the history of the city. I very much	
6	enjoyed do this job, and found that in spite of not speaking	
7	their language I could communicate well with my clients.	
8	I was regularly received compliments and gifts from them.	
9	The job which advertised by you seems to be very similar	
10	to my previous one, and I hope so that you will invite	
11	me for an interview, in order that we can discuss the	
12	possibility of my working for you. I can come to London at	
13	any time during for the next two weeks. If you would like	
14	to meet me, would you be so kind as to tell me how	
15	to get there to your office from the station?	

I look forward to hearing from you soon.

UNIT 5 *Word formation*

Paper 3 Part 5

> **INFORMATION**
>
> In Part 5 of the Use of English paper, you are given a text containing ten gaps. You must use the 'stem' word in CAPITALS at the end of each line to form a word that fits in the space in the same line.
>
> - The missing words are all 'content' words – nouns, adjectives, adverbs, and sometimes verbs.
> - As in all gap filling tests, you need to read and understand the whole text before trying to answer the questions.
> - You may have to look for clues in other parts of the text in order to find out what a missing word should be.

Familiarisation exercise

For Questions 1–4, read the text below. Use the word given in capitals at the end of each line to form a word that fits in the space in the same line. There is an example at the beginning (0).

ONE WAY TO MAKE MONEY

A man known as 'the human fly' climbed two thousand (0) *buildings*	**BUILD**
in the USA to earn money when he became (1)	**EMPLOY**
After he lost his job as an (2) .... , he decided to use his	**ENGINE**
(3) .... of mountaineering to help him, until he could find	**KNOW**
a more (4) .... job.	**PROFIT**

Checklist: What kind of word is it?
- a concrete noun (*friend*)? singular or plural?
- an abstract noun (*friendship*)?
- a 'positive' adjective (*successful*) or a 'negative' one (*unsuccessful*)?
- a comparative adjective (*greater*) or a superlative one (*biggest*)?
- a 'positive' adverb (*happily*) or a 'negative' one (*unhappily*)?
- a 'positive' verb (*encourage*) or a 'negative' one (*discourage*)? what part of the verb (*appears, appearing*)?

Exercise 1

The aim of this exercise is for you to see what kind of changes may be needed when you form a new word from the 'stem' word.

Read the following text. Look at the words in green, and decide what 'stem' word the examiners might have put at the end of each line. Then say what the function of the word in the text is. (Use the checklist on page 150 to help.) The first word has been done for you.

(1) The stem word must have been 'friend'; 'friendship' is an abstract noun.

ANIMALS AND MAN

Pets in the house help us relax and provide a kind of (**1**) friendship. In fact, they can do much more than that – the (**2**) presence of a pet is also believed to be good for our health. A recent American study (**3**) interestingly found that pet (**4**) ownership can be an important factor in the possible (**5**) survival of people with heart disease.

FRIEND

Health care workers often (**6**) encourage lonely or elderly people, or those with time to spare, to think about (**7**) getting a pet. In 18th century England, an (**8**) unusually forward-looking hospital for the mentally ill used to give its patients small animals to look after – having other creatures (**9**) dependent on them improved the patients' (**10**) feelings of importance and responsibility.

More recently, doctors have started to make (**11**) systematic use of pets for therapy, and even allow dogs to (**12**) accompany their owners to hospital.

Exercise 2

Read the following text about a school for stuntmen and women (actors who do the dangerous scenes in films). Decide what kind of word would fit in each gap – use the checklist on page 150 to help you. Then write a word that could logically fit in the gap. Here is an example of the kind of thinking process you should work through.

(1) The missing word describes the training school so it must be an adjective, and possibly in the superlative form because 'the world's' means 'in the world'. It could describe the size, quality or age of the training school. Reading to the end of the passage it's clear that the adjective must be 'positive' rather than 'negative.' Possible answers: 'best', 'biggest', 'newest'.

ACTION ACADEMY

The world's (**1**) *newest* training academy for stuntmen and women is in Australia. It's located on a (**2**) .... part of the Queensland coast, and movie (**3**) .... are coming here from all over the world to make their action films. On their (**4**) ...., they find a wonderful climate, with (**5**) .... air and great scenery. The Academy itself checks (**6**) .... for its courses carefully; they do not want to waste their time training (**7**) .... people.

Look at the following list of 'stem' words for the gaps in the text on page 151; some of the words may be ones you've already chosen. Put them in the correct form in the appropriate gap. They are already in the correct order.

NEW   SUN   PRODUCE   ARRIVE   POLLUTE   APPLY   SUIT

Exercise 3

Read the following text. The missing words have been filled in but, unfortunately, **six** of them are **wrong**. Make the necessary corrections. Think about:

- function of the word
- positive/negative
- singular/plural
- verb endings

The first word has been done for you as an example.

(1) Wrong. The form of the verb should be the past participle: 'identified'.

THE LANGUAGES OF NEW GUINEA

750 languages have been (1) *identifying* in New Guinea and the   **IDENTITY**
(2) *surrounding* islands. This represents by far the greatest single   **SURROUND**
(3) *concentration* of languages in the world. More than half the   **CONCENTRATE**
languages have (4) *similarly.* to each other, often very close ones.   **SIMILAR**
Others, mainly in the (5) *mountain..* interior, are spoken   **MOUNTAIN**
by just a few hundred people. Almost (6) *certainly.*, there are   **CERTAIN**
tribes that remain (7) *discovered* in the remote parts of this   **DISCOVER**
land, and (8) *scientific.* believe that these people too may   **SCIENCE**
speak other languages. So the total of 750 is (9) *likely..* to   **LIKE**
stay the same if further (10) *exploration* of the country takes place.   **EXPLORE**

Exercise 4

The words in green in the following sentence can be used to form other words with different grammatical functions. Fill in the numbered spaces in the table below. Use a dictionary to help you. Watch out for possible changes in spelling. The first one has been done for you.

My advice to tourists when visiting a foreign country is to behave naturally.

Concrete noun	Abstract noun	Verb	'Positive' adjective	'Negative' adjective
	advice	(1) *to advise*	(2)	(3)
tourists	(4)	(5)		
(6)	(7)	to visit		
(8)			foreign	
	(9)	to (mis)behave		

Now read the text below. Use the word in capitals at the end of each line to form a word that fits in the space in the same line.

Although (**10**) **....** is a very important industry in many countries, the bad (**11**) **....** of some people on holiday has turned them into unwelcome (**12**) **....** in some places.

TOUR
BEHAVE
VISIT

Exercise 5

Now do the same with the following sentence. Fill in the numbered spaces in the table and then complete the text below it.

> The scientist was dismissed by his employer for making the wrong decision

Concrete noun	Abstract noun	Verb	'Positive' adjective	'Negative' adjective
scientist	(**1**) *science*		(**2**)	(**3**)
	(**4**)	to dismiss		
employer	(**5**)	(**6**)	(**7**)	(**8**)
	decision	(**9**)	(**10**)	(**11**)

My (**12**) .... in public relations didn't last long, as I was not only weak and (**13**) .... in my dealings with clients, but also hopelessly (**14**) .... in my research methods.

EMPLOY
DECIDE
SCIENCE

SUMMARY

⇑ You have:
- practised identifying the 'function' of missing words
- thought about what kind of 'stem' words you will be given
- looked at the sort of changes you'll need to make before your new word will fit in the gap

⇓ You are now going to:
- look at a reference list which can help you to 'word build'
- practise two particular aspects of word building which often cause problems
- be aware of how one word can lead you to many others, and can help you build up your vocabulary

USE OF ENGLISH

The following word formation table shows the most common noun and adjective endings, prefixes and other suffixes. Use it for reference.

Word formation table

Noun (people)	Abstract noun	Adjective
-or (visitor) -er (teacher) -ist (cyclist) -ian (politician)	-ment (argument) -tion (attention) -sion (permission) -(i)ty (poverty) -ance (importance) -ence (independence) -ry (misery) -ness (sadness) -al (arrival) -age (shortage) -ism (racism) -dom (freedom)	-ive (attractive) -ical (practical) -(i)ous (generous) -ful (beautiful) -y (happy) -ar (popular) -ised (centralised) -ly (weekly) -ic (economic) -ing (interesting) -ed (interested) -able/-ible (capable)
Prefixes	**Miscellaneous suffixes**	**Verbs**
un- (unhappy) in- (inability) im- (impractical) ir- (irregular) il- (illegal) dis- (disappear) mis- (misbehave) over- (oversleep)	-less (homeless) -hood (childhood) -ship (leadership) -proof (windproof)	-en (strengthen) -ate (educate) -ify (horrify) -ise/ize (criticise) un- (undo) dis- (disagree) de- (centralise)

Exercise 6

Use the table above to help you complete the sentences below.

Nouns (people)
1 A person who practises law is a _____lawyer_____ .
2 A person who plays the piano is a

   _____ .

3 A person who lives in Brazil is a

   _____ .

Abstract nouns
4 A factory that pollutes the river is causing

   _____ .

5 A person who is generous shows

   _____ .

6 A person who is kind shows _____ .

Adjectives
7 Someone who is naturally good at music is described as _____ .
8 Someone who shows great skill is described as _____ .

Prefixes
9 The opposite of understand is _____ .
10 The opposite of practical is _____ .

Miscellaneous suffixes

11 People who do not have a home are described as _____ .

12 The area where your neighbours live is your _____ .

Verbs

13 You put something sweet in your coffee in order to _____ it.

14 The opposite of to like is _____ .

Exercise 7

Spelling changes

Some words need more spelling changes than others. Complete the following, paying particular attention to spelling.

1 A person who is happy is full of ___happiness___ .

2 If someone is very poor, they are living in _____ .

3 Someone who feels anxious often shows their _____ .

4 If you make a pair of trousers longer, you _____ them.

5 If you ask someone to explain something, they'll give you an _____ .

6 A newspaper that's printed every day can be bought _____ .

7 When you ask how high a thing is, you want to know its _____ .

8 If you're proud of how strong you are, you show off your _____ .

9 When the police want to prove something, they look for _____ .

10 A builder needs the ground to be flat, so he _____ it.

Exercise 8

Negative prefixes

Negative prefixes can cause problems. First, when you're reading the text it's easy to miss the need for a negative, and secondly it's difficult to choose the right prefix. Use the word in capitals at the end of each sentence to form an appropriate negative word which fits in each gap. You'll sometimes have to make grammatical changes as well. (Look at the table on page 154 if you need help.)

1 Teachers found Mario's ___disobedience___ quite hard to deal with. OBEY
2 The Beacon Hotel is very good and surprisingly _____ . EXPENSE
3 Ralph got lost because the map he had with him was _____ . ACCURATE
4 By the end of his college days Max was going to lectures _____ . REGULAR
5 The police believe that Lauren _____ last Friday night. APPEAR
6 Ben fell 30 metres down the mountain but amazingly was _____ . INJURY
7 Some friends turned up _____ for dinner last night. EXPECT
8 In the UK it's _____ to buy cigarettes if you're under 16. LEGAL
9 Carrie is rather _____ considering she's already 21. MATURE
10 Megan's _____ made everybody feel very nervous. PATIENT
11 Harry left his keys in the car and had to get it _____ by the police. LOCK
12 The boss gave me a _____ look when I arrived two hours late. APPROVE

USE OF ENGLISH

SUGGESTED APPROACH FOR PART 5 OF THE USE OF ENGLISH PAPER

1 Look at the title – it'll help with your general understanding of the text.
2 Read the text.
3 For each gap, decide the function of the missing word.
4 Look out for negative meanings, plurals and verb endings.
5 If you've worked out the kind of word you need but don't know the word itself, have an intelligent guess! (Remember the possible endings, prefixes and suffixes.)
6 Remember that spelling can change when a word changes its form.
7 Check that the word fits with the meaning of the whole text.

Exercise 9   Exam practice

For Questions 1–10, read the text below. Use the word given in capitals at the end of each line to form a word that fits in the space in the same line. There is an example at the beginning (0).

HOWARD HUGHES: A SAD END

The American (0) *millionaire* Howard Hughes once knew the world's	MILLION
most (1) .... movie stars, but for the last 15 years of his life	ATTRACT
he had almost no (2) .... with the outside world. He	COMMUNICATE
became so (3) .... of illness that nobody else was permitted to	TERROR
touch his food, and no (4) .... were allowed to see him. He	VISIT
(5) .... moved from hotel to hotel, and in his room	SECRET
the only item of (6) .... , apart from a bed and a chair, was a screen	FURNISH
and projection (7) .... so that he could watch films. For days	EQUIP
he would eat only ice cream, and when he died his (8) .... had	WEIGH
gone down to only 40 kg because he ate so (9) .... . Despite	HEALTH
his huge wealth, he seems to have been a very (10) .... man.	HAPPY

Listening

The Listening chapter is in two sections.

Section A Listening and understanding teaches general listening skills which you'll need for all parts of the exam.

Section B Listening and answering exam questions applies these skills to the Paper 4 exam format. In this section you'll get help and practice in tackling the four parts of this paper.

SECTION A

Listening and understanding

Unit 1 Improving your understanding
Unit 2 Identifying and using the context
Unit 3 Keeping a clear head

SECTION B

Listening and answering exam questions

Unit 4 Short texts with multiple choice
Unit 5 Gap filling
Unit 6 Multiple matching
Unit 7 Two- or three-option answers

EXAM OVERVIEW PAPER 4 LISTENING (about 40 minutes)

Paper 4 has four parts:

PART 1	Multiple choice 8 questions	1 mark per question
PART 2	Note taking or gap filling 10 questions	1 mark per question
PART 3	Multiple matching 5 questions	1 mark per question
PART 4	Two- or three-option answers 7 questions	1 mark per question
Total:	30 questions	

UNIT 1 *Improving your understanding*

This unit gives you practice in:

- ► listening for the most important words
- ► getting ideas before you listen
- ► hearing the same thing said in a different way
- ► listening for general understanding and for specific details

Listening for the most important words

Exercise A1

Aim: to listen for the stressed words, which carry the information; to build up complete sentences from the stressed words.

When you're listening it's not necessary to hear and understand every word that's spoken. Your ears need to focus on the words that are **stressed**, that is, the words that come across most strongly. These words carry the main parts of the message. If you can hear these, you should have a good idea of what the piece is about.

You'll hear Zoe talking about her last family holiday. But you'll only hear the important words in each sentence, the rest has disappeared! Write down the words and phrases you hear for each sentence.

Sentence 1: *rented*   *house*   *small village* ....

Sentence 2: ....

Sentence 3: ....

Sentence 4: ....

Sentence 5: ....

Sentence 6: ....

Sentence 7: ....

Look at the words you've written down and guess what the woman was saying. Remember, Zoe was describing her last family holiday. Build the rest of the sentence around the words.

Sentence 1: *We rented a house in a small village in the hills about 30 minutes' drive from the coast.*

Now listen to the full recording of what Zoe said and check it against what you have written down. (Look at the tapescript on page 207 if you're not sure.)

Exercise A2

Aim: to listen for stressed words in order to complete a paragraph.

Look at what Zoe says next about her holiday. The stressed words have been removed so it's impossible to understand what she says: the stressed words are all 'content' words – nouns, verbs, adjectives – and they carry the meaning of what she's saying.

Listen to the recording once without stopping the tape. Then listen again and fill in the gaps. You will need to stop the tape to give yourself time to write.

When either _____ *John* _____ or _____ were not on _____ we _____ and _____ the _____. Then we'd all _____ for _____. The _____ there was _____, especially the _____. And the _____ couldn't believe their _____ with the _____. They came in _____ with _____ of _____, and little _____ in, and on the _____ we were there, the ice creams came _____ with _____. That was the _____ of the _____ two weeks for _____, I can tell you!

Exercise A3

Aim: to listen for stressed words in order to help you answer general comprehension questions.

You're going to hear a man talking about a course he went on. Listen once without stopping the tape. Remember to focus on hearing the stressed words to get a general idea of what he's talking about. Then, read Questions 1–5 below. Listen again and notice how the stressed words give you the answers to the questions.

1 Who wanted him to go on the course? *his boss*
2 Why?
3 What parts of the course did he enjoy?
4 How long was the course?
5 What positive result did the course have for him?

From your general understanding of the extract, answer these questions.

6 What kind of course was it?
7 How would you describe his feelings about the course – before, during and after?

159

Getting ideas before you listen

In real life (not classroom or exam life) you listen when you want to know something, e.g. from the TV news, having a conversation with a friend, on the telephone, and so on. You know what the topic is, and if you're not interested, you can choose not to listen.

In a listening test, you have to listen to whatever the examiner has chosen to put on the cassette. So you must use any information you're given – the instructions, the questions etc. – to start you thinking. In this way, when the tape starts playing you'll be prepared.

For example, you are told that you are going to hear two people talking about a film they both went to see. You should start imagining:

– who the two speakers are
– where they are having this conversation
– whether they both enjoyed the film (maybe one did and the other didn't)

Exercise A4

Aim: to think about what you are going to hear before you hear it.

Extract 1
Before you listen, look at the following words.

excursion   overbooked   sorry   refund

1 In what situation might you hear these words?
2 Who would you expect to hear using them?

Listen, and answer the following questions.

3 What is the problem?
4 How is the matter settled?

Extract 2
You're going to hear part of a talk about domestic cats. Before you listen, read the following incomplete statements about cats and decide how you could complete them. You may not know certain facts, but have a guess.

1 There are approximately ___*seven million*___ domestic cats in Britain.
2 The ancestors of all domestic cats came from _____ .
3 Cats became domesticated when _____ .
4 They were thought of as gods by _____ .
5 Cats express themselves most through the use of their _____ .
6 Before a fight, they often _____ in order to threaten their enemy.
7 When another cat comes into their territory, they sometimes _____ for hours.
8 The purring sound a cat makes is its way of saying

_____ .

Now listen and check your predictions against what the woman says. Stop the tape to give yourself time to write.

Extract 3

Two friends went to a party last night where they met some people they hadn't seen for a long time. You'll hear part of their conversation in which the friends talk about Robert and Paula, and how they have changed. Write two or three things you think you might hear in the conversation.

Paula doesn't seem as happy as she used to be.

🔊 Listen to the conversation and identify Robert and Paula, before and now, from the illustrations on the right. There are two extra illustrations which you do not need to use.

What did you hear that made you choose these particular illustrations? Listen again and complete the table below.

	Before	Now
Robert	*fatter*	
Paula		

Hearing the same thing said in a different way

Exercise A5

Aim: to listen for the ways in which things are expressed differently.

You're going to hear a woman reading from a story about an unemployed man. Look at sentences 1–14 below. These are not the words which the woman uses in the extract. You'll hear the same ideas but expressed differently.

🔊 Listen and match the phrases below with those you hear. They are in the same order as on the tape. Listen to the whole extract once without stopping, then play it again, stopping to give yourself time to write down what you hear. The first phrase has been done for you.

1 preparing for work
   getting ready for work
2 he didn't think there was a good reason
3 he gave him his tea
4 I don't think there's any chance
5 only been out of work for ...
6 he didn't look forward to this
7 he really wanted to

8 he washed the dishes
9 not making any effort
10 he'd welcome the opportunity
11 he was making a useful contribution
12 what was going to happen
13 it made him feel depressed
14 he picked up his briefcase

UNIT 2 — *Identifying and using the context*

This unit focuses on:

▶ the context from which a listening extract is taken – who's talking, to whom, what they're speaking about and why, how they're feeling etc.

▶ ways of picking up clues which will help you get a more complete picture of what you're listening to

Exercise A1

Aim: to decide what kind of extract you are listening to.

🔊 You are going to listen to 12 extracts. Stop the tape after each one and match it to one of the descriptions in the table below. The first extract has been done for you.

Description	Extract
general conversation	2
weather forecast	7
lecture or talk	4
interview	3
telephone conversation	5
news bulletin	
telephone information line	4
extract from film/book/play	6
public announcement	1
advert	8
commentary	12
speech	9

Exercise A2

Aim: to understand the circumstances surrounding the extracts.

You're going to listen again to the 12 extracts in Exercise A1. You know what kind of extracts these are. Now you are going to concentrate on:

– who is talking and who is listening
– where the 'talking' takes place
– what might have led up to this happening
– the feelings being expressed
– the relationship between the speakers

🔊 Listen to the extracts, one by one, and answer the following questions in note form. The first extract has been done for you.

Extract 1

1 Where did this take place?
   in a shop/department store
2 What words/phrases did you hear that helped you decide?
   'office', 'customer services department', 'second floor'

Extract 2

1 Where did this conversation take place?
2 What phrase gave you the answer?
3 What's the probable relationship between the speakers?
4 How do you know this?

Extract 3

1 How well do you think they know each other?
2 What impression do you have of the second speaker's character, and why do you think this?

Extract 4

1 Why did the listener call this number?

Extract 5

1 Who's she speaking to?
2 What is she going to do?

Extract 6

1 Where might you have heard this?
2 How does Gino feel about his walk to Anna's table?

Extract 7

1 Who might be interested in this?
2 What are the key information words for an interested listener?

Extract 8

1 What impression/mood does the speaker want to give?

Extract 9

1 What has led up to the speaker's words?
2 How does the speaker make a (small) joke?

Extract 10

1 Who might be listening to this speaker?

Extract 11

1 Who's speaking?
2 Who answered his question?

Extract 12

1 What detail might Milton Davies give?

If you're feeling imaginative, rewind the tape and listen to the 12 extracts again with your eyes closed. Can you 'see' the people who are talking? Are they young, old, standing, sitting, smiling or looking stressed? What are they wearing? What's the room like where they are talking? What's the expression on the listener's face?

Exercise A3

Aim: to understand the speaker's mood.

You're going to hear eight different extracts. Listen to each one in turn and answer the following questions. The first extract has been done for you.

1 What is the extract about?
2 How does the person feel? Choose one of the adjectives below.
   -excited- pleased annoyed sorry disappointed surprised nervous worried
3 What words did (s)he say that gave you this impression?

Example with Extract 1:
1) *the speaker's first helicopter flight*
2) *excited*
3) *'I'm really looking forward to it.'*

Exercise A4

Aim: to get further practice in using clues to help you understand the context, relationships, references etc. – this time with a longer extract.

Before you listen, read the questions below.

1 Where does the conversation take place? What 'clues' led you to this conclusion?
2 What are the two people doing?
3 Who's the man talking about when he says 'She didn't seem too pleased about that, did she?'
4 The man said, 'I stood at the stop and three went past …' Three what?
5 What did the woman buy last week?
6 Why does the man say 'as usual'?
7 What can you guess about the person who arrives in the car?
8 What impression do you have of the woman's character?
9 and of the man's character?

Listen to the conversation between Kathy and Philip once, without stopping the tape. See if you can answer any of the above questions. Listen again, stopping the tape where you need to, to write down your answers.

Keeping a clear head

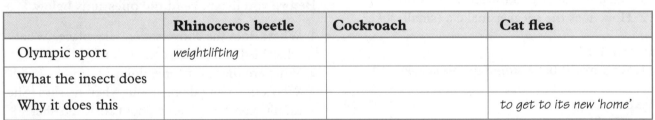

This unit gives you practice in:

▶ making brief notes about the information you hear
▶ identifying who says what

Exercise A1

Aim: to make notes about what you hear.

Extract 1

You're going to listen to an extract entitled 'Who would win the insect Olympics?' This tells you about the physical strengths of three insects, and imagines what sports they would do well in if they were Olympic athletes.

🎧 Listen and complete the table below.

	Rhinoceros beetle	**Cockroach**	**Cat flea**
Olympic sport	*weightlifting*		
What the insect does			
Why it does this			*to get to its new 'home'*

Extract 2

You're going to hear seven people talking outside a 24-hour supermarket. They're talking about what they've just bought and why they are there at that time. Before you listen, think of some reasons why people would shop in the middle of the night.

🎧 Listen and complete the table below.

	Bob	**Bettina**	**Carol**	**George**	**Stella**	**David**	**Anna**
What did (s)he buy?	*something to drink*						
Why was (s)he shopping?	*on his way to see a friend*						

Exercise A2

Aim: to write notes from a more complicated extract.

In the extracts in Exercise A1, the information you were listening for was presented separately – that is, you heard first about the rhinoceros beetle, then the cockroach, then the cat flea. Now you're going to listen to two friends discussing fish cookbooks. This time the information about each book is mixed up, not presented book by book.

Listen to the conversation, twice if necessary, and make notes about what each book offers. Use the following checklist.

price	what it contains	what it doesn't contain
photos	organisation	opinion

Tasty Fish	Something Fishy	Worldwide Fish
£15.99 lots of colour pictures		

Now use your notes to help you answer the questions below. Don't try this until you've made the notes!

Which book (or books):
1 doesn't have recipes for spicy fish?
2 does one of the speakers like and the other dislike?
3 has good photos in?
4 is the most expensive?
5 does the woman decide to buy?

Exercise A3

Aim: to decide which feeling or opinion is expressed by which speaker.

You're going to hear a conversation between three people talking about a picture in an exhibition. Look at Questions 1–9 in the table below. Listen to the conversation and tick (✓) whether it is Jack, Sarah and/or Maria who expresses each fact or opinion. It may be one, two or all three of them. Listen to the conversation as many times as you need. Pay attention when the speakers use each other's names so that you know who is who. It may also help if you make your own notes as you're listening, under the name of each speaker.

Who:	Jack	Sarah	Maria
1 has seen the picture?		✓	
2 advises their friend to see it?			
3 sympathises with the families' situation?			
4 feels it shouldn't be on display?			
5 didn't think it was very good?	✓		✓
6 was moved by the picture?	✓	✓	
7 thinks the artist had a selfish motive?			
8 suggests the artist's motive may have been good?			
9 changes their mind about going to see it?			✓

165

UNIT 4 *Short texts with multiple choice*

Paper 4 Part 1

> ### INFORMATION
>
> In Part 1 of the Listening paper, you will hear eight short unrelated recordings (each about 30 seconds) of people talking in different situations. Before you hear each extract, you'll hear a question and three alternative answers, only one of which is correct. The eight questions are presented both on the question paper and on the tape. You hear each recording twice.
>
> * The extracts are very short so you need to get used to switching your mind from one situation to another quickly.
> * There is only one question for each extract.
> * You need to listen for 'clues' which will enable you to work out who is talking, what the speakers are talking about and how they feel.

Familiarisation exercise

You will hear people talking in two different situations. For each question, choose the best answer, **A**, **B** or **C**.

1 You hear a woman talking about her job.
   What does she do?
   A She works in a hospital.
   B She teaches children.
   C She does the same as her parents. ☐ 1

2 You hear this conversation between two friends in a café.
   What kind of person are they talking about?
   A a friend of theirs
   B someone who works in a shop
   C somebody famous ☐ 2

> The exercises in this unit concentrate on:
>
> ▶ different kinds of questions that you will be asked (Exercise B1)
> ▶ why a particular answer is right (Exercise B2)
> ▶ multiple choice answers (Exercise B3)

Exercise B1

🔲 You'll hear people talking in six different situations. Listen and answer the questions.

What to do:
- Read the questions for each extract.
- Listen once.
- Note down any answers that you can.
- Listen again.
- Complete your answers in your own words.

Extract 1
Focus on When …?
You hear this conversation outside the cinema.

1 When did Mark arrive? *At 7.00.*
2 When does the film start? *7.30.*
3 When did Sarah arrive?
4 When did Sarah meet Jane?

Extract 2
Focus on What …?
You overhear a man talking on his mobile phone.

1 What is the reason for his call?
2 What does he want his wife to do?
3 What does he intend to do in about 50 minutes?
4 What is he wearing?

Extract 3
Focus on Who …?
Listen to this hotel manager talking.

1 Who is the manager talking to?
2 Who should show the guests to their rooms?
3 Who can guests ask about the leisure facilities?

Extract 4
Focus on Where …?
Listen to this woman giving instructions to her babysitter.

1 Where can Lisa find a telephone number for emergencies?
2 Where is the baby's special drink?
3 Where is the drink Lisa prefers?

Extract 5
Focus on How …?
Listen to these two colleagues talking at work.

1 How will the company save money?
2 How will the necessary decisions be made?
3 How do the speakers feel about the future?

Extract 6
Focus on Why …?
You hear a doctor's receptionist talking on the phone.

1 Why is Mrs Fleming ringing?
2 Why can't Dr Thompson see her on Thursday morning?
3 Why do they keep the first appointment free?

Exercise B2

🔲 You'll hear five short recordings. Before each, there is one question about the main point. The correct answer is given. Listen to each extract and say **why** you think the answer is right.

What to do:
- Read the question.
- Read the answer.
- Listen once.
- Note down the things you heard which gave you the answer.
- Listen again.

Extract 1
You overhear two people talking about a report while waiting for the bus.

What is the report about?
Answer: poor standards in reading and maths

What did you hear that led to this answer?

'One in six adults can't read or do simple adding up.'

Extract 2
You hear a man talking on the phone.
What does he want the other person to do?
  Answer: He wants her to sell his spare ticket.
  What did you hear that led to this answer?

Extract 3
You hear someone talking about a shopping expedition.
What did she buy?
  Answer: nothing
  What did you hear that led to this answer?
  (two things)

Extract 4
You hear a woman talking on the phone.
What's the woman's job?
  Answer: a police officer
  What did you hear that led to this answer?
  (two things)

Extract 5
You hear two people discussing a play during the interval.
What's the woman's opinion of the play?
  Answer: She finds the story quite depressing.
  What did you hear that led to this answer?
  (two things)

Exercise B3

⌨ You'll hear five short recordings of people talking. Listen and answer the questions.

What to do:
- Read the question before each one.
- Think about what you need to listen for (underline the key word(s) to help focus your eye and your attention).
- Listen once.
- Think about your answer in your own words (either note it down, or say it to yourself).
- Listen again.
- Turn to page 169, where you'll see three possible answers, A, B, C.
- Choose the answer closest to your own.
- Decide what made the other two choices wrong, according to what you heard.

Extract 1
You hear this conversation between two people on a bus.
What does the woman want the man to do?

Extract 2
You overhear this conversation.
Where is the conversation taking place?

Extract 3
You hear someone introducing a speaker at a conference.
What's the conference about?

Extract 4
Listen to this woman talking to a friend.
Why doesn't she want to apologise?

Extract 5
In a hotel, a man is talking to the receptionist.
What has he lost?

Now choose the answer closest to your own and explain why the other two are wrong The first extract has been done for you.

Extract 1
What does the woman want the man to do?

A watch a sports programme
B repair the video
C record a wildlife programme

C is right: she wants him to record 'Animals of the Andes' so she can watch the football live.
A is wrong: <u>she</u> wants to watch the sports programme.
B is wrong: there's nothing wrong with the video – it's the remote control thing that needs new batteries.

Extract 2
Where is the conversation taking place?

A at a gym
B in a bank
C on the street

Extract 3
What's the conference about?

A publishing books
B history
C unidentified flying objects

Extract 4
Why doesn't she want to apologise?

A She wasn't to blame.
B She has never liked him.
C She'll never see him again.

Extract 5
What has he lost?

A a beach bag
B a camera
C a towel

SUGGESTED APPROACH FOR PART 1 OF THE LISTENING TEST

1 Quickly read the first question.
2 Mark (underline or highlight) the important words.
3 Focus on what you have to listen for – What? Who? etc.
4 Don't think too much about the A, B, C choices yet.
5 Listen once, keeping the Wh…? in your head.
6 Answer in your mind, and check the A, B, C choices.
7 Listen again to confirm your choice.

Exercise B4   Exam practice

You will hear people talking in eight different situations. For Questions 1–8, choose the best answer, **A**, **B** or **C**.

1 While visiting a fitness club, you hear this man talking.
   What is his main reason for joining the club?
   A to get fit
   B the running machine | 1 |
   C for social reasons

2 Listen to these people talking about a book.
   What kind of book are they discussing?
   A a love story
   B a thriller | 2 |
   C a science book

3 You are listening to a radio phone-in
  programme.
  Why has the woman called?
  A to criticise the famous
  B to put a different point of view   3
  C to sympathise with photographers

4 You hear part of a radio programme about
  jeans.
  What did this man want his mother to do?
  A make his jeans narrower
  B make his jeans wider   4
  C stop quarrelling with him

5 You hear two people discussing the menu in a
  Chinese restaurant.
  Which dish are they going to have?
  A fish
  B duck   5
  C beef

6 A woman is talking on the phone to a friend.
  How does she feel about losing her job?
  A pleased
  B depressed   6
  C sorry

7 A man is talking on the phone about a medical
  problem.
  Who is he talking to?
  A a friend
  B his boss   7
  C a doctor

8 You hear a man trying to persuade his friend to
  come to the cinema.
  Why isn't she coming to the cinema tonight?
  A She is too busy.
  B She hasn't got any money.   8
  C She doesn't like the cinema.

UNIT 5 *Gap filling*

Paper 4 Part 2

Familiarisation exercise

You will hear part of a local radio programme about things to do and places to see in Oldcaster. For Questions 1–4, fill in the notes. For Questions 5–8, complete the sentences. (In the exam, you'll have to **either** fill in notes **or** complete sentences. They are together in this exercise to give you practice in both.)

VISITING *OLDCASTER*

- Best way to start: take tour in [Open-top bus] **1**

- Things you will see: [castle] **2**
  and [Old market] **3** Hall

- Recorded commentary in [other languages] **4**

- There is an art exhibition at [the Central] **5**
  by local painters. [Library]

- They have reconstructed a bottle factory at
  [with Museum] **6**

- The swimming pool opens from
  [8.0'clock] **7** to 7.00 pm.

- Tickets for the football match cost
  [£10] **8** OK.

CHAPTER 4

LISTENING

The exercises in this unit concentrate on:

> ► making your answer 'fit' the gap (Exercise B1)
> ► getting help from the questions before you listen (Exercise B2)
> ► listening for specific information (Exercise B3)
> ► keeping a clear mind, i.e. not being confused by 'distractors' (Exercise B4)

Exercise B1

Whether you are asked to fill in the notes or to complete the sentences, the task is the same: to write the missing information so that it fits. This is particularly important in sentence completion. The candidate who wrote the answers below understood what (s)he heard but made some mistakes. What do you think the correct answers might have been? (There is no tape to listen to.)

Beth put her toys back | the box | 1 |

There's something missing; to make sense there must be a preposition before 'the box'.
Probable answer: 'in the box'

An important part of my life is | play tennis | 2 |

There were | problem | 3 | with the brakes.

The table was too | weighed a lot | 4 | for David to move.

After school, Susie started studying at | Chicago | 5 |

The artist believes her work will make people | positive feeling | 6 |

Exercise B2

In the exam, it is important to read the questions carefully before you start listening, so that you have some idea in your mind of what to listen for. You'll hear an interview with Barbara Currie, who is talking about her work as a dentist.

What to do:

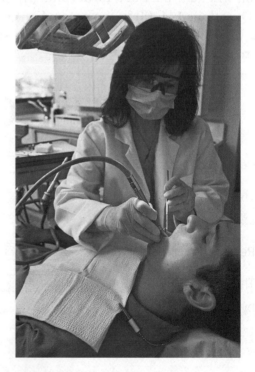

- Read Questions 1–11 on page 173.
- Before you listen, complete the sentences in pencil in ways that you think make sense and fit grammatically with the rest of the sentence. Write no more than three words. For practice only, try to think of more than one possible way of filling the gap.
- When you've finished writing, listen to the interview and see how close your predictions were.

Barbara was | living in London/quite old/unemployed | 1 | when her interest in dentistry began.

She now has her gold tooth on [   ] 2

At school and university, she studied [   ] 3 subjects.

She has been a dentist for [_no years_   ] 4

The number of women dentists [_Is not a big_   ] 5

Some very frightened patients are not treated during [   ] 6

Helping people to overcome their fear takes [   ] 7 and patience.

Dentists can create a relaxing atmosphere by using music, [   ] 8

and [   ] 9

Introduction of new treatments has meant a reduction in the use of

[   ] 10

One of her hopes for the future is to be able to buy [   ] 11

 Now listen to the interview. How close were your predictions to the real answers?

SUMMARY

⇑ You have:
- looked at how the words you put in a gap must 'fit'
- used the questions to help you predict possible answers

⇓ You are now going to:
- fill in gaps with specific information – times, numbers, names, dates etc.
- look at how distracting information can make you write a wrong answer

Exercise B3

You'll hear four short recorded messages. For Questions 1–11, complete the notes. In the exam, you may be asked questions like these as part of a larger gap filling task.

What to do:
- Read the question(s).
- Be clear what you are going to listen for.
- Listen to the recorded messages, and complete the gap(s).
- Listen again.

Extract 1
Old number: 012 7978 New number: [_____ 1]

Extract 2
Office open from [____ *to* ___ 2] on weekdays

Office open from [____ *to* ___ 3] on Saturdays

For London trains ring [____ 4]

Extract 3
Date of move: [____ 5]

New telephone number: [____ 6]

New address: [____ 7] Lane

Postcode: [____ 8]

Extract 4
John Bellino exhibition from [____ *to* ___ 9]

Alexandra Bruton exhibition from [____ *to* ___ 10]

Sculpture seminar at [____ *on* ___ 11]

If you had any problems taking down names or addresses, you need to check that you know how the alphabet is spoken in English – particularly the following letters: A, E, I, U, G, J, V, W, H, K, Q, Y, Z. For numbers, the main listening problem is probably hearing the difference between *fifteen* and *fifty* for example.

Exercise B4

You'll hear part of a radio programme in which two people are talking about a competition. For Questions 1–10, complete the notes.

What to do:

- Read Questions 1–10 in the notes on the right.
- Think what kind of information you have to listen for.
- Listen once, and answer what you can.
- Be careful! The speakers change their mind or contradict themselves sometimes, so the first piece of information you hear is not necessarily the right answer. Which questions does this particularly affect?
- Listen again.

Name of competition: [____ 1]

Winner had [____ 2] correct answers.

First prize worth: [____ 3]

Answers on [____ 4] page of paper.

Correct answer to Question 3: [____ 5]

Question about cathedral was number:
[____ 6]

Question 6 – most common incorrect answer:
[____ 7]

Most difficult question of all: number
[____ 8]

Name of next competition: [____ 9]

Entries in by: [____ 10]

1 Check whether you have to complete notes or sentences.
2 Read each question carefully.
3 Think what could logically fit in the gap – a name, a number, a place etc.
4 Listen and begin to fill in – one, two or three words are usually enough.
5 Make sure your words fit grammatically with what comes **before** and, in sentence completion particularly, **what comes after**.
6 Listen again, finish answering and check what you've written.

Exercise B5   Exam practice

You will hear part of a radio talk about inventions. For Questions 1–10, complete the sentences. You will need to write a word or short phrase in each box.

SOME USEFUL INVENTIONS

The wire coat-hanger

The company was already making wire frames for ⬚ 1

Before, the employees had to put their coats ⬚ 2

Albert Parkhouse ⬚ 3 made any money from the idea.

Rubber tyres

Rubber tyres were first invented by ⬚ 4

The reason they failed was because of ⬚ 5 of rubber.

John Dunlop added ⬚ 6 to his tyres.

An aid for night drivers

The idea came from seeing ⬚ 7 in his headlights.

The lens has ⬚ 8 behind it.

It took Percy Shaw ⬚ 9 to develop the idea.

His invention made him ⬚ and ⬚ 10

UNIT 6 *Multiple matching*

Paper 4 Part 3

> ### INFORMATION
>
> In Part 3 of the Listening paper, you will hear five short extracts with five different people talking. Each extract will last about 30 seconds, and they will all be related in some way. You have to match what each of the five speakers says to one of six summary words or sentences (there is always one extra). There are five questions in this part. You'll hear the whole recording twice.
>
> - You need a strategy to help you remember what each speaker says.
> - The speakers may all be speaking about aspects of the same subject, e.g. travel, or about similar experiences, or the link may be 'functional', e.g. all speakers may be apologising for something.
> - The second listening is important for checking (one wrong answer can affect the others).

Familiarisation exercise

You will hear three people talking about their last holidays. For Questions 1–3, choose from the list **A–D** where each person spent their last holiday. Use the letters only once. There is an extra letter which you don't need to use.

A in the mountains

B on a farm   Speaker 1 [ ] [1]

C in a city   Speaker 2 [ ] [2]

D by the seaside   Speaker 3 [ ] [3]

> The exercises in this unit give you practice in:
>
> ► using the instructions to help you predict (Exercise B1)
> ► collecting information about what each speaker says, and picking up 'clues' to help you choose the correct answer (Exercise B2)
> ► being aware of distracting information that might make you choose the wrong answer (Exercise B3)
> ► answering without an extra option to worry about (Exercise B4)

Exercise B1

You are going to think about the initial **question** contained in the instructions and predict the **items** that you might see in the list of six options.

What to do:
- Look at the following situations/experiences.
- Read the questions.
- Write possible answers to these questions. Ideally, try to think of up to five different answers. Use your imagination!

1 Five people talking about their recent holiday. What went wrong?
   their luggage got lost / the car broke down / they quarrelled / the hotel was awful / the food was terrible

2 Five people talking about something that happened during childhood.
   Which story does each speaker tell?

3 Five people asking for information.
   What do they want to know?

4 Five people talking about a party they went to.
   What aspect of it did each enjoy?

5 Five people talking at an airport.
  What are they doing there?
6 Five people talking in a restaurant.
  What do they think of it?
7 Five people complaining.
  What are they complaining about?

Exercise B2

📼 You'll hear five speakers talking about films they have seen. Each speaker expresses an opinion about his or her chosen film. The speakers (1–5) and their opinions (A–E) have already been matched. What did you hear that led to these answers?

What to do:

- Listen to the first speaker, and check you agree with the matching.
- Play the same speaker again and stop the tape where necessary in order to write down the words and phrases you hear which give 'clues' to the answer. (The first one has been done for you as an example.)
- Do the same for the next four speakers.

Speaker 1:   **C** The action was really exciting.

'the car chase … was … breath-taking'
'the bit where he tried to escape by jumping off the bridge …
I could hardly bear to look'

A The scenery was wonderful. ——————— Speaker 1
B The star was excellent. ——————— Speaker 2
C The action was really exciting. ——— Speaker 3
D The story was very moving. ——————— Speaker 4
E The acting was very good. ——————— Speaker 5

Exercise B3

📼 You'll hear the five speakers from Exercise B2 again. This time, listen for how some information could lead you to make a **wrong** choice. The first speaker has been done for you.

What to do:

- Look at the A–E choices in Exercise B2 and underline the key words – the ones which tell you what to listen for.
- When you listen this time, make a note of any words or phrases you hear that relate to one of the **other** choices. These pieces of distracting information can sometimes lead you to make the wrong choice.

Speaker 1:   didn't think much of the story (choice D mentions story)
*   actors did their best (choice E mentions acting)*

CHAPTER 4

LISTENING

Exercise B4

📻 You'll hear five people talking about the travelling they have to do in connection with their work. Decide which of the five statements (**A–E**) matches what each speaker says. There is no extra statement.

What to do:

- Look at statements A–E first.
- Underline the key words.
- Remember to listen for helpful 'clues' and not to be distracted by unhelpful ones!

A	I'm afraid of flying.	Speaker 1	D	1
B	I sleep to pass the time.	Speaker 2	C	2
C	I have special routines when I fly.	Speaker 3	B	3
D	I sometimes don't know where I am.	Speaker 4	E	4
E	I don't like to be ready too soon.	Speaker 5	A	5

SUGGESTED APPROACH FOR PART 3 OF THE LISTENING TEST

1 Read and listen to the instructions carefully. You should be clear about what the general context is – what the five speakers have in common. You should also be clear what question you are going to answer: simple (What job does each speaker do? Which of the opinions does each speaker express?) or more complex (What did each person think was the best thing about … ?).
2 Read the list A–F. Highlight or underline the bits that you have to listen for.
3 As you listen the first time, note for each speaker anything which will help to fix them in your mind (age, gender) and any words/phrases that correspond to what you're listening for.
4 Remember that the extracts may contain distracting information so you should listen to the whole piece before you make a decision. Don't decide too quickly. The word *but* may be the most important word on the tape!

Exercise B5   Exam practice

📻 You will hear five people talking about holiday disasters. For Questions 1–5, choose from the list **A–F** what spoiled their holiday. Use the letters only once. There is one extra letter which you do not need to use.

A	a crime	Speaker 1		1
B	a disco	Speaker 2		2
C	an illness	Speaker 3	D	3
D	the weather	Speaker 4	D	4
E	an accident	Speaker 5		5
F	the hotel			

UNIT 7 — *Two- or three-option answers*

Paper 4 Part 4

Familiarisation exercise 1 (Two-option answers)

You will hear a conversation between two people in which they are talking about a newspaper article. For Questions 1–4, decide which of the statements are **TRUE** and which are **FALSE**. Write **T** for True or **F** for False in the boxes provided.

1 Mr Flowers left £84,000 when he died. `T` [1]

2 The man does not approve of what Mr Flowers did. [2]

3 Mr Flowers had four children. [3]

4 The woman is annoyed about this report. [4]

Familiarisation exercise 2 (Three-option answers)

You will hear a conversation in a shop between a shop assistant and two customers, Tom and Carol. Answer Questions 1–4 by writing **S** for shop assistant, **T** for Tom, or **C** for Carol in the boxes provided.

1 Who feels embarrassed? [1]

2 Who has left the receipt at home? [2]

3 Who doesn't accept the situation? [3]

4 Who wants the manager to come? [4]

179

The exercises in this unit focus on:

▶ two-option answers:
  – justifying a yes/no answer (Exercise B1)
  – what makes an answer false (Exercise B2)
▶ three-option answers:
  – answering questions before looking at the choices (Exercise B4)
  – identifying who is expressing what (Exercise B5)

Two-option answers

Exercise B1

🎧 You'll hear a conversation between two people about an electricity bill they have just received. Some of the statements 1–6 below contain information which was given on the tape (shown as Yes) but others do not (shown as No). What did you hear which led to the Yes/No answers?

What to do:

- Read statements 1–6 below together with their answers.
- Listen to the extract once to make sure you agree with the Yes/No answers.
- Listen again, stop the tape at the right moment and write what you heard to justify the Yes/No answer.

1 The weather has been warm during the last
   three months.   **No**
   'it's been pretty cold'
2 They've needed the heating a lot.   **Yes**
3 Their electricity bill is bigger than last
   year's.   **Yes**
4 He's going to pay the bill immediately.   **No**
5 Electricity prices are higher than last year. **Yes**
6 She is surprised at the size of the bill.   **No**

Things to look for which may mean the answer is 'No' or 'False':

- The tense or time reference is wrong.
- The statement is too extreme for the situation, e.g. it includes a word like *always*, *nobody*, or *totally*.
- The statement is saying something which you might assume but which is not actually mentioned in the discussion.
- The statement contains information which is mentioned in the discussion but in connection with another situation or person.
- A word or phrase is introduced with a negative such as, 'It's not as if …', 'It doesn't necessarily mean …'.

Exercise B2

🎧 You'll hear part of a radio programme about the amount of money some people earn for the jobs they do. Decide whether the statements on page 181 are true or false.

What to do:

- Read statements 1–9 on page 181; **six** are false (**F**), **three** are true (**T**).
- Listen to the extract. Try and answer some of the questions as you're listening. Write **T** or **F** in the space provided.
- Think about what can make a statement false (look at the notes in the box above).
- Listen again. What is it that makes six of the statements false?

1 Mr Teacher doesn't know what he earns. ☐ 1

2 Some people have already lost their jobs at BritElectric. ☐ 2

3 Mr Teacher doesn't enjoy making any decisions. ☐ 3

4 Mr Johnson thinks the difference between the two salaries is too big. ☐ 4

5 Mr Johnson doesn't think Mr Teacher has a responsible job. ☐ 5

6 They both have to work at weekends. ☐ 6

7 Mr Teacher worked for BritElectric when he was at college. ☐ 7

8 Mr Teacher's lifestyle is the same as it was. ☐ 8

9 They are both satisfied with the amount they're paid. ☐ 9

SUGGESTED APPROACH FOR TWO-OPTION ANSWERS IN PART 4 OF THE LISTENING TEST

1 Read and listen to what the extract is going to be about. It's important to get yourself into the situation as soon as possible.

2 Read the statements – you have on average 45 seconds to do this.

3 Underline any key words to help you focus on what to listen for.

4 If any of the statements are connected with feelings/opinions, think about how these might be expressed.

5 Listen and begin answering. Don't expect to be able to answer everything during the first listening.

6 Listen again and finish answering.

7 Check your answers – have you answered every question?

Exercise B3   Exam practice

You will hear part of a radio programme in which Frank, a policeman, talks about his forthcoming retirement. For Questions 1–7, decide whether the information is stated or not, and write **Y** for Yes or **N** for No in the boxes provided.

1 Frank is retiring before he has to. ☐ 1

2 He disapproves of the new technology in the office. ☐ 2

3 Frank is not against DNA testing. ☐ 3

4 Getting respect from the public is now more difficult. ☐ 4

5 He believes that women will soon make up 50% of the force. ☐ 5

6 The first thing Frank wants is a holiday. ☐ 6

7 He thinks Jessie would like him to do night security work. ☐ 7

Three-option answers

It's important to understand what you have to do by reading the instructions carefully. They may come in a variety of different forms. For example:

- For Questions **1–7**, decide which of the choices, **A**, **B** or **C** is the best answer (multiple choice).
- Answer Questions **1–7** by writing **J** for John, **S** for Sam or **A** for Anne ('who said what', 'who expressed the idea' etc.).
- For Questions **1–7**, decide which school each statement refers to. Write **A** for Avalon School, **B** for Brewer School, **C** for Chaucer School.

Exercise B4

You'll hear a conversation about the dangers of sharks. Complete the statements below then turn to page 183 and choose the best answer, A, B or C.

What to do:

- Read the incomplete statements, 1–5 below.
- Listen to the conversation about sharks, once without stopping the tape.
- Listen again, and stop the tape when necessary in order to complete statements 1–5 in your own words.
- Turn to page 183 where you'll see the A, B, C choices.
- Match your own answer to the best answer.

1 This was the first time Jenny had …
2 Jenny thinks the number of people killed by sharks is …
3 Sharks usually only kill people who …
4 To reduce the possibility of a shark attack, you should swim …
5 If you think a shark is going to attack you, you should …

1 This was the first time Jenny had
   A been diving.
   B been to Australia.
   C seen a shark.

2 Jenny thinks the number of people killed by sharks is
   A quite high.
   B about what she expected.
   C surprisingly low.

3 Sharks usually only kill people who
   A try to catch them with spears.
   B make a lot of movement in the water.
   C make them think of a sea creature.

4 To reduce the possibility of a shark attack, you should swim
   A at certain times of the day.
   B only in deep water.
   C in unclear water.

5 If you think a shark is going to attack you, you should
   A make a loud noise.
   B wait for someone to rescue you.
   C swim away from it.

Exercise B5

You'll hear four short conversations on different subjects. Each conversation contains **two** ideas from the list 1–8 below. First, think what language might express each of these eight ideas. The first one has been done for you.

1 some encouragement *Go on, you can do it! Try it and see.*
2 an apology
3 a denial or an accusation
4 a dislike of something
5 a regret
6 a promise
7 a suggestion
8 a reminder about something

⌨Now listen to the four conversations and decide which two from the list 1–8 apply to each conversation. Write two numbers in the boxes in the table below. The first box has been done for you.

	List 1–8	Person
Extract 1	☑ 4 ☐	(Woman)/Son/David Woman/Son/David
Extract 2	☐ ☐	Man/Woman/Sue Man/Woman/Sue
Extract 3	☐ ☐	Mike/Jane/Helen Mike/Jane/Helen
Extract 4	☐ ☐	Woman/Man/Tony Woman/Man/Tony

Listen to the four conversations again. This time decide which person expressed each idea or feeling. Circle the appropriate names in the table above. The first one has been done for you.

SUGGESTED APPROACH FOR PART 4 OF THE LISTENING TEST

1 Read and listen to the instructions very carefully, so you know what the extract is about and what form of answer you have to give (T/F, A, B, C etc.).

2 Read the questions and underline any key words.

3 For complex three-option answers (three different people, three different places etc.) write down the relevant letters (e.g. **J** for John, **P** for Paula and **C** for Carol); if you have time during the first listening, note down under each letter anything which will help you remember who said what.

4 Answer what you can during the first listening. (Remember the questions follow the order of information on the tape.)

5 Use the second listening to complete your answers, and to check.

Exercise B6   Exam practice

You will hear a conversation about choosing a language school. For Questions 1–7, decide which school each of the following statements refers to. Write **G** for Goya Academy, **I** for Iberia International, or **M** for Martinez School.

1 The charge for accommodation is not included in the price. | 1 |

2 A colleague recommended this school. | 2 |

3 The brochure is well illustrated. | 3 |

4 This school offers the most intensive programme. | 4 |

5 It is near the centre of town. | 5 |

6 Accommodation is guaranteed close to the school. | 6 |

7 It's unsuitable because of the age of the students. | 7 |

CHAPTER 5

Speaking

The organisation of the Speaking chapter follows the format of the Speaking Test itself.

> Questions and answers about the Speaking Test
> Functional phrases
> **Unit 1** Socialising
> **Unit 2** Individual long turn
> **Unit 3** Two- and three-way discussion

EXAM OVERVIEW   PAPER 5 SPEAKING (about 14 minutes)

Paper 5 has four parts:

PART 1	Socialising	3 minutes
PART 2	Individual long turn with photographs	4 minutes
PART 3	Two-way discussion with task	3 minutes
PART 4	Three-way discussion leading on from Part 3	4 minutes

Questions and answers about the Speaking Test

1 How is it organised?

There are two candidates and two examiners. One examiner controls the test by asking the questions and listening. (S)he gives an overall mark for each candidate at the end of the test. The other examiner doesn't speak – (s)he listens and assesses your language.

2 Can I do the test alone?

No, unless there are exceptional circumstances where permission from the University of Cambridge Local Examinations Syndicate (UCLES) has been given. A 'paired' format means that the test is less of a one-to-one 'interview' and more of an exchange of information and ideas in a controlled but friendly environment! Talking with someone is also more natural than responding in a question-answer format. Very often in the test, as in real life, you may not have anything to say at a particular moment but the person you're with does say something, which you can then react to.

3 Can I choose 'my pair'?

It depends on the centre where you enter. When you enrol for the exam, you are given a candidate number and for the Speaking Test you are often paired with the person who has the number before or after yours. Check with your teacher or your centre for the situation in your area. Occasionally, if there is an uneven number of candidates for any reason, three candidates may be examined together. If this happens, the timing of the test is extended to 20 minutes maximum.

4 What if my partner and I don't know each other?

It doesn't matter whether you know each other or not. There is not much time for 'personal' chat during the test so you don't need to know anything about the other person.

5 What if my partner either talks too much or doesn't talk at all?

The examiner controls the test and will not allow this to happen. Each candidate has strictly timed 'turns' for speaking, particularly in Parts 1 and 2.

6 What if I can't understand what my partner is saying?

It is only in Part 3, and a bit in Part 4, that you have to work together, so first of all you can ask your partner to repeat what (s)he said. You'll know what you should be doing in Part 3 so just carry on even if you haven't understood everything. If there is a real breakdown in understanding, the examiner may step in and re-direct the situation.

7 What does it mean if the examiner stops me in the middle of my turn, when I haven't finished what I want to say?

It means that the time for that bit is over. Each part of the test has a time limit which the examiner tells you before each task. It doesn't mean that you've done something wrong. Don't worry!

8 How do I know whether I have to talk to my partner or the examiner?

The examiner tells you. But if for any reason you're not sure, ask.

9 What happens in the different parts of the test?

Part 1: Socialising (three minutes)
The examiner asks each candidate in turn questions about themselves.
Part 2: Individual long turn (four minutes)
Each candidate is given a different pair of photographs to talk about. Each candidate has a turn of one minute followed by a brief response from the other candidate.
Part 3: Two-way discussion (three minutes)
Candidates are given some visual material to discuss together, without the examiner joining in.
Part 4: Three-way discussion (four minutes)
This is an expansion of the activity in Part 3. The examiner joins in by asking questions in order to stimulate discussion.
There are more details about each part of the Speaking Test on the following pages.

10 How is my performance marked?

The examiner gives an overall impression mark for each candidate at the end of the test, after you've left the room. The second person (the assessor) listens and assesses throughout the test, recording the marks on a computer mark sheet. Candidates are assessed on:
- accurate and appropriate grammar and vocabulary
- the way ideas and language are linked together to form connected speech
- pronunciation, stress and rhythms of speech
- the ability to communicate, that is to speak, respond, react and take turns

NOTE

If you're studying for the exam on your own, it is obviously difficult to practise speaking because you need to work with a partner. If possible, therefore, find someone else in your town (ask your enrolment centre for the information) to work with, particularly to practise Parts 2 and 3.

Some of the work that follows is recorded on the cassettes that accompany this book – in those exercises, you can use the cassette, or the tapescript, as your partner!

Functional phrases

You will need the following phrases, and other similar ones, at various stages in the Speaking Test. The phrases are divided into different functional groups. As you work through this chapter, use this phrase bank for reference.

Asking for clarification

Sorry, I'm not sure what you mean.
I don't (really) understand.
Can I ask a question?
Do you want me to ...?
Can you say that again please? I'm not (quite) sure what I have to do.

Correcting yourself

I don't think I explained that very well!
What I mean is ...
What I meant was ...
What I'm trying to say is ...

If you don't know the word for something

I don't know what you call it, but ... (followed by some attempt to describe or define the object)
It's like a ...
You use it to **open** ...
It's used for **opening** ...
It's used to **open** ...
It's what you do when you ... (if you don't know the verb)

Compare and contrast (expressing similarity or difference)

They both **show, have** etc.

They're quite similar because they both **show, have** etc.

There are … in both of them.

Both of them have got … in them.

There are some differences. One … and the other …

The top one looks more … than the bottom one.

The one on the left **is/shows/has** … but the one on the right is …

This one is not as … as the other one.

It's quite difficult to compare them.

Expressing your likes, dislikes, preferences

I (really) like/love/enjoy **tennis / walking by the sea.**

I don't (really) like **football.**

I'm not very keen on **baseball.**

I much prefer **reading.**

I'd prefer **something to eat / to go swimming.**

I'd (much) rather **stay at home.**

My favourite pastime is **walking.**

The thing/one I like best is **cooking.**

Expressing your opinions/feelings/reactions

I don't think **he's very happy / she's going to buy anything.**

I'm not sure whether **he would enjoy it / people believe …**

I think it'd be better if **they chose … / we didn't go …**

I think we should **pay less / choose …**

It makes me **angry/worried/smile/want to …**

I find it really **interesting/awful.**

It looks a bit **strange/difficult.**

She looks as if **she's enjoying it / she hasn't slept.**

Agreeing or disagreeing with your partner (Parts 3 and 4)

I agree.

That sounds like a good idea.

That's a great idea.

(You're) right!

(That's) true.

I'm not sure about that.

I don't (really) agree.

Yes, but …

Involving your partner (Part 3)

What do you think?

Do you think we should …?

Why don't we …?

Perhaps we should …

Let's decide about … first, shall we?

What shall we do first?

Expressing 'for' and 'against' views

The good/bad thing(s) is/are …

One advantage/disadvantage is …

On the other hand … (to introduce a contrast to something that's already been said)

Speculating

He could/might be **on holiday / explaining something.**

I think this **would be good for him / might not help in the situation / could cause problems.**

What'll happen if **we don't go?**

What would happen if **people didn't do anything?**

What if **there was no opportunity to change?**

Reaching a conclusion with your partner (Part 3)

(What) have we decided then?

So, let's decide which one …

I think that's it, don't you?

UNIT 1 *Socialising*

Paper 5 Part 1

> ### ℹ INFORMATION
> Part 1 of the Speaking Test gives you the chance to relax, and get to know a little bit about your partner. In this part you answer questions from the examiner about yourself and you listen to your partner doing the same.
>
> - You go into the room with your partner and hand over your marksheets (which you've been given earlier).
> - The examiner introduces herself/himself and also introduces the assessor.
> - The examiner asks each of you in turn some questions about yourselves. The examiner chooses questions from a selection in her/his script.
> - You are each given an equal chance to speak. The examiner may ask you questions alternately, or (s)he may put a few questions to you, then a few to your partner.
> - There is no need for you to talk to each other in this part, but sometimes a reaction or comment is natural. The examiner controls this interaction.

Exercise 1

The purpose of the questions in Part 1 is to get you to **talk about yourself**. Imagine yourself as the examiner. Write two questions that you might ask under each of the headings below. One of your questions should ask for factual information and the other should ask about feelings, likes and dislikes, opinions etc.

1 Your home town/country
   Factual: Where are you from?
   Opinion: Do you enjoy living there?
2 Your work/study etc.
3 Your family
4 Interests/hobbies/leisure time
5 English – when? how long? why? etc.
6 Your plans for the future

Exercise 2

The questions that the examiner asks will give you the opportunity to use different verb tenses. Look again at the questions you wrote in Exercise 1. Do your questions use a variety of tenses? If not, add some more questions, using past, present and future where possible.

> *Where do you live? (present simple)*
> *How long have you lived there? (present perfect)*
> *When did you move to Athens? (past simple)*
> *Where do you think you'll be living in 20 years' time? (future continuous)*

Make sure **you** can answer all your questions! If you are working with a partner, ask her/him the questions you have written in Exercises 1 and 2. Then answer your partner's questions. Think about how to make your answers as interesting as possible.

Examiner   Candidate

This candidate's answer is not very exciting! It would be much more interesting to say something like this instead:

Candidate

Exercise 3

Listen to the cassette and practise Part 1 of the test by answering the examiner's questions. There is space on the cassette for you to speak your answers out loud. You may also want to refer to the tapescript on page 218.

UNIT 2 *Individual long turn*

Paper 5 Part 2

INFORMATION

In Part 2 of the Speaking Test, you will have a chance to speak without interruption for about one minute.

- The examiner will give you a pair of photographs and (s)he will tell you to let your partner see the photos as well. Then (s)he will ask you to compare and contrast them and give some personal reaction to them. You will only have one minute to do this.
- Your partner will listen during that minute and then will be asked a question to which (s)he should make a short response or comment. 'Short' means short – a one or two sentence response is enough! (Only 20 seconds is allowed here.) Don't be surprised if the photos are taken away while this takes place – it's to stop your partner referring in detail to the pictures.
- Then the same thing happens with your partner: (s)he speaks about two different photos for a minute. You listen, and respond briefly at the end. Don't interrupt when your partner is speaking.

Exercise 1

Look at this pair of photographs of people involved in the world of art. Can you say **briefly** what is in each photograph?

> The photo on the right shows a young girl painting. I'm not sure what she's painting. She could be at home, or maybe in school. She's made a bit of a mess, but she looks as if she's enjoying herself.

Describe the second photograph in the same way. Remember, you are not being asked to give a **detailed** description. Talk about the main action, where it might be taking place and the feelings shown by the people in the picture.

Exercise 2

What are the similarities and differences between the two photos in Exercise 1? Add at least one sentence of your own to each of the examples below. (Use some of the phrases from the list of functional phrases on page 188 to **compare** and **contrast** the two art photos.)

Similarities

Both are about some kind of art – painting and sculpture.

Differences

In the top one the child is actually doing a painting but in the bottom one the people are just looking at the statue.

Exercise 3

As part of your task you'll be asked by the examiner to give some kind of personal reaction to your two photos. The instruction (s)he gives will be: 'I'd like you to compare and contrast these photographs and say …'

1 how much you think the people are enjoying these activities.
2 how you think the people are feeling.
3 whether art is important for you.
4 how much enjoyment you get from art.
5 what kind of art you prefer.

(You will only be asked **one** of these questions.)

Listen carefully to the **second** part of what the examiner says. Remember, the first instruction will always be 'compare and contrast' – it's the second part that varies and therefore needs more attention.

Look again at the two art photos in Exercise 1 and decide what you would say in answer to Questions 1–5 above. Don't forget to refer to the functional phrases on page 188.

Exercise 4

The candidate who has been listening to the one-minute long turn is now asked **one** direct question, and has about 20 seconds to answer. Here are some possible questions about the two art photos in Exercise 1.

1 Do you enjoy/like art?
2 Do you ever go to art exhibitions?
3 When did you last go to an art exhibition?
4 Are you artistic?
5 Which activity in the photos looks more enjoyable?

Look at the example below and then think of two-sentence answers to Questions 2–5.

Examiner *Do you like art?*

Candidate *Well, some art, yes. I like paintings but not particularly modern ones.*

Do make sure that you answer the question, and try to say a little more than just *yes* or *no*. **Don't** start describing the photographs.

Exercise 5

Look at these two photos showing people doing different sports. The examiner will say:

> I'd like you to compare and contrast these photographs and say what kind of sport you prefer. Remember, you have only about a minute to do this, so don't worry if I interrupt you. All right?

You're going to listen to the instructions on the cassette and speak out loud. There is a space on the cassette of just over one minute.

Remember:

  – give a brief description (where it is, what the main action is)
  – compare and contrast
  – say what kind of sport you prefer

🔊 Now play the cassette.

How long did one minute feel?

🔊 Now, start the cassette again and listen to Candidate A doing the task you've just done. (If you're not working with a cassette, look at the tapescript on page 218.)

1 Do you think the candidate you have heard has done the task well? Why/Why not? Check the three points above. (There are one or two very minor grammatical mistakes which would not affect the marks.)

🔊 If you're working with a partner, (s)he will now play the part of Candidate B and answer the follow-up question on the cassette. There is a 20-second space on the cassette for Candidate B to speak the answer. If you're working alone, you take the part of Candidate B.

🔊 Now listen to a candidate doing the same task.

2 How well do you think Candidate B did?

Exercise 6

📼Practise with another pair of photographs of people selling goods. Follow the instructions on the cassette, or look at the tapescript on page 218. If you're working with a partner, change roles.

For further practice (This material is not on the cassette.)

1   Learning

These photographs show people learning in different situations.

Examiner *Candidate A, compare and contrast the two photographs, saying which you think is the better way of learning.*

(Time yourself: you only have one minute to do this.)

Examiner *Candidate B, are you good with your hands?*

(Time yourself: you only have about 20 seconds to answer this question.)

2 Places to live

These photographs show people living in different places.

Examiner   *Candidate A, compare and contrast the two photographs saying what the advantages or disadvantages are of living in these places.*

    (Time yourself: you only have one minute to do this.)

Examiner   *Candidate B, what kind of building do you live in?*

    (Time yourself: you only have about 20 seconds to answer this question.)

3 Feelings

These photographs show people looking happy.

Examiner   *Candidate A, compare and contrast the two photographs, saying what might have happened to make these people feel like this.*

    (Time yourself: you only have one minute to do this.)

Examiner   *Candidate B, what makes you happy?*

    (Time yourself: you only have about 20 seconds to answer this question.)

UNIT 3 *Two- and three-way discussion*

Paper 5 Parts 3 and 4

INFORMATION

For Part 3 of the Speaking Test, the examiner will give you and your partner a sheet on which there will be several pictures or illustrations. You will be asked to talk about something together for about three minutes and to come to a decision.

- The examiner will give you your instructions and then will say nothing more until the three minutes are finished, unless you need further guidance.
- After the three minutes (s)he will then ask you some questions which make up Part 4 of the Speaking Test. Part 4 lasts approximately four minutes.

To do well in Part 3 you need to do a number of things:
- Say what you think and why you think this.
- Ask your partner for her/his opinion.
- Listen to your partner and follow up on things (s)he says, e.g. add something more or a contrast, or agree or disagree.
- Make suggestions or give information.
- Speculate, e.g. say what might happen, or how this could affect someone.
- Come to a decision.

Exercise 1

In Part 3 of the Speaking Test the examiner will ask you and your partner to talk about something together. Look at the illustration on page 197 and the examiner's instructions below.

> *I'd like you to imagine that a local college is running a variety of evening classes. Here are some of the courses they are offering. Talk to each other about the attractions of attending these different evening classes. Then choose the most suitable one for a 17-year-old, a 35-year-old and a 65-year-old.*

At this stage, if you're not clear what you should do, you can ask the examiner to explain again. (Look at the ways of asking for clarification in the list of functional phrases on page 187.)

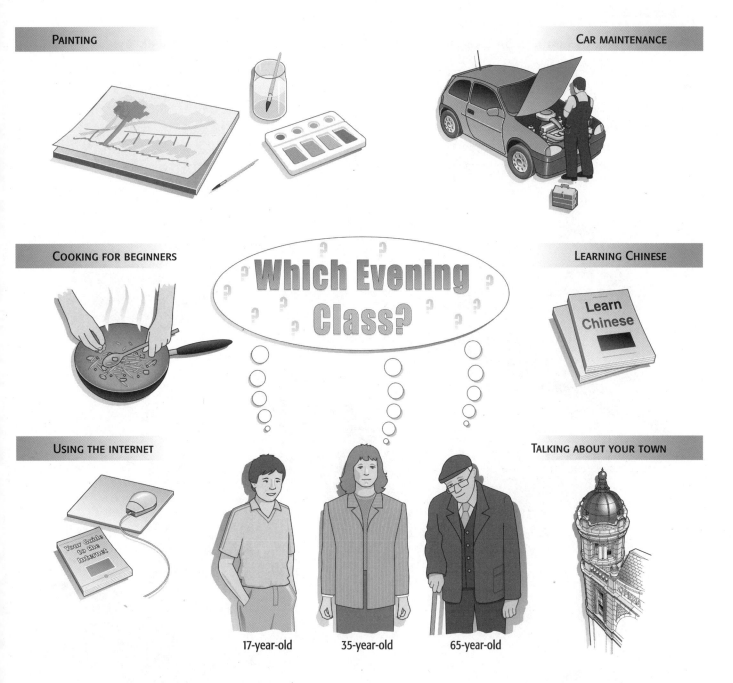

PAINTING

CAR MAINTENANCE

COOKING FOR BEGINNERS

Which Evening Class?

LEARNING CHINESE

Learn Chinese

USING THE INTERNET

Your Guide to the Internet

TALKING ABOUT YOUR TOWN

17-year-old   35-year-old   65-year-old

🎧 Listen to the discussion between two candidates. When you've heard the whole discussion, answer the questions below.

1 Did they talk about all/most/some of the classes?
2 Did they talk about the attractions of all/most/some of the classes?
3 Did they decide on a suitable course for all three people?
4 Did they reach these decisions during the conversation or at the end?
5 Did the candidates take turns to speak?
6 Did the candidates involve each other? How?
7 What do you think about the man's question to the examiner?
8 Was there anything about their 'performance' that you particularly liked or didn't like?

SPEAKING

Exercise 2

Practise doing the same as in Exercise 1, but with another task. The examiner will say:

> An environmental charity is designing a poster to encourage people to give money to their organisation. Here are some of the ideas. Talk to each other about the environmental problems that are represented by these illustrations, and then choose one design for the poster that you think will be most effective.

What to do:
If you're working by yourself:

- Make a brief note of what you think about each illustration.
- Decide how you would ask your partner for his/her ideas.
- Decide what you could say to make your partner feel good about his/her contribution.
- Decide what you could say to bring the discussion to a conclusion.
- Reach a decision.

What to do:
If you're working with someone else:
- Do the task together, allowing yourself three minutes.
- When you've finished, answer these questions (or get a third person to listen to you and answer the questions for you):

  – Did we do what we were supposed to do?
  – Did we run out of time or the opposite?
  – Did either of us speak too much or too little?
  – Did we ask each other questions?
  – Did we reach a decision?

Exercise 3

After your three-minute discussion of the task in Part 3 the examiner will ask some questions on the same theme. These questions make up Part 4 of the Speaking Test. Now you need to face towards the examiner and be prepared to be part of a three-way discussion which will last about four minutes.

Sometimes the examiner will direct a question to one candidate by name, and at other times the

question is open for either candidate to answer.

If you feel you want to comment or react to something your partner has said, feel free to do so. This is all part of natural conversation and is very appropriate in this part of the Speaking Test.

Listen to the follow-up questions that the examiner might ask after the discussion about evening classes on page 197. There is space on the cassette for you to speak your answers aloud.

Exercise 4

Think of some questions the examiner might ask you, following on from the 'Environmental Poster' decision in Exercise 2 on page 198. If you can't think of anything, use the ideas on the right and make complete questions.

– Which poster design …?
– Do you think posters …?
– In your country, what are the worst …?
– Do most people care …?
– What can individuals …?
– What do you think will …?
– How can city life …?

Now decide how you would answer your questions.

CHAPTER 5

SPEAKING

For further practice

> I'd like you to imagine that you are going on a short holiday to one of the world's tropical rain forests. Here are some things that you might take with you. Talk to each other about how useful some of these things are and then decide which three things you would definitely take with you, and which two you wouldn't. Remember you only have about three minutes to do this.

Then the examiner will move on to Part 4. Below are some possible questions that (s)he could ask you. Decide how you would answer and respond out loud.

1 Would you enjoy going on a holiday like this?
2 What do you think would be the best and worst things about it?
3 Do you think people should be encouraged to go to unusual places? Why/Why not?
4 What region of your country would you like to go to for holidays? Why?
5 What kind of holidays do you think people will want in the future?

Some final advice about the Speaking Test

1 Listen to the examiner's instructions.
2 If you're not sure what to do, or don't understand something, **ask** for clarification.
3 Be aware of the timings of the different parts, and know when you should speak, listen, interact with your partner, interact with the examiner etc.
4 It's a **speaking** test, not a listening test. So speak as much as possible when it's appropriate. Don't just give one-word answers. The assessor needs some language to assess.

5 However, you must be sensitive to turn-taking. There has to be a balance between saying too little and saying too much.
6 The examiner's responsibility is to give clear instructions and to manage the interview; your responsibility is to bring the instructions/task to life – to put flesh on the bones!
7 Think about your body language, particularly when you are talking with your partner. Turn towards each other a little, look at your partner when (s)he is speaking. Look interested.
8 There are no right and wrong answers to the tasks.

Word + preposition combinations

Verbs	Adjectives	Nouns
accuse s'one of	acceptable to	advantage of
agree with	accustomed to	agreement about/with
apologise for	afraid of	apology for
appeal to	amazed/astonished at/by	application for
apply for	annoyed with/about	approval of
approve of	anxious about	argument about
argue with/about	ashamed of	attack on
arrest s'one for	attached to	attitude to(wards)
arrive in/at	aware of	attraction to(wards)
be on		belief in
believe in		
belong to		
blame s'one for		(put the) blame on s'one
boast about		
borrow s'thg from s'one		
charge s'one with	capable of	choice between
choose between	characteristic of	combination of
combine with	conscious of	comparison between
comment on/about	crazy about	complaint about
compare with	curious about	congratulations on
complain about		connection between
concentrate on		cruelty to(wards)
congratulate on		
consist of		
decide about/on	dependent on	decision about/on
depend on	different from	decrease in
differ from	dissatisfied with	delay in
disagree with/about	doubtful about	difference between
divide into		(have) difficulty in/with
		disadvantage of
		disagreement with/about
		(have) doubts about
excuse s'one for	enthusiastic about	experience of/in
	envious of	expert at/in
	excited about	
face up to	famous for	
forgive s'one for	fed up with	
	fond of	
	friendly with	
	frightened of	

Verbs	Adjectives	Nouns
	good at	
	guilty of	
hear of/about/from	helpful to s'one	(no) hope for
insist on	incapable of	increase in
interfere with	interested in	information about
		(have no) intention of
		interest in
joke about	jealous of	
	keen on	knowledge of
laugh at/about		lack of
lend s'thg to s'one		
listen to		
mistake s'one for	married to	
object to	opposed to	objection to
		opinion of
		opposition to
pay for	pleased with	(have/take) pleasure in
prepare for	popular with	preference for
prevent s'one from	proud of	preparation for
protest about		(have/take) pride in
provide s'one with		
punish s'one for		
quarrel about		
refer to	related to	reaction to
rely on	respected for	reason for
result in	responsible for	report on/about
		responsibility for
		result of
		rise in
		room for
save s'one from	satisfied with	similarity between
sentence s'one to	sensitive to(wards)	solution to
smile at	serious about	(have/show) sympathy for
stand for	sick of	
succeed in	similar to	
suffer from	sorry for/about	
	suspicious of	
	sympathetic to(wards)	
talk to s'one about s'thg	tired of	trouble with
thank s'one for	typical of	
think of/about		
	used to	use of
wait for		
warn s'one about		
worry about		

APPENDIX 2

Preposition + word combinations

at dawn/night
at a distance
at first
at first sight
at a glance
at a guess
at gunpoint
at home/school
at a later stage
at last
at the latest
at least
at once
at peace/war
at present
at a profit
at random
at risk
at sea
at the same time
at a time of
at times
at work

by accident
by bus/car/plane/bike
by chance
by cheque
by day/night
by far
by hand
by heart
by land/sea/air
by all means
by means of
by mistake
by oneself
by (25)%
by phone/post/fax
by return
by sight
(take) by surprise
by yourself
bit by bit/one by one etc.

for ages/ever
for your birthday
for a change
for the first/last time
for good
for hire
for life
for nothing
for once
for sale
for s'one's sake
for the time being
for a visit/holiday
for a while

from now on
from time to time

in addition (to)
in advance
in agreement with
in answer to
in bed
in bloom
in any case
in charge
in common (with)
in danger (of)
in the dark
in (great) detail
in difficulty
in the end
in fact
in fashion
in favour of
in flames
in general
in half/two
in honour of
in a hurry
in ink/pencil
in Italian/Chinese etc.
in length/height etc.
in love
in a good/bad mood
in the news
in s'one's opinion

in pain
in pieces
in practice/theory
in prison
in private/public
in relation to
in safety
in secret
in self-defence
in stock
in the sun/shade
in tears
in (good) time
in touch
in the town/countryside
in tune
in turn
in (your) twenties etc.
in uniform
in use
in view of
in a way
in other words
in writing

off duty
off work

on account of
on behalf of
on business
on a diet
on duty
on fire
on foot
on the other hand
on holiday
on the increase
on a journey
on loan
on s'one's mind
on order
on the phone
on purpose
on sale
on second thoughts
on strike

on time
on trial
on TV/the radio
on the Internet
on the whole

out of breath
out of control
out of danger
out of date
out of order
out of place
out of practice
out of print
out of the question
out of reach
out of sight
out of stock
three/six etc. out of ten
out of work

under age
under attack
under your breath
under control
under pressure

up to and including
up to date

with a smile/laugh etc.
within reach (of)
without fail
without success
without warning

APPENDIX 3

Model answers for Writing chapter

Unit 6

Exercise B1, Sample Question 1, page 84 (also referred to in the 'further practice' section on page 90)

Dear Sir/Madam

I saw your advertisement for walking holidays in the Himalayas and would be grateful for some more information.

First of all, I should tell you a bit about myself so you can decide whether I might be a suitable person to join an expedition like this. I am in my mid-twenties and have done quite a lot of long-distance walking, but not very much at high altitudes. How high will the expedition be going? I consider myself to be very fit, so I hope this will not be a problem. As for offering a useful skill to the group, the only thing I can think of is that I am good at drawing, so I could record what we see.

I would like to know more about the expedition. Your advertisement did not mention the dates, nor the cost and obviously these are very important. I am also interested to know something about the group itself – how many people will there be and what qualifications do your guides have?

I look forward to hearing from you soon.

Yours faithfully

(180 words)

Unit 7

Exercise B9, Exam practice, page 95

A student magazine is organising a short story competition. Entrants must write a short story about a day when something surprising happened. The **story** must begin like this: 'Sonya put the letter on the table and left the room.'

Sonya put the letter on the table and left the room. She walked slowly into the kitchen and stood looking out of the window. Next door's cat was digging a hole in her garden, but for once she didn't care. She couldn't believe what she'd just read in John's letter. He was getting married. How dare he write and tell her that!

She and John had been together for three years. They'd been thinking about getting married when she finished her university course, but then John's firm had offered him a great opportunity to work in Sri Lanka and he felt he couldn't turn it down. It was a two-year contract and Sonya had encouraged him to accept. She knew he would regret it if he didn't.

At first, it was fine – they E-mailed each other more or less every day. But recently there had been some silences from his end. And now this. She knew she had to phone John immediately, so she walked back into the sitting room, picked up the letter and began to dial.

(180 words)

Unit 8

Exercise B10, Exam practice, page 101 (Question 2 from the Information Box on page 96)

You have been invited to write a short **article** for your college magazine on a teacher who has been important in your life. Write the article. Include details of the teacher's character and say why the person is/was important.

<u>My French teacher</u>

Mrs Griffiths was the first teacher I had who filled me with a love of language. Up until that point I had never enjoyed speaking a foreign language. Like most children, I had always felt rather self-conscious.

What I liked most about Mrs Griffiths was her enthusiasm. She obviously loved the French language and somehow she managed to communicate this to a class of thirty 12-year-olds. She made speaking French fun, rather than agony.

As well as this, she had a wonderfully vivid imagination; she made up lots of stories or situations that seemed exciting, and then made us act some of them out. We were hopeless, but she never made us feel we were. I still remember the encouragement she gave to us all.

As a result of her teaching, my love of language was born. I am here at college studying French and Spanish, and I am thinking of training to be a teacher. So you can see, she was responsible for a lot!

(170 words)

Unit 9

Exercise B7, Exam practice, page 106 (Question 2 from the Information Box on page 102)

Your college is starting a video library. You have been asked to report on a film you've seen recently with a view to including the video in the library. Write your **report**: give a brief description of the film, comment on the level of language difficulty, and say who the film might appeal to.

Report on: <u>'Elizabeth'</u>

Description: A historical drama. It tells the story of how Elizabeth 1 becomes queen of England in the sixteenth century, and how she has to fight against all the male prejudice. The acting, particularly by the main characters, is fantastic – there's even a small role for Eric Cantona, more famous as a footballer in France. The best thing about the film is it is wonderfully visual – the colours, scenes, costumes are memorable.

Language: I found it very clear and easy to understand – maybe because it's historical and the language is not so colloquial. Most of our students will have no difficulty with the level of language.

Appeal to: Most people, but particularly the students who are studying European history – they'll know more about that period than the rest of us do. There were one or two points when a knowledge of British history would have been helpful, but not essential.

Comment: I think it would be a great addition to our video library. Let's get it!

(170 words)

205

APPENDIX 4

How to show your answers

You show your answers in a different way in each of the four exam papers.

1	A B C D E F G H I
2	A B C D E F G H I
3	A B C D E F G H I
4	A B C D E F G H I

Paper 1 Reading

For Paper 1 you mark **all** your answers in pencil on a special answer sheet.

Paper 2 Writing

For Paper 2 you write your answers in pen on empty pages of the question sheet. Remember to write clearly.

Paper 3 Use of English

For Paper 3 you mark or write your answers in pencil on special answer sheets.

> For Part 1 you fill in a 'lozenge' as you did in the Reading paper.
> For Part 2 you write **one** word in each space.
> For Part 3 you write between **two** and **five** words in each space.
> For Part 4 you write **one** word or put a tick (✓) in each space.
> For Part 5 you write **one** word in each space.

Part 2		Do not write here
16	*although*	16
17		17
18		18
19		19
20		20

Paper 4 Listening

During the Listening Test, you write your answers on the question paper. At the end of the test, you have five minutes to copy your answers in pencil onto a special answer sheet.

> For Part 1 you fill in a 'lozenge' to show your answer (A, B or C).
> For Part 2 you write your answer in each space.
> For Part 3 you fill in lozenges as in Part 1.
> For Part 4, depending on the question, you write T(rue)/F(alse), or Y(es)/N(o), or A/B/C, or other letters.

Part 4		Do not write here
24	*T*	24
25		25
26		26
27		27

For Papers 1, 3 and 4:

- You must complete the answer sheet in pencil.
- If you change your mind about an answer, rub it out and rewrite it.
- If you change one answer, you may have to change others.
- Make sure that you put an answer for **every** question. Don't leave any answers blank; if you are not sure, guess!
- Don't write the example (0) item by mistake.
- Don't write more words than you are supposed to.
- Check that you've put your answers against the right question numbers.

For all papers:
- Write as clearly as possible.

APPENDIX 5 *Tapescripts*

Chapter 4 Listening

The material in Section A is on the cassette once. The material in Section B is on twice.

LISTENING SECTION A UNIT 1

Exercise A1 Page 158
Sentence 1: We **rented** a **house** in a **small village** in the **hills** about **30 minutes' drive** from the **coast**.
Sentence 2: There were **six** of us so the **house** was **quite big**.
Sentence 3: But the **best thing** about it was the **garden**.
Sentence 4: It was **huge**.
Sentence 5: We spent a **lot** of **time** there and in the **evenings** we had **barbecues outside**.
Sentence 6: The **kids** wanted to **go** to the **sea**, of course.
Sentence 7: So **every morning** we **took** them **there** and John and **I took** it in **turns** to **stay** with them on the **beach**.

Exercise A2 Page 159
ZOE: When either **John** or **I** were not on **duty** we **went off** and **explored** the **town**. Then we'd all **meet** for **lunch**. The **food** there was **wonderful**, especially the **fresh fish**. And the **kids** couldn't believe their **luck** with the **ice creams**. They came in **huge dishes** with **lots** of **fruit**, and little **umbrellas** in, and on the **last day** we were there, the ice creams came **lit up** with **sparklers**. That was the **highlight** of the **whole** two weeks for **Jamie**, I can tell you!

Exercise A3 Page 159
MAN: I never imagined myself ever going on that kind of course. I mean I'm just not the type. But it was my boss, actually, who asked me to go – he thought someone in the office should know what to do in an emergency. And I suppose he's right. Anyway, to my surprise, I found some of it really interesting – particularly the practical bits like dealing with people when they faint, or what to do if someone cuts themselves really badly. It was only a weekend course, so I'm not an expert, but I think I'd have a good idea what to do – and more than anything I guess, I wouldn't panic now.

Exercise A4 Page 160

Extract 1
MAN: No look, it just isn't right. We've paid to go on the excursion to the cathedral and we want to go.
WOMAN: I'm really sorry, Mr Carstairs. There's a problem. You see the person who took your booking shouldn't have, because the coach was already full.
MAN: So, you're saying you've overbooked. That's not very clever, is it?
WOMAN: No, but there'll be another excursion – exactly the same – tomorrow. You'd be the first on the list for that.
MAN: That's not much good to me – we're leaving tomorrow.
WOMAN: Well all I can say is that I'm really sorry. I'll give you a full refund of course.

Extract 2
WOMAN: Any of the owners of Britain's 7 million cats will tell you that these creatures are absolutely wonderful, but probably most owners don't really realise how wonderful their pet is. The ancestor of all domestic cats is the African tabby. Regardless of whether we're talking about the elegant Siamese or the cat that lives in the street, they all come from the same origins. When humans began living together in towns and villages, that's when cats decided to join them. They realised very quickly that food was to be found near humans, and they became domesticated. In ancient Egypt, cats were regarded as gods and they had a very comfortable life.

To find out what a cat is thinking, watch its tail. The tail is the most expressive part. If it's in the up position, the cat is greeting you, but if the tail starts to swing, it's a sign of aggression. Sometimes, before a fight, a cat makes its tail bigger by fluffing it up. This is done to frighten the opposition. When cats meet, they also communicate with their eyes. A cat will sometimes sit for hours, more or less without moving, and just stare threateningly at another cat that has entered its territory. And then there's the purr – you know that wonderful sound a cat makes, and we think they're letting us know how happy we have made them. In fact, they're more likely to be purring for themselves, simply to say 'I'm here'.

Extract 3
WOMAN: Well, that was an interesting evening last night. How long has it been since we last saw all those people?
MAN: Must be at least ten years. Longer in some cases.
WOMAN: I'm glad you introduced me to Robert. I'd never have remembered him. He's changed such a lot, hasn't he?
MAN: Certainly has! Slimmed down a bit. And do you remember his hair?
WOMAN: Oh yes, it was incredibly long and he wore it tied back.
MAN: He'd have got some strange looks from his office if he'd kept it like that. In fact, he's going a bit thin on top. He'll be bald soon. And he's lost his earring as well.
WOMAN: No he hasn't. It's still there, just smaller and more discreet, that's all.
MAN: Thank goodness he hasn't changed everything. Anyway, what about Paula?
WOMAN: Didn't she look great? Never used to though. Do you remember she had big front teeth, and her hair was really curly, like a bubble bath. Her mother was really strict about how she dressed and the make-up she wore and everything. And she had horrible rows with her about wanting to have her ears pierced. Her mother just refused to let her!
MAN: When was that, then?
WOMAN: When she was about 16.
MAN: Well, she's certainly made up for it now. Those things she was wearing in her ears must have weighed a ton!
WOMAN: Actually, she's put on a bit of weight, hasn't she?
MAN: Mmm, but it suits her. It would have been impossible for her to stay as thin as she was.
WOMAN: True. Isn't this awful? We sound like two old gossips.
MAN: I know. I wonder what they're saying about us?

Exercise A5 Page 161

WOMAN: John lay in bed listening to the sounds of his mates in the apartment getting ready for work. He knew he should get up, but couldn't see the point. What was there to do?
'Cup of tea, John?' called out Paul, who was always the last to leave.
'Please,' said John.
'Got anything on today?' asked Paul as he handed over a steaming mug of tea.
'Not really. Thought I'd go down the job club and see if anything new has come in. But I'm not very hopeful.'
'Don't give up, you've only been unemployed for three weeks. Something'll turn up soon.'

When everyone had left, the place seemed unnaturally quiet. This was the moment that John dreaded. It seemed as if he was the only person in the world who had no purpose. It was tempting to pull the covers up over his head and hide, but he didn't.
'Get going, move, make an effort. Today may be the one that changes your useless life,' John muttered to himself as he banged about the flat. He did the washing up, which the others had left behind. Interesting that – that they'd started not bothering to do things around the apartment. Nobody said anything but John knew they all thought he'd got nothing to do so he'd jump at the chance to make himself useful. Well, damn it, they were right. He did feel that by clearing up after them he was at least doing his bit in some way. But it still all seemed like a dream. Why was he standing in the kitchen on a Monday morning when he should be discussing the fall in share prices on the stock market? That's what he was doing a month ago. If anyone'd told him then what was just around the corner, he wouldn't have believed it. John knew thinking about the past was the worst thing he could do. It just got him down – or made him bitter. So he deliberately made himself hurry. He grabbed his briefcase, made sure the answerphone was on – someone might phone with an amazing offer – and left the apartment to face the world as seen through the eyes of the unemployed.

LISTENING SECTION A UNIT 2

Exercises A1 and A2 Page 162

Extract 1

WOMAN: Could we have your attention please? We have here in our office, a little boy who says his name is Daniel, and he's lost his Mum and Dad. Could Daniel's Mum and Dad come to the customer services department on the second floor to collect him?

Extract 2

WOMAN: Well, anyway, I phoned Gary and told him I couldn't make it.
MAN: And? What did he say?
WOMAN: Nothing much. He seemed to accept it. Pass the salt.
MAN: Didn't he even try to persuade you to change your mind?

Extract 3

MAN: Do you feel you made the right choice?
WOMAN: Yes, I think I knew from a very early age that music was going to be my life in some way or another.
MAN: What was your parents' attitude to your decision?
WOMAN: They knew me well enough not to try to dissuade me!

Extract 4

WOMAN: Thank you for calling the Los Angeles Bus Company hotline today, August 14th. If you are speaking on a touch-tone telephone, please use the buttons. If at any stage you make a mistake, press zero to take you back to the beginning.

Extract 5

WOMAN: I'm sorry, she's not in at the moment ... No, she didn't say ... Yes, sure, just let me get a pen ... OK, go ahead.

Extract 6

WOMAN: Gino pushed open the door and walked into the restaurant. He fully expected to be met by silence, and he was not disappointed. Fifty heads turned in his direction and all conversation died. His walk from the door to Anna's table was the longest he could remember.

Extract 7

MAN: So, get the old umbrellas out today, we're in for a soaking, especially in the north and west of the country. And it looks set to stay that way for the next few days, I'm afraid.

Extract 8

MAN: Poulton's After Dinner Mints. What a ridiculous name! They're not after dinner mints, they're during the morning, after lunch, before going out, while watching TV mints. Whenever you feel like a cool, chocolatey mint, Poulton's are the ones.

Extract 9

WOMAN: And so finally, I'd like to thank everyone for coming and for making my parents' silver wedding anniversary a special day. And I'd just like to say thanks, Mum and Dad, you've been great ... so far!

Extract 10

MAN: Most scientists believe that in the beginning there was nothing. It may seem absurd to believe that something – indeed everything in the universe, including the earth, sun, moon and all the planets and stars – could come from nothing, but astronomers and physicists assert this with increasing confidence.

Extract 11

MAN: Over on the left, you'll see the famous Sears Tower, which was, until recently, the world's tallest building. Does anyone know which building has taken over the record? ... Yes, that's right. Anyway, the Sears Tower is the biggest on our continent.

Extract 12

WOMAN: At the International Environment Conference in Athens today, delegates were told that unless drastic measures were taken, the quality of life in our cities would become unbearable. Over to our correspondent in Athens, Milton Davies, for more detail. Milton ...

Exercise A3 Page 163

Extract 1

MAN: I've never been in a helicopter before. I'm lucky to have the chance, really. I'm really looking forward to it.

Extract 2

WOMAN: Yes, I think it looks good, too. Just the right colour. I'm happy with it.

Extract 3

WOMAN: He just doesn't know where he can find the money from. He's thought of everything, but nothing's come up so far. I don't know how long he can carry on like this.

Extract 4

MAN: Well, I'm sorry, but if you'd given me all the facts in the first place, I wouldn't have had to ring you again, would I?

Extract 5

WOMAN: I was expecting more, actually. All the magazines kept going on about how good it was, but it didn't strike me as anything special.

Extract 6

MAN: I know I shouldn't have told her, but I didn't realise how she'd react. I feel bad about it now.

Extract 7

MAN: She didn't fail, did she? I don't believe it. She was the best one in the group.

Extract 8

WOMAN: I guess it'll all be over in about half an hour – then I can relax a bit. Oh, my turn – here goes. Do I look all right?

Exercise A4 Page 163

KATHY: Philip! I'm over here. Come on, you can come in here.

PHILIP: Excuse me, do you mind if I join my friend? … Thanks … She didn't seem too pleased about that, did she? Cor, I can't believe it's taken so long to get here. I had to walk from home.

KATHY: Why? What was wrong with the bus?

PHILIP: I stood at the stop for ten minutes and three went past completely full so I gave up. Anyway, I'm here now. How long have you been waiting?

KATHY: Since about 9.00. I couldn't believe the number of people who'd arrived even earlier. How many do you think there are ahead of us?

PHILIP: About a hundred or so, I guess. Look, do you want to go and see if there's any sign of movement up front? I'll hang on here.

KATHY: OK.

PHILIP: And see if you can bring back some coffee or something. I didn't have time for breakfast.

KATHY: Oh you poor thing! Neither did I … Here you are. Black, no sugar.

PHILIP: Thanks. What news?

KATHY: Well, there's a lot of activity inside. The lights are all on and there are loads of assistants standing round, but the doors aren't open yet.

PHILIP: They've got to wait for him to arrive first and get settled.

KATHY: Suppose so. Have you got your book with you?

PHILIP: No, I thought I'd buy one quickly when we get in.

KATHY: I bought mine last week when I knew he was coming. Thought it'd save time.

PHILIP: Very sensible – as usual. Hey look, there's a big car pulling up now.

KATHY: Oh yes, this is getting exciting.

PHILIP: It's him – I think. I can't really see, can you?

KATHY: Too many large men surrounding him, but it must be.

PHILIP: Good, so not long now.

KATHY: Look, we'll have to separate when we get in, 'cos I'm going to get mine signed straight away, so the best thing is if we arrange to meet after in the café round the corner.

PHILIP: OK, I'll take longer than you, so that's probably a good idea. Hey, we're moving. Great.

LISTENING SECTION A UNIT 3

Exercise A1 Page 164

Extract 1

WOMAN: Who'd win the insect Olympics?
The gold medal for weightlifting would go to the rhinoceros beetle, which can support up to 850 times its own weight. There are many different kinds of rhinoceros beetle from small to large, but the strongest and largest are the African variety. They have to be strong enough to dig out large amounts of earth and big stones in order to make their nests.

MAN: The insect champion of the 100 metres would be the cockroach. One particular kind of cockroach has been timed at 5.4 kilometres per hour, which is like a human running the 100 metres in just over a second. At this speed, the cockroach actually runs just on its back two legs. They have developed this style of running in order to escape as quickly as possible from things that eat them – rats and spiders. But they can only keep it up for a short time.

WOMAN: The high jump master is the cat flea, which can jump 130 times its own height – the equivalent of a human jumping over a 50-storey building. This jumping talent enables a flea to jump from one animal that it lives on to another. But jumping this high can be dangerous because of the pressure the flea experiences on his body. So nature designed a kind of outer shell for him, which acts as a pressure suit, so he can hop about happily.

Extract 2

BOB: A friend of mine just phoned for a chat about a problem he's got, and I've agreed to go and see him. You can't have a serious discussion without something to drink, so I've come to get some.

BETTINA: We've just invited friends for supper. Then we discovered we had nothing in the fridge. It's so convenient to be able to pop out and buy just about anything at any time of the day or night. We've just bought all the stuff for spaghetti bolognese.

CAROL: I was on my way home after having dinner with a friend, when my babysitter rang me on my mobile phone. She's changed my baby daughter's nappy and used the last one in the packet. I don't know what I'd have done if the supermarket hadn't been open. I normally have a really good stock of nappies, so I haven't a clue how I managed to run out. I felt a bit embarrassed buying nappies at midnight, but no one gave me a second look.

GEORGE: I regularly work nights at the ambulance station and never have time to prepare a meal to take with me. I normally cook something in the staff kitchen at four in the morning. I've just got some steak and salad today. The 24-hour supermarket is next door to where I work. Since it started staying open all the time, I do most of my shopping here in the early hours.

STELLA: I work at the hospital nearby, and we've just run out of coffee. This place is so handy. I'm constantly amazed at the number of people who are shopping in the middle of the night. I even came at 4 o'clock in the morning once, and there was a woman doing her big weekly shop.

DAVID: I usually get up at 5 o'clock to go to work. This morning I turned on the bathroom light and the bulb blew. I didn't have a spare. Luckily I live nearby, so I ran to get a replacement. I couldn't have shaved in the dark!

ANNA: I'm just coming home from a club. I've been out all night and had a great time. I stopped here to buy a carton of fruit juice. I come from Australia and lots of big stores open 24 hours there. It's perfectly normal and loads of people take advantage of them.

Exercise A2 Page 165

WOMAN: Heavens above! I didn't realise there were so many fish cookbooks. Which one do you think Kate'd like?

MAN: No idea. How about this one, 'Tasty Fish'? £15.99. It's got loads of colour pictures in it so at least you know what you should be aiming at.

WOMAN: So has this one, 'Something Fishy'. Has your one got any recipes for spicy fish – you know – Thai or Indonesian cooking? Kate's really into that at the moment.

MAN: Noooo, I don't think so. Seems to be mainly fairly traditional stuff. But this one must have: 'Worldwide Fish' – that's bound to have some oriental recipes in.

WOMAN: Sounds interesting – let's have a look … Oh I don't like it so much. It looks more like a reference book rather than a cookbook – a lot of reading and not many pictures.

MAN: It's interesting though, isn't it, the way it's organised fish by fish. Who would have thought there were so many things you could do with a piece of salmon. I'd like this one – it'd be easy to find what you wanted.

WOMAN: True. How much is it?

MAN: £12 – not very expensive

WOMAN: And the one I picked up first – where did I put it … ?

MAN: Which one?

WOMAN: 'Something Fishy'… oh here it is. That's £17.99. What do you think?

MAN: It's got some Thai recipes in, which is what you want – but they're a bit buried in all the others. You'd have to search through to find them.

WOMAN: Mmm. It's a bit of a muddle, isn't it? I'm not sure it's very useful being organised season by season. Still, it's got a good index at the back. Well, we can't spend all day doing this. I'm going to get it. She can always change it if she doesn't like it.

Exercise A3 Page 165

JACK: Look Sarah, here's another article about that picture in the summer exhibition.

SARAH: D'you mean the 'Portrait of a Murderer'?

JACK: Yes.

MARIA: Have you been to see it, Sarah?

SARAH: Yes, and it's pretty powerful. It's just his head and shoulders, but it's sort of made up of bits of paper with writing on.

MARIA: Well that doesn't sound anything special.

JACK: It's what's on the bits of paper that everyone is talking about, Maria. The words are taken from letters he wrote to his intended victims. This reporter says it shouldn't be on public display, that it's unfair to the victims' families, and I must say I think I agree with him. And I guess you do too, don't you Maria?

MARIA: Yes, but I don't imagine any of the families will go to see it.

SARAH: So, neither of you has actually seen it, right?

JACK: Yes, I have, actually.

MARIA: No, and I don't think I want to either, Sarah.

SARAH: I think you should. And I bet that reporter hasn't seen it either. What strikes me as unfair is the way people keep expressing opinions about it without having seen it.

MARIA: True. What did you think of it, Jack?

JACK: I thought, as a piece of art, it was nothing special. I mean, people have been making picures out of torn up paper for ages. It was the subject matter that was shocking, and I just thought the artist did it to get all this free publicity – and he's succeeded, hasn't he? We're all talking about it, aren't we, Sarah?

SARAH: Mm, but I had a different reaction. I can understand that the families might be upset by it, but it's an amazing experience looking at it. People were getting up close so they could read what was written. And quite a few people were obviously very moved by it – including me.

MARIA: I suppose one thing is that those horrible murders will never just fade into the background – if that was the artist's intention – you know, to make people remember for always that particular crime. Maybe I should go and see it.

LISTENING SECTION B UNIT 4

Familiarisation exercise Page 166

Extract 1

WOMAN: Well, it wasn't what I'd planned to do. In fact, I was never particularly interested in kids. When I was little, I quite liked the idea of being a doctor – you know, walking around in a white coat looking important – and of course my parents were keen for me to go into the bank, like them. But then after school I did a year of voluntary work abroad, and I discovered I actually enjoyed working with little ones and helping them to learn. So I trained, and here I am.

Extract 2

WOMAN: So where were you when you saw him, then?

MAN: Outside the supermarket in Collins Street. I'd just come out in a rush as usual, and he was going in.

WOMAN: And? Did he look like he did in 'Wallgame'?

MAN: Well, no he didn't, unfortunately. If I hadn't almost knocked him over, I wouldn't have noticed him. He looked ever so small and ordinary, and he had a tiny –

WOMAN: Stop! Don't tell me any more. Leave me with my dreams. You'll be saying he didn't have blue eyes next.

MAN: Well, funny you should mention that …

Exercise B1 Page 167

Extract 1

SARAH: Hi Mark. Sorry I'm a bit late. I missed the bus. You haven't been here long, have you?

MARK: Since 7.00, actually.

SARAH: I thought we said 7.30.

MARK: No, we can't have. The film starts at half past.

SARAH: I'm sure we said 7.30. Don't you remember, I said I was meeting Jane after work and I couldn't get here earlier?

MARK: That's news to me! Anyway, do you want to go to this film, or not? We've probably only missed the first few minutes.

SARAH: OK.

Extract 2

MAN: Yes, I know, I'm sorry, darling, but it's not my fault. Anyway, I'm on the way now. I'll be there in another hour or so … What time are they expecting us? … Well, it'd be quicker if you could pick me up at the station … I'll ring you again when we're about ten minutes away … No, I don't need to, do I? A suit isn't too formal for John and Penny, is it? … OK, speak to you soon.

Extract 3

WOMAN: Now remember, when guests arrive late at night, their first priority is to get to their rooms and get to bed, so they don't want a lot of fuss from us. They're tired, they've probably been travelling all day. So keep all the paperwork short. Just get them to register, give them their room number, and get one of the porters to take them up. Don't start giving them details of when the swimming pool is open or how to use the fitness room. That's the entertainment officer's job anyway. OK?

Extract 4

MRS B: Now, you know where everything is, don't you Lisa? And I've left the number of the restaurant we're going to by the phone in case you need to get hold of us urgently.

LISA: That's fine, Mrs Bentham. You go and enjoy yourself.

MRS B: If he wakes up, he might just need a drink. His special juice is in the fridge. But if he doesn't go back to sleep after that, you may have to read him a story. His favourite at the moment is 'Animal Wood'. It's on top of the bookcase somewhere.

LISA: Don't worry, I'll find it.

MRS B: And help yourself to coffee or whatever. It's on the worktop in the kitchen. Oh, I've just remembered, you'd rather have tea, wouldn't you? That's in the right-hand cupboard.

Extract 5

MAN: What did you think about last night's meeting? I really feel we're in for a rough time.

WOMAN: Yes, the sales forecast for the next 18 months isn't good, is it? They didn't actually say it, but it obviously means they're going to have to make cutbacks and get rid of some people.

MAN: Yes, and you know how they're going to do it, don't you?

WOMAN: No, how?

MAN: They'll use the results of those personnel assessment tests we all had to do in February. I remember at the time wondering why they were suddenly introducing new American-style management techniques.

WOMAN: Well, now we know.

Extract 6

WOMAN: Well, Thursday's a bit difficult, actually Mrs Fleming. Dr Thompson's at his other surgery all morning and the afternoon's more or less full. What about Friday? We could do mid-morning … Yes, I see, it is tricky sometimes. Well, could you manage first appointment on Friday? … 8 o'clock. We try to keep that one free for people like you who don't want to take time off work … Fine. I'll put you down for that then, Mrs Fleming.

Exercise B2 Page 167

Extract 1

MAN: Have you seen this latest report?

WOMAN: Yes, makes depressing reading, doesn't it? I really felt like giving up when I read it.

MAN: It made me angry. I mean, where do they get all these statistics from? I can't believe that one in six adults can't read or do simple adding up.

WOMAN: Well, I'm sure they haven't just made it up. Do you think it makes us seem useless or the people we're trying to teach?

MAN: Both, probably.

WOMAN: Oh dear! I think I've chosen the wrong job.

Extract 2

MAN: No, I don't want to book, I've already got two tickets. The thing is, the person I was coming with can't come now, so I was hoping to return her ticket to you to sell … OK, I'll bring it in this lunchtime … I see, but there's a good chance, you think … Right, so after the show, to the box office … Thank you ma'am.

Extract 3

WOMAN: They were lovely, dark brown lace-ups with a good thick sole, but they were too tight round the toes. I'd never have been able to wear them in the winter with thick socks. Anyway, just as I was leaving the shop, I bumped into Emily and she'd just bought the most amazing dress for Frank's wedding. It's red with a really low back. It'll look great with her colouring.

Extract 4

WOMAN: So you think it was the video camera, the TV and the stereo that they took. Anything else, do you think – jewellery, watches, ornaments, money? … No, I appreciate it's difficult to be sure. The best thing to do is stand in each room and look round slowly and try to remember what's normally there. And if you could come down to the station to give us a full report, you know, makes, serial numbers and so on.

Extract 5

WOMAN: Cor, I thought it was meant to be a comedy.

MAN: Well, there are some funny bits.

WOMAN: Mm. Not yet there aren't. I couldn't believe it when Jessica started talking about her childhood. I mean, do you think anyone has such a bad time as that?

MAN: Yes, I'm sure they do. Anyway, it's supposed to be based on the writer's own life, isn't it?

WOMAN: Is it? Gosh, poor woman!

Exercise B3 Page 168

Extract 1

MAN: Oh good, 8.30, 'Animals of the Andes', BBC 1.

WOMAN: Same time as the football.

MAN: We can record that.

WOMAN: No, it's much better live. Record your animal progamme instead.

MAN: We can't do either until we get some new batteries for the remote control thing.

WOMAN: Course we can. You can programme directly onto the video.

Extract 2

MAN: Can I have a current statement, please?

TOGETHER: Oh, hello!

MAN: Didn't I see you at the gym last night?

WOMAN: Yes, … training for next month's marathon.

MAN: How long have you been at it, then?

WOMAN: Oh, every day for about six weeks now, I guess. Seems longer though.

MAN: I bet.

WOMAN: The mornings are the worst, pounding the streets for miles. Still, they're very good here. They don't seem to mind if I arrive a bit late sometimes. In fact, my boss is going to sponsor me. Perhaps you'd like to, too?

MAN: Sure. You can take it straight out of my account!

Extract 3

MAN: Our final speaker is someone I'm sure you all know from his books – 12 of them to date, and he's working on the next. He is the voice when it comes to trying to explain the mysterious things we see. His ideas are based on records of thousands of unexplained sightings over the past years. Ladies and gentlemen, I can think of no better person to wrap up this final session of our conference.

Extract 4

WOMAN: I couldn't believe it. I mean, I know he's under pressure – we all are. But that's no reason to be so rude. It's so unlike him. Apparently, I've got to apologise then he'll forget all about it. Well, I don't see why I should. It wasn't me who forgot to make the stupid reservation. Honestly, I really don't feel like facing him again.

Extract 5

MAN: I put my bag down here, just by the desk, to speak to you. Do you remember? I was asking you about the bus to the beach.

WOMAN: Yes, about ten minutes ago.

MAN: That's right. I went outside to wait for the number ten, and I was thinking to myself – I hope I don't see too many interesting sights today 'cos I haven't got a spare film, and I was feeling about in the bag, under my beach towel – I'm always careful to put something on top of it so it's not too easy to steal – and I realised it wasn't there anymore.

Exercise B4 Exam practice Page 169

Extract 1

MAN: It seems a great club – lots of hi-tech equipment. I like the look of that running machine particularly, and I certainly need something to help me get fitter. But you know, I haven't been in Oxford very long, so really I'm just hoping I'll be able to get to know some new people here.

Extract 2

MAN: I thought it was an awful book. Honestly, just because it's set in the future doesn't mean it has to be so strange. I mean, for a romance, it was pretty weird, don't you think?

WOMAN: No, not really. I enjoyed all the action around their relationship. I thought it was really exciting.

MAN: Yeah, maybe, but it took you away from what should've been the main point of the story – the way they came together.

Extract 3

MAN: OK, Mary from Glasgow, go ahead, put your point.

MARY: Well, I can't believe what your last caller said. How would she like it if she was on a beach and some photographer stuck his camera in her face. I mean …

MAN: But these people are famous – they must expect it, surely?

MARY: Yes, but not all the time. Not when they're not on duty, so to speak. Everybody on your programme seems to think that these photographers can do anything, but I just want to set the record straight, I don't. There should be some respect for people's privacy.

Extract 4

MAN: In the 1980s we were into heavy metal music and the great trend then was to wear jeans so tight they really almost stopped your circulation. Well, my Mum made my jeans at that time and they were deeply unfashionable. I used to insist on her taking them in and this was a cause of great conflict at home. I refused to go out in jeans that were more than ten centimetres wider than my ankles.

Extract 5

WOMAN: These ones here are really good. You see where it says 'sizzling dishes'?

MAN: Mm.

WOMAN: They come to the table all bubbling and spitting. I had the beef one last time.

MAN: Worth having again, then.

WOMAN: Well, I'd rather try something different – like fish.

MAN: Mm, I'm not too keen on that, actually … What about this duck thing, it seems to be a sort of speciality?

WOMAN: Mm, 'crispy duck with an aromatic sauce' – yum.

MAN: OK, well that's one, then. And I quite like the sound of this rice, it seems to have a bit of everything in it.

WOMAN: I think the noodles are better actually.

Extract 6

WOMAN: … Yes, I know, but in the end I didn't really have any choice, did I? The sad thing is I'd only been there three months and I was actually beginning to enjoy it. But making me work for two bosses instead of just the one, well, that wasn't fair. I didn't know whether I was coming or going … No, I couldn't, I knew it wouldn't have worked. Still, it's a pity.

Extract 7

MAN: Well, I dunno really. I just got up this morning and I couldn't walk. It feels like hot knives sticking into my right knee … No, I can't move. Oh I've just thought – you couldn't ring my boss and tell him what's happened, could you? I really don't feel like talking to him today … Thanks, that's great. And tonight's off, I'm afraid … That'd be nice … And bring some aspirin or something with you when you come.

Extract 8

MAN: Come on, you'll enjoy it.

WOMAN: No really I can't. I must get this report finished by tomorrow if I want to get paid this month – and I do as my bank balance is not in a healthy state at the moment!

MAN: But you'd be better after a break.

WOMAN: Oh I know, but in any case, I don't like big Hollywood-type films, you know that.

MAN: OK. Well if I can't persuade you …

LISTENING SECTION B UNIT 5

Familiarisation exercise Page 171

KEVIN: And now it's time for our regular weekly guide for visitors to the city. Here's Sue Ashcroft with some suggestions.

SUE: Thanks, Kevin. Well, first of all, for those of you who don't know Oldcaster at all, the best way to start is with one of the open-top bus tours. You get a wonderful view of the most interesting sights, such as the castle and the old royal palace, and at the same time you'll hear all about the town's history from the guide. If your English isn't too good, you can hear a recorded commentary in a choice of four other languages. For those of you interested in art, there's an interesting exhibition this week at the Central Library of work by local painters, and there's a marvellous reconstruction of a 19th-century bottle factory. That's not at the library – it's at the City Museum.

KEVIN: What about sport, Sue, is there anything for visitors to do or see?

SUE: Yes, there's the swimming pool, which is open from 8 o'clock every day until 7.00, or, if you prefer your sport sitting down, Oldcaster Rovers football team are playing this Saturday, kick-off 3 o'clock, and seats are still available for £10.

Exercise B2 Page 172

MAN: Good evening and welcome to 'Hardlife', the programme that talks to ordinary people about their jobs. Today's guest is Barbara Currie, who's a dentist. Welcome, Barbara.

BARBARA: Thank you.

MAN: I suppose I should start by asking you how you became interested in dentistry?

BARBARA: Well, I suppose it started when I was eight, really. My older brother tripped me up and I smashed my front tooth. The dentist put in a gold one, which I thought was wonderful. I had it until I was 17. Well, in fact I've still got it, but not in my mouth. I wear it on this chain here, see.

MAN: Oh yes, how unusual! But in a way a good advertisement for your job.

BARBARA: True. Anyway, after that early fascination with my gold tooth, I suppose I kind of followed the normal course – you know, science subjects at school, university and so on.

MAN: And you've been practising now for … what … ten years or so?

BARBARA: Fifteen now.

MAN: And would you say that dentistry is still a man's world? I mean, I can't remember ever having a woman dentist in my life.

BARBARA: Well it used to be a totally male profession. It's getting better, but you still find only a few women who own their own practices. Most of them are junior partners or employees in a man's business.

MAN: I pride myself on being a very good patient for the dentist, but others in my family are awful. In your experience, is it common for people to be frightened of the dentist?

BARBARA: Well, not really the dentist him or herself, but more the whole experience, and yes, some really frightened people only make it as far as the front door by themselves. I have to go through a long process of getting them to come in, walk around, sit down and then leave.

MAN: You mean you don't actually do any work on their teeth?

BARBARA: No that's right. Sometimes, as I say, if people are really scared, the first visit is simply helping them to feel a bit more comfortable with the place, the furniture, the smell etcetera. Then, hopefully, when they come back next time, we move on to the next stage, walking them round my room with all the instruments, and explaining what everything is and what it does. It's a very time-consuming process. We've come a long way in recent years in helping people to cope with this experience. Music – great for relaxing – is common nowadays. In fact, you see a whole range of things in dentists' surgeries, from video games to TV. Anything to stop the patient worrying about what's happening in their mouth.

MAN: But that's certainly progress from the days of out-of-date magazines in the waiting room.

BARBARA: Yeah, well, even our magazines are current.

MAN: So, would you say you enjoyed your work?

BARBARA: Oh yes, I think so, on the whole. I mean there are some pretty awful bits. I'm still not used to some of the horrors I see when people open their mouths, and bad breath is not pleasant to deal with. And another thing which actually I find difficult – and I know this sounds surprising from a dentist – it's the noise of the drill. But laser treatment is now doing a lot of the work we had to use the drill for, so now it's not so much of a problem. But really I enjoy the technical side of the job and also the people side. I think I'm quite good at making a potentially unpleasant experience pleasant.

MAN: It sounds it. And the future, Barbara, what do you want for that?

BARBARA: More of the same, I think. And perhaps a bit more money to help develop the practice more, and to make sure we can afford the latest technology.

MAN: Barbara Currie, thank you for coming to the studio today.

Exercise B3 Page 173

Extract 1

MAN: This is a telephone company recording. The code and number you have dialled have been changed. Please dial again, using the new code 0123 and putting a seven before the telephone number. If you require assistance, please hold. You have not been charged for this call.

Extract 2

WOMAN: Thank you for calling the Southwest Railway Company. Office hours are from 9.00 until 5.30 Monday to Friday, and from 10.00 until 12.00 at weekends. Timetables showing details of train times can be obtained from all Southwest ticket offices during opening hours. For direct trains to London, please ring 0171 0396418 for a recorded message.

Extract 3

MAN: Hello, this is a message from Dick and Celia. Sorry we can't take your call right now. Please note that we're moving house on October the 14th, and from that date our new number will be 23547. If you'd like to visit us, our new address is 50, Leisure Lane, that's L-E-I-S-U-R-E, and the postcode is AJ4 3GY. Thanks for calling.

Extract 4

WOMAN: Thanks for calling the Arts Centre hotline. There are two special exhibitions during May. From the 3rd to the 13th, we shall be celebrating the life and work of the painter John Bellino, and then from the 16th to the 27th, Alexandra Bruton's sculptures will be shown and she herself will be talking about her work at a special evening seminar at 6.15 on Friday the 20th. Admission is free, but space is limited so do come early.

Exercise B4 Page 174

WOMAN: Well, now it's time for the results of last month's competition, which was called 'People and Places', and the winner was Carol Sutton, who answered all but one of the ten questions correctly. Well done, Carol!

MAN: Yes, great stuff. Now you may remember that the competition was sponsored by the local shopkeepers' federation, so as her prize Carol gets gift vouchers to the value of £100, which she can spend at any of about 30 local shops. Happy shopping Carol.

WOMAN: We'll just run through a few of the trickier questions, shall we? Of course, the full list of answers is printed in this week's Evening Chronicle – though you won't find them in the usual place on the back page. For some reason this week they've been moved to the front, so you can't miss them. Well, pretty well everyone got the first two questions right, about the most famous person associated with the town and where her father worked, but question three confused a lot of you, who thought she had been a scientist before she became well known.

MAN: Yes, waitress was an unlikely answer, wasn't it, but that's what she was, and I'm sure she was very good at it.

WOMAN: Moving on, number four was straightforward, but the one after it about when the cathedral was built, caused lots of problems – quite a few incorrect answers there. And then number six, well, a lot of people seem to have misheard this one and thought we were asking about the worst hotel in the town, when in fact we wanted to know the first hotel built here. So although the poor old late-lamented King's Hotel was the most popular choice, what we were after was the Queen's Arms.

MAN: Yes, and talking of tricky questions, I myself would have expected number seven to be the most difficult one, but actually that honour went to number ten, which not even our winner, Carol, got. You'll kick yourselves when you see the answer in tonight's Evening Chronicle! And just to keep you in suspense a bit longer, we're not going to tell you until the end of the programme.

WOMAN: Bit unfair that, but anyway it's time to think about this month's competition, so get your pencils ready. We had lots of suggestions for names, including 'Plays and Players' and 'Heroes and Villains', which we particularly liked, but in the end we settled for 'Past and Present', and the questions will be coming up in a minute. Remember, entries must be in, actually here in the studio, by the 30th of June. The 1st or the 2nd of July won't do – we've got to be firm about that because the results come out on the 15th.

Exercise B5 Exam practice Page 175

WOMAN: Have you ever dreamt of inventing something so beautifully simple, yet essential, that the world marvels and says 'Now why didn't I think of that?' Tom Shanks has been investigating the world of inventions and the highs and lows for their makers.

TOM: It's true, a flash of inspiration doesn't necessarily bring a happy future, and a wonderful example of this is what happened to the creator of the world's first wire coat-hanger. At the beginning of the 20th century, a man called Albert Parkhouse was working for a company in Michigan, in the States. They manufactured wire lamp-shade frames. The firm was too mean to provide enough hooks for its employees to hang up their coats, so, one day, rather than throw his coat on the floor as usual, Parkhouse twisted a piece of wire into the now familiar shape of a hanger. His employer noticed what he'd done, realised it was a good idea and registered it with the patent office. Parkhouse just went on working on the shop floor of the factory and never received any money for his clever invention. And there are many stories like this.

Another invention which people cannot imagine life without is the pneumatic rubber tyre. Most people think that John Dunlop invented that, but in fact he re-invented it. It was first invented in 1845 by a London engineer for use on the wheels of carriages, but it didn't succeed because rubber was so expensive at the time. So it wasn't until about 40 years later that Dunlop came up with the same idea, and this time it was an immediate success. He'd noticed how the solid rubber tyres on his son's bicycle bumped over the rough streets. So he changed them for tyres filled with air and patented his invention. He should have been a millionaire from this but he sold his interest in the business and got nothing from the invention that made his name famous throughout the world.

But in terms of having a simple and successful idea, you have to admire Percy Shaw. One dark, foggy night in 1933, he saw a cat's eyes shining brightly in the light of his headlights. This everyday experience gave him the idea for a revolutionary form of road-marking for night driving – a convex lens backed by a mirror. These were put into a rubber pad, which was protected by an iron case, and set into the middle of the road. The lens and mirror are positioned so that they will reflect the light from a car's headlights back to the driver. This simple device made life so much easier for drivers at night. A year after he first had the idea, Shaw was ready to patent his invention. He opened a factory to manufacture his 'catseyes' and became rich and famous. So a success story for Percy Shaw.

LISTENING SECTION B UNIT 6

Familiarisation exercise Page 176

SPEAKER 1: So, we really enjoyed it, actually. The weather was marvellous and the view inland to the mountains was great. And having the beach right on your doorstep meant you could spend all day in the sea if you wanted, or you could just wander up and down and look at the people.

SPEAKER 2: It was such a beautiful place, and so unspoilt, and we just loved the views. You could even see the sea in the distance. And I'd come all prepared for it to be cold but actually, it was really warm even though it was so high. And I just loved all the wildlife, of course.

SPEAKER 3: I didn't miss the usual holiday things at all. I mean, in the past it's always been the seaside in the summer and the mountains to ski in spring, but this was the first time we'd done anything like this and there was just so much to do that I was quite exhausted at the end of the day, not to mention a lot poorer!

Exercises B2 and B3 Page 177

SPEAKER 1: To be honest, I didn't think much of the story – just not very believable really, and I don't think the actors believed it either, though they did their best. But some individual scenes were great – the car chase through San Francisco was, I don't know – breath-taking, and the bit where he tried to escape by jumping off the bridge – ooh – I could hardly bear to look at one point. Pity about the story though.

SPEAKER 2: I always like watching Ralph Fiennes, although this wasn't perhaps him at his very best. But for me the setting was what made the film, rather than the love interest, which I can't say I found very moving. Anyway, it was shot in North Africa somewhere, and it looked marvellous, made me want to go there. All the action took place in the desert against a background of beautiful sandhills and impossibly glorious sunsets over the mountains in the distance. Wonderful!

SPEAKER 3: There was lots of action of course and some spectacular camerawork in the mountains, but the thing that appealed to me most was the relationships between the two climbers. The scene when she got down to base camp and discovered that Geoff hadn't returned was so sad. She wasn't the only one in tears, I can tell you. There was hardly a dry eye in the house.

SPEAKER 4: He's an interesting director 'cos he tends to use lots of non-professional actors in all his films, and his latest one's the same. In fact, the main actor is a professional, but to be honest it was the unknown actors that were the stars. It's amazing what he got out of them. The scenes between Clare and her daughter, Lucy, were really exciting, I thought.

SPEAKER 5: It was certainly good to look at, and the setting was quite attractive, but for me it's not enough for a film to be just good visually. I want to be moved or excited when I go to the cinema, and I'm afraid this film didn't really do all that much for me. But I have to admit that Rupert Everett's performance was head and shoulders above the rest. And if this does turn out to be a big hit, it'll really all be down to him – apart from anything else, he's hardly off the screen all night.

Exercise B4 Page 178

SPEAKER 1: I travel an amazing amount, up to a hundred trips per year, and I'm not usually away for more than three days at a time, so I seem to spend half my life just packing and unpacking. In fact, I travel so much it takes a while for my mind to catch up with my body. I have to look for clues when I wake up. If I see a yellow cab, then I know I'm in New York.

SPEAKER 2: I've visited about 95 countries so far in my work for the BBC. I used to claim that I hadn't got any superstitions, but I do find myself thinking that if I look at a certain clock, then the trip will be all right. I can't explain why, it's not as if I'm frightened or anything, it's just habit. And another thing, when I'm in a place I want to go back to, I sing a little song. That means that I'll return.

SPEAKER 3: I'm often away for as long as three weeks at a time, but I don't have a family so travelling is not a major disruption. When I'm on a long-distance flight, I just get the eye mask on, get my head down and forget I'm there. Course they keep coming and waking you up every couple of hours to bring you meals, but actually I don't mind that. When you've been stuck somewhere eating beans and rice for several weeks, even airline food seems wonderful.

SPEAKER 4: I don't do that many trips and they're always to the same places. But I've been travelling like this for about 15 years and it's really tough. I miss my friends and family a lot. I always pack my luggage at the last possible moment. If I do it a day or two earlier, I feel like I'm on the plane already. To be honest, I'd be happy if I never saw another airline meal in my life.

SPEAKER 5: I've lost count of the number of trips I've made, the different places I've been to and all the different sort of planes I've been on, but it still seems to me an unnatural means of transport. However, no business meeting is going to wait for you to arrive by ship or whatever these days, so I close my eyes during take-off, keep my fingers crossed and hope.

Exercise B5 Exam practice Page 178

SPEAKER 1: We'd just loved the look of it in the brochure, you see, on the outskirts of the town with its own swimming pool and all those lovely grounds surrounding it, and the blue skies. So you can imagine how we felt when we arrived and found this. I mean look, if you compare my photo with theirs, you can see how they've deliberately angled it so you can't see the bit that hasn't got a roof on. And you see where those men are? Well they were doing that all day – you can just imagine the noise and the dust. Well it was just a nightmare.

SPEAKER 2: I had a funny feeling about it at the time, but I didn't say anything 'cos everyone else seemed to think it was delicious. It didn't really hit me until the middle of the night, but boy did I know about it then! I didn't sleep at all, and it was about three days before I felt well enough to stagger downstairs. And as for facing the outside world, well forget it. By the time I felt OK, it was time to come home.

SPEAKER 3: Well it didn't stop. Night and day for the best part of ten days. They said they'd never experienced anything like it before. Just our luck! The thing that surprised me was how much the noise got on your nerves. There was nothing we could do about it – no escape. It even seemed to follow you inside, you know, when someone opened the door. We spent most of the time in the lounge watching videos to take our minds off it. And when Paula did brave it outside, she was nearly blown off her feet.

SPEAKER 4: It was stupid really, but we were so keen to make the most of the place that we just felt we had to go out even on the one day it rained, and of course, I had to go and slip on the steps outside the hotel. The next I knew about it, there I was eating grapes and watching people sign their names on the plaster – do you want to add yours? It didn't really stop me doing most things. The only problem was sleeping at night, I just couldn't get comfortable.

SPEAKER 5: Well, what do you do in a situation like that? I mean for starters we had to stay in the hotel all day while they tried to sort things out, because obviously the first thought was that it was someone there, one of the staff for example; but then because of the disco there'd been the night before down in the basement, that meant it could really have been anyone, so we were no further forward.

LISTENING SECTION B UNIT 7

Familiarisation exercise 1 Page 179

MAN: Have you seen this? 'Man leaves fortune to dog. Eighty-four-year-old Stanley Flowers, who died last week, has left over £100,000 to Rover, his two-year-old German Shepherd. Rover is now being cared for by a next-door neighbour.' What a waste of money! Why do people do that?

WOMAN: Why not? Maybe he hasn't any family to leave it to.

MAN: Even if he hadn't, he could have left it to something a bit more worthwhile, like a charity. Anyway, he has got a family. It says here that he has two sons and four grandchildren.

WOMAN: Mmm. I wonder how they feel about it? I'd be a bit annoyed if it was me.

Familiarisation exercise 2 Page 179

TOM: Come on Carol. I'm just going into this department to ask for a refund on the sweater I bought last week.

CAROL: Oh, you can't do that. You wore it on Saturday at the disco. Look, I'm leaving you to it. I'm already getting all hot and bothered just thinking about it.

TOM: Too late now, here's the assistant. Um, excuse me, I'd like to return this sweater. It's got a hole in it, look here, just under the arm.

SHOP ASS: I see. And have you got the receipt?

TOM: Didn't I give it to you, Carol?

CAROL: No, you left it on the table in the kitchen.

SHOP ASS: Well, I'm sorry, we can't take anything back unless we have a receipt.

CAROL: That's fair enough. Come on Tom, we'll have to go home and get the receipt.

TOM: No, look, you can see I bought it here 'cos of the label. I mean it's obvious, isn't it?

SHOP ASS: I know it's one of ours, but as I said, it's policy to ask for the receipt. In any case, I'm fairly new here so I'm going to get the manager to come down and sort this out.

Exercise B1 Page 180

MAN: I can't believe it! There must be something wrong; £200 is ridiculous! .

WOMAN: Is that the electricity bill or the gas?

MAN: Electricity, but we can't have used £200's worth in three months, can we?

WOMAN: Well, it's been pretty cold so we've had the heating on much more than usual.

MAN: Yeah, but not all day and every day. In any case, it was colder this time last year and the bill was nothing like as big as this one. I'm going to ring up and ask about it.

WOMAN: Don't forget they put up electricity charges last month, so £200 is about what I was expecting.

Exercise B2 Page 180

WOMAN: Good evening and welcome to this week's edition of 'Right to Question'. Our subject tonight is how much should we earn for the work we do – in other words, what are we worth? And in the studio we have Bob Teacher, Chairman of BritElectric, who this week has been given a 75% pay rise, bringing his salary up to £680,000 a year. And David Johnson, a firefighter for the past 20 years and earning considerably less. Mr Teacher, can we start with you? Do you feel you're worth £680,000?

BT: I don't know whether that's exactly what I'm worth, but I do know I have a tremendously responsible job running an organisation that employs over 20,000 people.

WOMAN: Although I did read in the paper yesterday that your company is going to cut a thousand jobs. Or is that just a rumour?

BT: Nobody likes to be the one to make decisions like that, but I have a responsibility not only to our employees but to our shareholders. I have a duty to ensure profitability, and taking unpleasant decisions is part of what I'm paid to do. So, yes, for the first time in our history, we are going to have to make some redundancies.

WOMAN: So tough times ahead for some. Mr Johnson, if we could turn to you now. What do you feel? Do you think you're paid enough for the job you do?

DJ: Well, I did until I heard what Mr Teacher earns. Seriously though, it's not that I'm unhappy with my own salary – I mean I wouldn't mind a bit more, but basically I think it's fair. But what I don't understand is how somebody can be worth about £660,000 a year more than me. Mr Teacher talks about having a lot of responsibility – well I have a responsible job too – in some ways more. I mean, I'm responsible for saving people's lives sometimes, and my job can be very dangerous. But don't get me wrong, I'm not against people being paid well for the jobs they do, but Mr Teacher's salary is unrealistic. It sounds like a telephone number to me, not real money.

BT: I work extremely long hours – 60 hours a week minimum and even at the weekends I'm on duty. (DJ: So am I.) I'm often rung up at home if there are problems or if my colleagues feel there is a situation I should be aware of. My organisation does a lot of business overseas and I travel a lot – sometimes going there and back in a day. The stresses and strains are enormous. You know, when I first started at BritElectric I was 21, straight out of college, and I worked as a technician earning £8,000 a year. I've worked my way up to the top and now I get paid the going rate for the job. My lifestyle hasn't changed that much – I don't have a luxury yacht or rooms full of Picasso paintings and –

WOMAN: Do you think of yourself as rich, Mr Teacher? Do you think you've got enough money?

BT: No, I don't think of myself as rich, I think of myself as someone who earns a good salary for an honest, hard day's work. As to the second question, yes, I've got enough at the moment but –

WOMAN: And Mr Johnson?

DJ: Do I think of myself as rich? Well, no, obviously. But I'm not saying I think I'm underpaid, just that Mr Teacher is overpaid.

WOMAN: Well thank you, Bob Teacher and David Johnson for coming in tonight. Our telephone lines are now open for you to ring in with your comments and opinions on what you've heard tonight, so let's have your calls. Thank you and goodnight.

Exercise B3 Exam practice Page 181

INTERVIEWER: So Frank, how do you feel about retiring?

FRANK: I can't tell you how much I'm looking forward to the end of the month when I stop. I'll be 55. I know that's early to stop working for many people, but we had the chance to take early retirement and I jumped at it. It's hard work in the police force, I can tell you, and not just physically either. Nowadays you've got to keep up with all the changes in technology that are part and parcel of any office job. When I started as a boy of 17, paper and pencil were about all the office equipment we needed but now, well. We were all encouraged to go on training courses for the computer, of course. It was very interesting actually and there's no doubt that it saves us a lot of work. But sometimes I long for the old days when a PC meant a police constable, not a personal computer.

INTERVIEWER: What other changes have you seen?

FRANK: Well, you wouldn't recognise the forensic side of the job nowadays. One fantastic example of that – well it's fantastic to me, though I think the younger ones just accept it without question – is this DNA testing. If they can find a tiny piece of tissue, for instance, at the scene of the crime, they can build up the DNA profile and match it, or not, to a suspect's. Wonderful – even if I don't really understand it. Well, anyway, you can see why I'm happy to be retiring. I'm lucky too – we've got a good pension scheme in the police force and to be honest the pay is pretty good for everyone too, at least it is these days. When I first joined, very few, except those right at the top, got much money; but still we were respected in the community. Now we get much more but our position is worse in many ways. The public are more suspicious of us. I don't know, maybe I'm just falling into the trap of looking back and thinking everything was better.

INTERVIEWER: That's true for a lot of us, I think.

FRANK: Mm. I suppose you notice I've been talking about policemen – and that's another thing. Women are in the force today. Now I do approve of that change. Well, it makes sense, doesn't it? If we're supposed to reflect the composition of society, we ought to have 50% women. We're not there yet, but maybe we will be. I'm not too hopeful though. The police are a conservative lot. Anyway, as I was saying, money shouldn't be too much of a problem. But Jessie, my wife, she's more worried than I am about my retirement. Thinks I'll be hanging around the house all day getting bored. Getting in her way is probably what she's thinking. It's true though, it'll be very strange not having the daily discipline of a job – maybe not at first, that'll probably feel like a holiday, but after a few weeks. Still, if I get fed up, I can always try and find a little part-time work. Some mates of mine who left the force recently told me that ex-policemen can get security work – you know in a supermarket, or guarding a building at night. Don't think Jessie'd be too keen on that though, me working nights. Not sure I would, come to that, I've had enough of shift work over the last 30 years or so. It'll be nice to keep normal hours again.

INTERVIEWER: Thank you Frank, and good luck.

Exercise B4 Page 182

MAN: Jenny, you're back. Good time?

JENNY: Brilliant.

MAN: What did you do?

JENNY: I went diving, as usual.

MAN: Where did you go?

JENNY: Well, I always try to go somewhere different and everybody'd told me Australia's great for diving, so I thought I'd try there. I went to a place on the northern coast.

MAN: Cor, sounds a bit exotic. Was it dangerous? Meet any nice sharks?

JENNY: Do you know, that's the first thing everybody asks when I say I went diving in the tropics. They look really disappointed when I tell them I didn't.

MAN: Understandable really. Sharks have got a bad reputation ever since that film, 'Jaws'.

JENNY: Yeah right. In fact, I used to worry about them a bit when I was diving so I did a bit of research and discovered there are fewer than 50 deaths a year – remarkably few I thought compared with the millions who swim.

MAN: I dunno – sounds quite a lot to me.

JENNY: Nah. And most of them are either spear fishermen or surfboarders.

MAN: How come?

JENNY: Well, with the spear fishermen, the sharks are attracted by the wriggling movement of the fish on the end of the spear, and with the surfboarders – are you ready for this? It's the shape of the surfboard. It looks a bit like a sea lion to a Great White Shark and that means 'lunch'.

MAN: Lovely! But you didn't actually meet one.

JENNY: No, although there were a couple of days when the local people said to be careful.

MAN: Why was that?

JENNY: There had been sightings of sharks I guess, by the fishermen.

MAN: What does 'be careful' mean?

JENNY: Oh, things like not going in the water in the early morning or evenings, or swimming in unclear water, and the best bit of advice, not letting yourself think that just 'cos you're in shallow water you're safe. Sharks can swim almost up to the beach you know.

MAN: And what are you supposed to do if you're in the water and a shark appears and starts heading in your direction?

JENNY: Well, for a start, trying to swim away from them isn't much use, they're far too quick. Nor is hoping some brave soul is going to jump in and rescue you. There is actually a theory that shouting at them can scare them off. Anyway, enough about those monsters. D'you want to see my photos of the holiday?

Exercise B5 Page 183

Extract 1

WOMAN: We're going to be late if you two don't hurry up. And you know I hate it when we have to get everyone to stand up to let us get past.

SON: Don't panic, Mum, I'm nearly ready.

WOMAN: David, what about you?

DAVID: Three minutes. Look why don't you get the car out of the garage instead of nagging me? That'll save a bit of time.

WOMAN: OK, but don't be long.

Extract 2

MAN: I don't think I've got much chance, you know. I'm not just being pessimistic. I really haven't got the experience they're looking for.

WOMAN: Don't say that. You've got loads of ability and enthusiasm. That counts for a lot. We've got faith in you, haven't we Sue?

SUE: Yeah, I guess so.

MAN: You don't sound so sure. But thanks, anyway. If by any remote chance I do get it, I'll take you both out for a celebration dinner.

WOMAN: Great, can I choose where?

Extract 3

MIKE: Hey, hang on a minute, Helen. Honestly, you're always so quick to jump to conclusions. Come on, Jane, tell her it wasn't me.

JANE: Yeah Helen, Mike's right. It wasn't him who told me. In fact, if you think about it calmly it can't have been, 'cos he was in Germany at the time, if you remember.

HELEN: Oh God, you're right. I'm really sorry, both of you. Me and my big mouth. So who was it then?

Extract 4

WOMAN: You said you'd drop that video round at Lena's tonight, remember?

MAN: It's OK, I haven't forgotten. I wish I didn't have to, though. You know what she's like – chatter, chatter, chatter. I can't think why I said I would. Tony, you couldn't go for me, could you?

TONY: Nope, can't tonight. I'm out this evening. You'll just have to do it yourself.

MAN: Oh, hell.

Exercise B6 Exam practice Page 184

SIMON: Hi Peter, Oh good, you've brought the brochures with you.

PETER: Yes. I think all the schools sound quite interesting. We're definitely going to go, aren't we?

SIMON: Sure, it's just a matter of choosing the right one. Which one is the cheapest?

PETER: Well, the Martinez School looks as if it costs about £500 less than the other two, but that's tuition only – the other two include everything, tuition, room, food, excursions etcetera, so there probably isn't much in it.

SIMON: I didn't think the Goya Academy included everything – that was the only thing Mary – you know, my friend at work who did a course last year? – she wasn't happy about that, though she still thought it was the best place for us to go.

PETER: Maybe they've changed their pricing policy since she was there.

SIMON: Could be. Anyway, it looks good, doesn't it? The photographs of the building and the town make the place seem really attractive. Mary said it was an interesting city – very historic but with lots going on.

PETER: What about the courses themselves? I was looking last night and Iberia International and the Goya Academy both seem pretty serious – they both have courses for business people. The only thing is that the Goya doesn't seem to run really short courses, and they only have 25 hours a week. I'd rather go for the Iberia – they seem to pack a lot into each day.

SIMON: How do you feel about position? The Martinez School's the only one that isn't quite a long way out of town. Does that matter to you?

PETER: Not really. If we're only at school for ten days and in class for 60 hours of that, I'm not too worried about where the place is as long as it's not too far from my accommodation.

SIMON: Good point. So that means …?

PETER: Well, the only school that actually promises you'll be within walking distance is Iberia International.

SIMON: OK, so in terms of position that one looks good. What about classes? What do they say about the number of students in each group?

PETER: Well, they all say they have small classes, but I suppose it depends what you mean by small. Maybe that's one of the things we should check, that and the average age of the students.

SIMON: Mm, I don't think we need bother asking the Martinez School about that. Look, all their short courses seem to cater for teenagers on holiday courses.

PETER: Not really our scene. Shall we give the other two a ring and ask a few questions?

SIMON: Yes, let's.

Chapter 5 Speaking

SPEAKING UNIT 1

Exercise 3 Page 190

EXAMINER: Good morning. Could I have your marksheets please? Thank you. My name is Anne Dover and this is my colleague, Peter Principal. He is just going to be listening to us. So you are ... ? And ... ? Thank you. First of all, we'd like to know something about you, so I'm going to ask you some questions about yourselves.

Where do you come from?
How long have you lived there?
Have you got any brothers and sisters?
What do you do?
What do you enjoy about it?
When did you start learning English?
How do you think English will be useful for you in the future?

Now I'd like to ask you something about the things you like doing or things you don't like doing.

Are you interested in music?
What kind of music do you prefer?
What other things do you do in your spare time?

Thank you.

SPEAKING UNIT 2

Exercise 5 Page 193

EXAMINER: Now, I'd like each of you to talk on your own for about a minute. I'm going to give each of you two different photographs and I'd like you to talk about them. Candidate A, here are your two photos. They show people doing different sports. I'd like you to compare and contrast these photographs and say what kind of sport you prefer. Remember you have only about a minute to do this, so don't worry if I interrupt you. All right? ... Thank you.

PRESENTER: You will now hear a candidate giving her answer to the same task. Listen and answer the questions in your book.

CANDIDATE A: Well, on the picture on the left you can see two people swimming. Um ... they're in a swimming pool outside, it actually looks like a hotel pool. Well they could be on a holiday and ... it looks like they're enjoying themselves. They seem to be talking to each other. Um ... I think it's a very warm place or tropical place, er ... because you can see lots of palm trees in the background. It could be, for example, Thailand or something like that. And also, at the side of the pool you can see these chairs. I don't know what you call them. Now, in the second picture you can see some men playing basketball in a stadium and they look pretty serious. It looks like a professional game, and um ... well, the two photos both show different sports, or well, different forms of exercise, but the left one, the swimming one, is really relaxed and the right one, well, they're very concentrated and they try to win.

EXAMINER: Thank you.

EXAMINER: Now, Candidate B, do you enjoy team sports? ... Thank you.

PRESENTER: Now you'll hear a candidate answering the same question.

CANDIDATE B: Yes, I do. I play football quite a bit. It's fun playing with other people, but it's also serious. You have to play for each other as well as yourself.

EXAMINER: Thank you.

Exercise 6 Page 194

EXAMINER: Candidate A, here are your two photographs. They show people selling goods. Please let Candidate B see them. Candidate B, I'll give you your photographs in a minute. Candidate A, I'd like you to compare and contrast these photographs and say how much satisfaction you think these people get in their jobs. Remember, you have only about a minute for this so don't worry if I interrupt you. All right? ... Thank you.

Candidate B, do you buy food from street markets in your country? ... Thank you.

SPEAKING UNIT 3

Exercise 1 Page 196

EXAMINER: Now, I'd like you to talk about something together for about three minutes. I'm just going to listen. I'd like you to imagine that a local college is running a variety of evening classes. Here are some of the courses they are offering. Talk to each other about the attractions of attending these different evening classes. Then choose the most suitable one for a 17-year-old, a 35-year-old and a 65-year-old. All right? You have only about three minutes for this so, once again, don't worry if I stop you, and please speak so that we can hear you. All right?

CANDIDATE A: So, which course are we going to talk about first?

CANDIDATE B: Um ... I don't know. You decide.

CANDIDATE A: Ah ... 'Painting'? I think that would be quite good for older people, let's say 65-year-olds.

CANDIDATE B: Why?

CANDIDATE A: Because they've got plenty of time.

CANDIDATE B: Yes but on the other hand, painting is also something to relax people, so I could imagine that, that person that's 35-year-old would find it very useful um ... if they have a very stressful job.

CANDIDATE A: Yes, OK, OK, but you need to relax when you're older too ...

CANDIDATE B: Yes ...

CANDIDATE A: ... because you've got, you know, less to do. Otherwise, er ... 'Car Maintenance'. Oh, excuse me. Do we have to talk about all the courses?

CANDIDATE B: No, not necessarily. You decide.

CANDIDATE A: All right. Except that for car maintenance, you know, people go to the garage, so ...

CANDIDATE B: Yes, but on the other hand I mean, it's very expensive if you do that ...

CANDIDATE A: Yes.

CANDIDATE B: ... it's quite useful I think, to know a little bit about your car, but um ... Oh my God! What about 'Using the Internet'! I think, that's quite useful for all three of them, isn't it?

CANDIDATE A: Yes, but I think more so for, for young people because, I mean, they really will need to know about Internet.

CANDIDATE B: Yes, but the old ones have to catch up and maybe it makes them feel better if they think that they're sort of on top of developments if they ...

CANDIDATE A: Yes, but, you also have the right not to catch up ... when you're old.

CANDIDATE B: Yes, that's true!

CANDIDATE A: And what else?

CANDIDATE B: What about the 'Cooking for Beginners'? Who would that be suitable for? What do you think?

CANDIDATE A: For modern career woman! 'Cos I don't …

CANDIDATE B: Oh no! I think it's much better for that boy, that 17-year-old, so he can later cook for his girlfriends!

CANDIDATE A: All right, OK. That's fine. And … 'Talking about your Town' Oh no … my town … mind you, it would be interesting too because even, I mean, my town is quite dull but if you know the history, it could be really good.

CANDIDATE B: Yes, but I think that's something people can find out for themselves. You just have to read a … you don't have to do a course for that, I don't think.

CANDIDATE A: No, you're right. Yes, especially …

CANDIDATE B: You read a book or a good guide book and there you are. Now, what about 'Chinese'? Would you actually consider learning Chinese?

CANDIDATE A: Nope. I'm not very good at … English is, is hard enough.

CANDIDATE B: I find that too, yes. It's quite frightening, but maybe for that um … older man, that 65-year-old, because that is quite a good exercise for the brain.

CANDIDATE A: Yeah, that's a good idea.

CANDIDATE B: So, what do we say? So … for the old person, for the 65-year-old – 'Chinese'.

CANDIDATE A: Yes.

CANDIDATE B: What did we say for the 35-year-old?

CANDIDATE A: Er … we said 'Painting'.

CANDIDATE B: Yes, that's right – to relax. And for the 17-year-old?

CANDIDATE A: Internet. 'Using the Internet'.

CANDIDATE B: Yeah, I think that's quite good, isn't it?

CANDIDATE A: Yep.

EXAMINER: Thank you.

Exercise 3 Page 199

EXAMINER: What did you decide?
What kind of course would you like to attend? Why?
How popular are evening classes in your country?
What opportunities are there for older people to continue learning?
Did you enjoy learning at school? Why?
Do you think you'd be a good teacher? Why?

Chapter 1 Reading

READING SECTION A UNIT 1

nouns: Daniel, photograph, drawer
adjectives: old, sepia
verb: put
adverb: quickly

Exercise A1 Page 12
1 Can see: firefighter furniture finger plastic family flower water cow blackbird back factory beef pencil wool musician steel beetle
2 Can't see: problem love advice Marxism oxygen
3 Can count: problem firefighter finger family flower cow blackbird back factory pencil musician beetle
4 Can't count: furniture plastic love water beef advice wool Marxism steel oxygen
Collective word: family furniture **Person:** musician
Thing: suitcase pencil **Animal etc.:** blackbird beetle cow
Plant: flower **Part of person:** back finger **Building:** factory **Liquid etc.:** oxygen water **Other material:** plastic wool steel **Food:** beef **Abstract idea:** happiness love problem advice Marxism

Exercise A2 Page 13
Age/Time: last elderly former **Colour:** green dark cream
Material: glass wooden silk **'Positive':** attractive generous lovely exciting clever satisfied priceless **Shape:** round long square oval **Origin:** Chinese artificial **Size:** little wide
'Negative': careless stupid impatient destructive unimaginative

Exercise A3 Page 13
1 Usually with direct object: know hit carry find discuss surprise
2 Usually without direct object: smile sleep laugh lie talk
3 With or without direct object: fly eat read ring
Some of the above verbs can be used in different categories, e.g. *know* can be used without a direct object (*I don't know how to do it.*) but for the purposes of this exercise the above are the most useful categories.

Exercise A4 Page 13
How? carefully fortunately well fast badly
Where? away backwards here outside upstairs
When? late soon recently yesterday finally

Exercise A5 Page 14
2 adjective 3 adjective 4 noun 5 verb 6 adjective
7 noun 8 verb 9 adjective 10 adjective 11 verb
12 verb; noun 13 adjective; noun 14 verb 15 verb

Exercise A6 Page 14
2 noun – some kind of animal because they're living there: birds, animals, snakes
3 verb – without direct object, some kind of activity: playing, running, shouting
4 noun – person because we chatted: man, woman, lawyer
5 adjective – positive – something that makes us sit on the edge of our seats: thrilling, exciting, scary
6 adverb – describes the way she talked: quietly, interestingly, slowly
7 verb – with direct object: greet, kiss, hit
8 noun – the name of a place, because it's easy to get to: Spain, London, Athens
9 adjective – describing him: old, short, unhappy
10 noun – place or building in the local area: pub, cinema, supermarket
11 noun – abstract: love, lying, work
12 noun – 'negative' material or substance because it is referred to as *that*: mud, oil, vomit
13 adverb – negative because of *unfortunately*: quickly, badly, untidily
14 noun – person because of *he*: Tony, Carlos, Adonis
15 noun – an abstract idea, probably 'negative': complaint, problem, suggestion
16 participle – without a direct object: crying, eating, working

Exercise A7 Page 15
2 verb with *-ing*: walking, running
3 adverb: slowly, carefully
4 noun – small thing: paper, cassette
5 abstract noun: happiness, laughter
6 negative adjective: horrible, disastrous
7 noun – female person: Jane, Clare
8 noun – uncountable: rubbish, dirt
9 adverb: well, nearly
10 participle: crying, screaming
11 plural noun – must be able to run: rabbits, deer (not trees!)
12 noun – collective: group, crowd

Exercise A8 Page 16
2 C 3 B 4 B 5 D 6 D 7 A 8 A 9 D 10 C 11 A
12 B

Exercise A9 Page 17
1 some time after midnight
2 They were looking for badgers.
3 They felt very depressed.

b verb; must mean putting some part of your body (maybe your knees?) on the piece of wood; it caused pain
c noun; something that made the badger run away; must be a sound that he made because he was in pain
d participle; something to do with movement because the badger heard the noise and so it would be natural for it to hurry away
e noun (after *its*); must be the place where it lives – a natural place to go if in danger
f adverb; describes the way Simon looked at the writer; obviously they were both disappointed so it probably means something like *sadly*
g adjective; the clue is the rain; what else could the ground be other than wet or very wet?

h adjective; the clouds that covered the moon made it difficult for them to see; must mean *very thick* or *very dark*

i verb in past tense; they couldn't see the fallen tree in the dark so Simon sort of fell

j noun; some sort of substance; probably the wet ground, which we know made him look awful

k verb in past tense; it was dark, he didn't see the low branch and as a result it went into his eye

l verb in past tense; some kind of movement, walking, probably in a tired way

m noun; is related to their hotel in some way, which they must have been glad to see after all their problems; probably means *comforting place* or something like that

n adverb describing how fed up they were, so it probably means *very fed up*

READING SECTION A UNIT 2

Exercise A1 Page 18
1 e 2 d 3 a 4 b 5 c

Exercise A2 Page 18
2 f 3 h 4 c 5 j 6 a 7 b 8 i 9 g 10 e

Exercise A3 Page 19
2 something to do with 3 become of 4 couldn't stand
5 stand in for 6 ten to one 7 put me right off
8 born and bred in 9 just the job 10 try it out

Exercise A4 Page 19
2 expect 3 he realised 4 much 5 heard about
6 enough to start 7 affect 8 find 9 dominates
10 I wasn't certain whether the deal would succeed or not

Exercise A5 Page 21
2 B 3 A 4 C 5 C 6 A 7 B 8 B 9 A 10 C 11 B
12 A 13 B 14 B

READING SECTION A UNIT 3

Exercise A1 Page 22
2 *they* refers to *dreams*
3 *them* refers to *daylight-feeding animals*
4 *those* refers to *people*
 this refers to the fact that *people who eat breakfast tend to be slimmer*
 it refers to *missing food early in the day*
5 *it* refers to the fact that *many of us have felt dizzy*
 this refers to *a fear of heights*
6 *that time* refers to *Christmas*
 their refers to *the shopkeepers* and *the economists*
7 *So* refers to the fact that his clothes *are everywhere*

Exercise A2 Page 23
2 remarkable changes 3a a good reason to visit Dublin (Ireland's capital) 3b reasons/aspects/features/attractions etc.
4a it was 4b where 4c to be seen 4d in order / so as
5b the fact that it is fashionable this year

Exercise A3 Page 23
1b the knowledge 2 Charlie Chaplin 3 the monster flower
4a this hot, yellow spice; the ready-made condiment 4b Dijon
5a insects 5b wounds 5c covered with maggots

Exercise A4 Page 24
2 Rebecca; nobody else was surprised 3 quite a lot, certainly a lot more than big insects 4a language 4b that we pay so little attention to the correct use of English 5a a means of mass-producing books (printing) 5b it changed the way of spreading knowledge more than any other invention

Exercise A5 Page 25
(possible answers)
2 (contrast) … were not happy about it
3 (contrast) … wasting it on silly things
4 (additional information) … but of broadening your mind *or* … it's about broadening your mind
5 (explanation) … is that the fish is not so fresh
6 (explanation/contrast) … their professional lives are short, so they need it
7 (additional information) … and success in later life
8 (additional information/contrast) … he couldn't understand anything
9 (contrast) … on reality
10 (explanation) … found I couldn't hit the ball straight

Exercise A6 Page 25
1 the increased chance of being injured
2 health care for footballers has improved
3 players feel there is pressure on them to play even if they're not fully fit
4 main point: there's not much time between seasons
 supporting point: the season finishes in May and starts again in July
5 mental difficulties
6 the work of footballers

Exercise A7 Page 27
2 it does / it depends 3 salt 4 they discovered that salt could preserve meat or fish; it's introduced by *however* to show the contrast – that until that discovery they were not aware of how much they needed salt 5 it (salt) had a very practical use
6 food 7 the fact that salt could preserve food 8 Britain
9 no, *hardly* has a negative meaning 10 were 11 salt

READING SECTION B UNIT 4

Familiarisation exercise Page 28
1 D 2 A 3 C 4 B

Exercise B1 Page 29
2 A 3 C 4 B

Exercise B2 Page 30
Summary sentences
2 B 3 B 4 A 5 B
Headings
2 A 3 B 4 B 5 B

Exercise B3 Page 31
2 It's getting worse. It can damage your health.
3 They never turn off – the rest of the paragraph emphasises that our ears are always at work – *register the sound, never let's us relax.*
4 noise from neighbours
5 The second one because it almost dismisses the first sentence (*regardless of decibel level*) in order to make a more important point – the problem with certain sounds.
6 because it is very irregular in speed etc.
7 Reduction in concentration is less with a third person because there is a more constant babble of noise which is less distracting.

8 It's supposed to make you feel relaxed.
9 People either hate it or don't even hear it.
10 the good effects that some music can have

A Para 2   B Para 6   C Para 1   D Para 8   E Para 5
F Para 3   G Para 4   H Para 7

Exercise B4   Page 33
1 E: We are told not to lie from the moment we learn how to do it.
2 C: In childhood, the line between imagination and lying is often not clear.
3 A: … we have definite ideas …
4 B: … there are three types …
5 G: … what they want to hear; … you get something
6 J: You cannot be blamed
7 F: more dangerous
8 H: verbal clues
9 I: body language

Exercise B5   Page 34
1 E: six months in isolation; were suffering from boredom
2 A: gorillas proved to be very keen on their new entertainment; … refused to eat … when their TV was temporarily removed
3 G: During the day they wander around their island; at night they return to … and watch TV
4 D: fond of sports coverage and animal programmes; keen on an advert for tyres; also cartoons
5 C: … just like we do
6 F: … seem to use their TV for their social life and sense of community

0 f   1 d   2 b   3 a   4 h   5 c   6 g
The extra heading (e) does not relate to anything in the text.

Exercise B6   Exam practice   Page 36
1 G   2 H   3 B   4 A   5 C   6 D   7 E

READING SECTION B UNIT 5

Familiarisation exercise   Page 38
1 C   2 B   3 A   4 C

Exercise B1   Page 39
She felt generally happier.

Exercise B2   Page 39
Mr Boggis is involved in the antique furniture business or something similar.

Paragraph 1: … by his ability to produce unusual and often quite rare items with astonishing regularity
own words: he was able to find good things regularly

Paragraph 2: … it had come to him as a result of … driving in the country
own words: by chance, he was driving around for another reason

Paragraph 2: if he could please have a jug of water
own words: he needed some water for his car

Paragraph 3: … he spotted something that made him so excited …
own words: he saw something that excited him

Paragraph 4: … of a type he had only seen once before in his life … this thing is late fifteenth century!
own words: it was rare and very old

2 B   3 D   4 C   5 A   6 D   7 B
8 C (A is wrong because he didn't get all his supply from this one source)

Exercise B3   Page 42
(possible answers)
2 begin right from the beginning
3 having to look at only white paint for a year
4 be very expensive
5 which costs as little as possible
6 employed
7 my back
8 the mark on the map which showed the island
9 it is very isolated, a long way from any other land, and it's very small
10 the idea of being isolated on a small island
11 C   12 B   13 A

Exercise B4   Exam practice   Page 44
1 C   2 A   3 B   4 D   5 C   6 B   7 D

READING SECTION B UNIT 6

Familiarisation exercise   Page 46
1 C   2 A   3 D

Exercise B1   Page 47
Paragraph 3: paragraphs 2 and 5
Paragraph 4: as an announcement
Paragraph 4: in paragraph 1
Paragraph 5: paragraph 2
Paragraph 7: the fact that she thinks astrology is complete nonsense
Paragraph 8: whether people will be able to manage or search for their perfect astrological partner if they are a new sign
Paragraph 8: the names of the zodiacal signs
Paragraph 8: in paragraph 6
Paragraph 9: in paragraph 5

Exercise B2   Page 48
(possible answers)
2 key words: *didn't think* in text; *didn't even see* in sentence
correct sentence: b (the other is wrong because there is no reference to lunchtime)
3 key words: *There* and *unknown* in sentence.
correct sentence: a (the other is wrong because Jim couldn't be congratulating someone if the winner was unknown)
4 key words: *the mystery winner* in sentence
correct sentence: a (the other is wrong because he didn't know she'd won £630,000 – that information comes later)
5 key words: *however* in sentence
correct sentence: b (the other is wrong because *so* is not a word of contrast which is needed after *it's wrong, and in some cases dangerous, to use information …*)

Exercise B3   Page 50
2 key phrase in text: *move around … between dry- and wet-season camps*
key phrase in paragraph: *Three to five families camp together* – continues description of camps
answer: A
3 key phrase in text: *In the long dry season … have to camp near a well of water*
key phrase in paragraph: *But once the first rains come …*
answer: D
4 key phrase in text: *changes are, however … in this traditional way of life*
key phrase in paragraph: *And political changes … too* – back reference
key phrase in next paragraph: *As a result of these changes …*
answer: B

Exercise B4 Page 51

B   key phrase: *can, of course, <u>only</u> carry* (negative point)
i   key phrase: *they also contribute ...* (negative point)
e   key phrase: *their biggest advantage is that they can travel from door to door ...*
C   key phrase: *worst form of urban transport ... those who use them*
v   key phrase: *ban them from their streets ... those who see it as an attack on their personal freedom*
c   key phrase: *parking is ...* (it's only private cars which have this problem)
D   key phrase: *the great advantage of ...* (positive point)
iv key phrase: *they are, unfortunately, extremely expensive to build* (negative contrast, and only things that can link to *build*)
f   key phrase: *however* (introduces positive contrast) *necessary investment* (links to *expensive to build*)
E   key phrase: *were once a common sight in most city streets*
vi key phrase: *they still are*
b   key phrase: *where this is the case* (refers back to *extended and modernised*)
F   key phrase: *danger ... from cars, buses and lorries*
iii key phrase: *if the latter were forbidden ...*
a   key phrase: *on the other hand* (contrast to positive point before) and the rest of the sentence which cannot relate to any other means of transport

Exercise B5   Exam practice Page 53
1 E   2 C   3 G   4 A   5 H   6 B   7 D
F is the extra one.

READING SECTION B UNIT 7

Familiarisation exercise Page 54
1 D   2 A   3 B   4 D   5/6 C/A (in any order)

Exercise B1 Page 55
2/3 B/F (in any order)   4 E   5 A   6 D

Exercise B2 Page 56
1 D   2/3 C/F (in any order)   4 B   5 A   6 E

Exercise B3 Page 57
1 B   2 E   3 A   4/5 B/C (in any order)   6 A   7 A   8 E
9 A   10/11 C/B (in any order)   12 D   13 C

Exercise B4 Page 58
1 C   2 A   3 E   4 A   5 D   6 E   7 D   8 B   9 A

Exercise B5   Exam practice Page 60
1 E   2 C   3 D   4 D   5 E   6 A   7/8 C/B(in any order)
9 C   10 E   11 A   12 E   13 C

Chapter 2 Writing

WRITING SECTION A UNIT 1

Exercise A1 Page 62
(student's own answers)

Exercise A2 Page 63
2 (possible answer) At the beginning of her presentation she was nervous. But then she began to relax and perhaps even enjoy it. Then her confidence left her when things began to go wrong. She was surprised when everyone clapped at the end, and began to feel hopeful again about her possible promotion.
3 past simple tense: the most common story-telling tense

4   past continuous: *... was sitting*
past perfect: *... this was the first time I had made a presentation*
... by the time I reached ... my earlier confidence had left me
conditional: *... if I did it well, my company would ...*
past participle: *having organised ...*
future in the past: *... I knew he was going to ask ...*

Exercise A3 Page 64
2 was pouring   3 was feeling   4 had left   5 was going to be
6 was really looking forward to   7 bumped   8 looked   9 knew
10 had last seen   11 hadn't changed   12 had been living
13 had met   14 had happened

Exercise A4 Page 64
2 enjoying   3 had   4 was blowing (*blew* possible but doesn't give the feeling of a longer action)   5 had been working
6 was looking   7 saw   8 attracted   9 carried on   10 stayed
11 had never seen   12 got   13 was actually driving
14 was surrounded   15 closed   16 stopped   17 woke
18 was bending   19 (was) saying   20 had happened
21 believed   22 had climbed

Exercise A5 Page 65
2 Having organised my papers in front of me, I started.
3 At the beginning my voice sounded a bit shaky, but gradually I began to relax.
4 ... during the next half hour I even managed to make the audience laugh occasionally.
5 I was in the middle of explaining my sales predictions when things started to go wrong.
6 First, half the lights in the hall went off and then, worse still, my boss interrupted.
7 As soon as he raised his hand, I knew he was going to ask a tricky question.
8 So, by the time I reached the end of my presentation, my earlier confidence had left me.
9 I sat down and, much to my surprise, the audience clapped.

Exercise A6 Page 66
2 while   3 before   4 At first   5 but gradually   6 During
7 suddenly   8 After   9 in the middle of   10 when suddenly
11 later   12 it wasn't until

Exercise A7 Page 67
1 Sue came home while I was making dinner. (or the other way round)
2 while
3 As she walked in the front door, the dog ran to greet her. (or the other way round)
When she walked in the front door, the dog ran to greet her. (or the other way round)
4 as
5 She told me she was leaving her job while we were eating dinner. (or other way round)
6 She told me she was leaving her job during dinner. (or other way round)
7 When/As soon as I looked at her face I knew she didn't really want to give up her work.
8 *As soon as* is more dramatic – it sounds more immediate.
9 Before she admitted the real reason, I had to ask her to tell me.
10 It wasn't until she told me about her boss that I realised how unfair he was.
11 ... until she told me about him.
12 She was telling me all the horrible details when the telephone rang.
13 She was in the middle of telling me all ...

14 *in the middle of* makes it more dramatic. The telephone call really interrupted the story.
15 She was just about to tell me … when the telephone rang.
16 (possible answer) At first, he was trying to be nice to her, but slowly he changed and became quite aggressive.
17 Eventually, she just put …

WRITING SECTION A UNIT 2

Exercises A1 and A2 Pages 68 and 69
(students' own answers based on their own ideas)

Exercise A3 Page 69
(possible answers)
2 … black clothes. He thinks they make him look more interesting.
3 … the way she always tells the truth. This sometimes gets her into trouble.
4 … his deep voice. It makes him sound very sincere.
5 … long black hair which reaches down to her waist. I don't think she has ever had it cut.
6 … of being a bit shy. But really I'm just the sort of person who prefers to think about things before I say anything.
7 … she's a bit aggressive. Actually, she's only like this with people she doesn't know.
8 … enjoys being with people. She's a good listener too, so people enjoy being with her.
9 … we enjoy doing similar things. It's great knowing that I'll always have someone to do things with.

Exercise A4 Page 69
(students' own answers based on model paragraph)

Exercise A5 Page 70
1 it's a watch
2 round
3 no information given
4 traditional
5 silvery metal
6 (answer obvious so not worth saying)
7 present from a friend
8 exactly right for her; it means a lot to her

Exercise A6 Page 70

not far from the station	Building
west of the capital	Town
with a view of the mountains	Room (possibly Building)
about 2 km from the university	Building
on the tenth floor	Room
within walking distance of the centre	Building
in Broad Street	Building
on the outskirts of the town	Building
on the site on an old church	Building
in the basement	Room
in the pedestrianised area	Building
quite close to the town hall	Building
surrounded by countryside	Town (possibly Building)
opposite the bathroom	Room
in the city centre	Building

(possible answers)
1 My room is on the second floor of an apartment block, near the lift. It has a view of the main street.
2 The building I'm in is near the city centre, in Mortimer Street; it's within walking distance of the station.
3 This town is 100 km north of London, surrounded by small villages.

Exercise A7 Page 71
(possible answers)
2 house, office, room of some sort
3 town, island
4 room, office, café
5 classroom, restaurant
6 house, hotel, museum
7 town, park, factory
8 bar, café, a town square
9 sports centre, gym
10 college, computer centre
11 art gallery, museum, shopping precinct
12 cinema, gallery, theatre
13 restaurant, café
14 office, jazz club, house
15 bar, disco
16 town, sports centre, holiday resort

(model answer)

Friends Café is in Walters Street, which is about 10 minutes' walk from the city centre. It used to be a small printing works and was made into a café about ten years ago. It's big enough to hold about 200 people who can sit at the tables or dance. It offers a limited range of food. It's a place where people go to be with their friends and to listen to live music.

Exercise A8 Page 71
lively – dull (or sleepy)
well-organised – chaotic
welcoming – unfriendly

(possible answers)
Museum: impressive – dull
Disco: lively – crowded
Bedroom: cosy – chaotic
Village: picturesque – sleepy
Restaurant: welcoming – dirty

Exercise A9 Page 71
(students' own answers based on example sentences)

Exercise A10 Page 72
place – attic; **where** – at the top of the house; **size** – not very big, but big enough for purpose; **use** – work room; **special features** – view of garden; **feelings/impressions** – peaceful, cheerful and welcoming; **why favourite**? – lots of natural light

Exercise A11 Page 72
2 until you come   3 turn right into   4 as far   5 you'll see
6 at the lights   7 carry on past   8 next   9 towards   10 take the second turning   11 into   12 on the left   13 reach/come to
14 go round   15 straight on   16 on your left   17 turn left
18 on the right/on the right hand side   19 opposite

Exercise A12 Page 72
(students' own answer based on example paragraphs)

WRITING SECTION A UNIT 3

Exercise A1 Page 73
(possible answers)
2 … one way of keeping up with current affairs.
3 … help you to get a better job.
4 It's difficult to imagine life without …
5 … smaller than they used to be.
6 … a way of processing what happened during the day.
7 … has a population of about 300,000.

8 In the last 20 years more people have become interested in ...
9 ... is statistically safer than travelling by car.
10 ... are much cheaper than they used to be.

Exercise A2 Page 73
(possible answers)
1 It is said that fewer people read books nowadays.
2 People believe that books help the reader's imagination to develop.
3 According to a recent report, books are the most popular gift for birthdays.
4 People say that shopping can sometimes help with depression.
5 It is believed that shopping can become addictive.
6 Shopping takes up 10% of most people's lives, according to experts.

Exercise A3 Page 74
(possible answers)
in support of keeping cats as pets
First of all, cats are easy to keep.
Secondly, they are very independent.
Another point in favour is that cats are quite clean animals.
Finally, they are good companions for old people or children.
against keeping cats as pets
To begin with, cats are not always very friendly.
Secondly, cats catch birds and mice and bring them into the house.
Another disadvantage of cats as pets is that, unlike dogs, you can't take them for a walk.
In conclusion, I believe that cats are not as loving as dogs and therefore not as suitable as pets.

Exercise A4 Page 74
(possible answers)
1 In addition to this, it is an exciting game to watch.
2 Moreover, they probably have to go to the nearest town for work.
3 What's more, some of them are quite violent.
4 They also don't need to be taken for walks.

Exercise A5 Page 75
(possible answers)
1 TV is entertaining as well as (being) educational.
Apart from being entertaining, TV is (also) educational.
Besides being entertaining, TV is (also) educational.
2 As well as being dangerous to ride in cities, bicycles are not good in the rain.
Apart from not being good in the rain, bicycles are (also) dangerous to ride in cities.
Besides not being good in the rain, bicycles are (also) dangerous to ride in cities.
3 Music helps you (to) relax as well as giving you pleasure.
Apart from helping you (to) relax, music gives you pleasure.
Besides giving you pleasure, music helps you (to) relax.

Exercise A6 Page 75
(model answer)

First of all, public phones are often out of order, or if they are not, there may be a queue of people waiting to use them. You also need to have the right coins or a phone card with you. A mobile phone is more convenient. It allows you to make calls wherever you are, a great advantage for business people for example.
As well as being very useful, a mobile phone can be a real life-saver in emergency situations, such as breaking down in your car. In addition, old people would probably feel safer if they had a mobile phone.

Exercise A7 Page 76
(possible answers)
2 ... not everybody enjoys it. or ... it can be a frightening experience for some people.
3 ... we stayed until the end because the cinema was nice and warm.
4 ... can help you to understand another culture.
5 ... is an essential meal.
6 ... in my country we drive on the right.
7 ... Sam loves going to the cinema.
8 ... you don't have to pay it if you don't want to. or ... they are not supposed to.
9 ... of them don't. or ... of them earn very little.
10 ... are a very convenient way of getting around.
11 ... most people still don't have one.
12 ... all the effort they put in.

Exercise A8 Page 77
(possible answers)
2 ... it's more convenient.
3 ... can go straight into the city centre.
4 ... on a train you can enjoy looking out of the window.
5 ... you have to carry your own luggage when you travel by train.
6 ... it can take a long time to get to or from the airport.
7 ... there's not much leg-room.
8 ... the fact that it's more expensive. or ... the expense.
9 ... it is more convenient in many ways.
10 ... the train is relatively slow ...

Exercise A9 Page 77
(students' own answers)

WRITING SECTION A UNIT 4

Exercise A1 Page 78
(possible answers)
2 ... be banned.
3 ... they are bored with politics.
4 ... a good way to escape.
5 ... displayed their menus outside.
6 ... people work hard.
7 ... one of the world's most exciting cities.
8 ... continue into adult life.
9 ... have difficulty finding good jobs these days.
10 ... stay open all night.
11 ... it helps me relax.
12 ... be taught in every school.

Exercise A2 Page 79
(possible answer)
In my view, there's too much violence on TV. I think programme makers should only include violent scenes if they are really necessary, and only after a certain time in the evening. This would mean that children couldn't see unsuitable images.

Exercise A3 Page 79
Letter 1
My personal view (opinion)
What I like about it most is (reason – why you like the club)
I believe (opinion)
all this would be lost if (result)
To my mind, it would be a much better idea to (opinion/suggestion)

Letter 2
I am most disappointed about (feeling)
and feel that they should (opinion/suggestion)
this is the reason why (reason)
My suggestion ... is that ... should (suggestion)

Letter 3
It seems to me (opinion)
In my opinion (opinion)
... appears to me (opinion)
Why don't (suggestion)
In this way (result)

Exercise A4 Page 80
(students' own answer based on letters 1 to 3 in Exercise A3)

Exercise A5 Page 80
Visiting the city
don't miss (fine architecture); you must go (largest museum outside London); I would certainly recommend (it's efficient, friendly and good value); it's well worth visiting (it's unique – there's nothing quite like it anywhere in the world); make sure you don't leave the city without (owner's personality and excellent coffee)

Activity weekend
I wouldn't really recommend; Don't bother trying; definitely not recommended; It was not worth spending

Exercise A6 Page 80
(students' own answers based on example)

Exercise A7 Page 80
(possible answers)
1 I think it's extremely ugly. or I think it should be knocked down.
2 I would recommend Berties Burgers. or You must try Berties – they're the best burgers in town.
3 Because it will destroy some beautiful countryside. or One reason is that it is not needed. or It'll mean an increase in pollution and noise.
4 No, I'm not. To my mind, the existing one is fine. or No, not really. It's not worth spending money on a new flag.
5 Why don't you look at the weather information in the paper before you decide? or I think you should take lots of thin, cotton things.
6 By doing this, they can help in a practical way. or Because without it, a lot of important research would not survive.
7 It's a good idea to eat something light before you get on board the ship. or Stay in the fresh air, if you can. This will make you feel better.
8 'English Grammar in Use'. What I particularly like about it is that it's very easy to understand. or Personally, I'd recommend ...

WRITING SECTION A UNIT 5

Exercise A1 Page 81
(possible answers)
1 Dear David 2 Dear Mr Spencer/Mrs Simmons
3 Dear Sir or Madam 4 Dear all

Exercise A2 Page 81
2 ↓ 3 ← 4 ← 5 → 6 ← 7 ← 8 →
9 ↓ 10 ← 11 ← 12 →
(some people may disagree with one or two of these, but the authors feel these answers are a useful guide)

Exercise A3 Page 82
(possible answers)
1 a person writing to a friend asking about the price of a ticket
2 As requested
3 I would like to add that the service we received was excellent.
4 So you see, it's just not possible. This is why it is not possible for us to come.

5 I don't think we should change our plans. I think it would be a good idea if we wrote to them. The best thing would be to tell him directly.
6 a holiday which was not up to his expectations; or goods or services supplied that did not do what was promised
7 It wasn't what we were expecting at all.
8 I understand how you feel. I'd feel the same.
You must be feeling very pleased about the results.
I was really surprised to hear your news about the job.
I am writing to apologise for not sending you all the information you requested.

Exercise A4 Page 83
(possible answers)
1 I was really sorry to hear you've lost your job. It must have been a terrible shock for you.
2 I have seen your advertisement for sports shoes in Student Monthly. I would be very interested to receive information about the model called 'Adtrak Tiger'.
3 You asked me about my Japanese holiday plans. Well, first of all, I'm going in July for three weeks.
4 I am writing to inform you that I have to cancel my reservation for June 2nd–16th in the Villa Begonia. Unfortunately, my company has asked me to go to South Africa at that time, and I have no choice but to do what they want.
5 Oh dear, you'll never believe this! The problems started when we got off the plane in the middle of a hurricane.
6 I am writing to tell you about the problems we had on our recent holiday in Florida which your company arranged. The most serious complaint concerns the hotel.

Exercise A5 Page 83
1 a Looking forward to seeing you in March. ('I' is missed out)
b I'm looking forward to meeting you next week. (present continuous is less formal than present simple – see below. Also the contraction 'I'm' makes it less business-like)
c I look forward to hearing from you soon.
2 Hope to hear from you soon.
Hoping to hear from you soon.
(We don't say: I'm hoping to hear from you.)
3 Both sentences mix informal and more formal language.
Drop me a line soon if there's anything else you'd like to know.
Please do not hesitate to contact me if you require any further information.
4 Dear Hilary: With love; Kind regards; With best wishes; Yours
Dear Mr Kinnock: Yours sincerely (if you know Mr Kinnock reasonably well, you might also use: With best wishes or Kind regards)
Dear Sir or Madam: Yours faithfully; Yours truly

Exercise A6 Page 83
(students' own answers)

WRITING SECTION B UNIT 6

Exercise B1 Page 84
1 Himalayan Expedition Company
2 You have read their advertisement.
3 You are writing to tell them something about yourself, so that they can see if you're a suitable person for the expedition, and also to get some more information.
4 business-like

Exercise B2 Page 85
1 yes 2 no 3 yes 4 yes 5 maybe 6 yes 7 no 8 yes
9 yes 10 no 11 maybe 12 no 13 yes 14 no 15 yes

ANSWERS

Exercise B3 Page 85

Sample answer 1 answers the question better.
Sample answer 2 is unsatisfactory for the following reasons:

content

one required point missing (no question about equipment)
irrelevant points: (studying Sociology; doctor's waiting room;
when my friends learnt to swim; working in my father's office)

style

language which is too informal (anyway, as I was saying; why
don't you drop me a line; sorry about all these questions)

effect on reader

the reader might well be a bit irritated by the tone, and also by
the unnecessary information that makes the letter rather wordy

Exercise B4 Page 86

(possible answers)

1 How much would it cost?
2 Because the person hiring the club doesn't want Europop
   style music.
3 Is the room big enough to take 100 or possibly as many as
   150 people?
4 Because it's an important feature; the hirer must check there
   is one.
5 The hirer is surprised that the club is only available until
   midnight. They probably want to ask for it to be available
   longer.

Exercise B5 Page 87

(possible answers)

2 It's better if you can speak a foreign language. We had a lot of
   South American teenagers so Spanish was really useful.
3 The people who work there stay in tents on the site, which
   might not be what you were expecting. But it's no problem if
   the weather is fine.
4 The pay isn't wonderful but it's enough to cover everything
   you need.
5 You do get some time off – usually one day a week and some
   evenings. So it's not all hard work.
6 It's a very friendly place to work – I made some really good
   friends.

Exercise B6 Page 88

(model answer)

First of all, yes, you do need to be qualified in your
sport. They're really strict about this but it won't be a problem
for you as I know you've got a swimming diploma. And being
able to speak another language is really useful. I'm sure I told
you before that lots of the kids came from South America, so I
was grateful for my Spanish. And you speak Spanish too,
don't you? The accommodation they provide is in tents! Not
very luxurious, but fun – the weather was wonderful and I got
on well with the other people working there. We actually spent
quite a bit of time together on our day off and when we were
free in the evenings. The only thing I didn't like was the pay –
not very good, I'm afraid. But the experience of working there
was something I wouldn't have missed. I know you'll enjoy it
too. Go on, apply now! Lots of love

Exercise B7 Page 89

1 C 2 A 3 E 4 G 5 B 6 F 7 D (possible to reverse 4
and 5)

Exercise B8 Page 90

(students' own answer)
See also Appendix 3 on page 204

WRITING SECTION B UNIT 7

Exercise B1 Page 91

2 other students 3 informal 4 a straightforward story 5 on
my own experience or imagination 6 the title, which could also
be the first line 7 one really good thing that's happened to me
8 'thing', i.e. only one

Exercise B2 Page 92

(possible answers for sports event)

Who?	me, some friends, the team
What?	final match of the season
When?	rainy evening in March
Where?	local stadium
Why?	if they win they get promotion to top division
How?	played badly in first half; second half was magic

Exercise B3 Page 92

(see sample answer in Exercise B4 for correct order)

Exercise B4 Page 93

Basic paragraph breaks

... my number one priority. // So six weeks ...
I've failed. // The rest of the test ...

Possible extra breaks

good at it. // Then one day ...
closed his notebook. // By this time ...
(Alternatively, it's also possible that the first and last sentences
could stand alone.)

Exercise B5 Page 94

(possible answers)

Tenses

... told me she and her family were moving ...
... passing my driving test ...
... I was sitting beside ...
After answering ...
... while I was reversing ...
'I've failed'
... what I'd done wrong
I was just about to ...
I couldn't wait to ...

Vocabulary

I wasn't particularly good at it.
my number one priority
my hands were shaking
reversing round a corner
take ages
convinced
couldn't wait to

Exercise B6 Page 94

(possible answers)

2 She telephoned Sam, who was her best friend, and asked her
   to come too.
   She knew that Sam – her closest friend for many years – also
   enjoyed swimming, so she rang and asked her to come too.
3 They met at the nearby lake, which was very popular.
   The lake where they met was surrounded by trees and was a
   popular place with young people in the summer.
4 Sam was wearing a new black swimsuit.
   Sam looked great in her new swimsuit.

5   The water was wonderfully warm.
    They were surprised at how warm the water was considering it was only early summer.
6   Afterwards, they had a really delicious picnic.
    After their swim, they sat on the grass eating the delicious picnic that Jenny had brought.
7   They decided they'd had such a pleasant time together that they'd do the same again the following week – if the weather was good enough.
    The afternoon had been an enjoyable one and they agreed to do it all again the following week – if the good weather continued.

Exercise B7 Page 94
(possible answers)
 2 completely/totally
 3 very well/clearly
 4 definitely/almost certainly
 5 immediately/at once
 6 efficiently/badly
 7 excitedly/quietly
 8 unusually/surprisingly
 9 slowly/quickly;   seriously/definitely
10 seldom/hardly ever

Exercise B8 Page 95
One day last winter, Pete Daniels left his office earlier than usual. He had an appointment, but he didn't want anybody to know about it. In fact, he was going to an interview with another company which had offered him a better job (or better work).

But while he was at his interview, his manager was looking for him back at the office. One of Pete's most important customers from Brazil had come to see him and everybody was trying desperately to find Pete. Nobody could find him. 'I'm sorry, Mr Cavalho,' said the manager, 'Pete seems to have disappeared.'

Mr Cavalho was very disappointed. He had to fly back to Rio the following day and he particularly wanted to see Pete.

The following day, Pete went into work as usual. He was feeling very pleased because his interview had been successful. When he sat down at his desk, his phone rang. It was his manager, who wanted to see him immediately in his office. Pete had no idea what it was about, but he wasn't worried – until he opened the door and saw the look on his boss's face.

Exercise B9 Page 95
(students' own answer)
See also Appendix 3 on page 204

WRITING SECTION B UNIT 8

Exercise B1 Page 96
Example 2
1 an article
2 college magazine
3 fellow students
4 no: 'A teacher who has been important in my life'
5 two: describe character of teacher and say why (s)he is/was important for you
6 personal views
7 might forget to say *why* this person is important

Example 3
1 a letter
2 local newspaper
3 local people
4 no: 'A park or an exhibition centre?'
5 three: which one, why, suggestions for what to include in it

6 bit of both: some things will be more factual, but reasons may be more personal
7 might find yourself discussing both proposals instead of choosing one

Example 4
1 a composition
2 your teacher
3 your teacher
4 no: 'The advantages and disadvantages of having a nationwide TV-free day'
5 one: the main discussion, which asks for the pros and cons
6 both: you can discuss objectively or subjectively
7 remember to discuss both sides of the argument

Exercise B2 Page 97
(possible answers)
1 Personal reaction: yes, on the whole, but there can be a lot of practical difficulties
2 Who?   old people themselves and the people who look after them
   Where?   my own country; other countries; cities or villages; size of house etc.
   What?   depends on how much looking after old person needs
   When?   part-time or full-time care
   Why?   duty of younger generation; useful as babysitters
   How?   with help from community; financial help from government
   But?   problems between generations; old people lose independence
3 Possible points: the alternative of putting them in a home is horrible; they looked after us, we should look after them
   but: need to work; size of modern houses makes it difficult

Exercises B3 and B4 Pages 97 and 98
(students' own answers)

Exercise B5 Page 98
(possible answers)

Advantages
1 gives you more time to do other things
2 people would have to talk to each other instead
3 might encourage people to be more active

Disadvantages
1 TV offers opportunity to learn, why reduce that opportunity?
2 busy parents would have to think of something else for their kids' entertainment
3 you might miss some important information or news

Exercise B6 Page 98
(possible answers)

Paragraph breaks
line 2: after … on the subject
line 6: after … many others too
line 9: after … makes it exciting

Exercise B7 Page 99
1b is better because it refers to the question but uses a different way to express it; it makes a choice and it gives you an idea of what's going to come next.
1a is not so good because although it answers the question, the words 'The plane' should be put in a sentence. It also introduces a first point which should be part of the body of the writing.

2a is better because it refers to the question; it acknowledges that there's another side to the question without wasting too many words. It's a general introduction.
2b goes straight into the points.
('How well do schools prepare students for their future?' – students' own answers)

Exercise B8 Page 99
1b is best because it is introduced by a concluding phrase; it refers back to the question.
1a is clearly the last thing, but uses exactly the same words as the question.
1c is a final point not a conclusion.
2a is best because it concludes with a summary of what has been said in the body of the writing.
2b seems to indicate that the body of the writing has been discussing the good and bad things about TV which is not what was asked.
2c is too personal, and a bit too chatty.

Exercise B9 Page 100
1 yes: that we could do more to stop crimes happening
2 two main positive points: improve security in our homes; be more aware on the streets
3 main negative point: can't do much against violent, professional criminals
4 support: burglar alarms; locks on doors and windows; a dog; don't walk in certain places at certain times; can't resist armed criminals
5 yes: you can do something but not much
6 yes: see above
7 yes: good vocabulary, e.g.: para 1 – *on the increase*; para 2 – *to make it hard for*; *excellent protection for*; *sensible*; para 3 – *not much … can do against*; *faced with*; para 4 – *aware*; *the legal system*
  yes: good structure, e.g.: para 1 – *It is true that*; *… it is also true that*; para 2 – *The first point*; *Even if we*; *As well as*; *In addition*; *If … then*; para 3 – *On the other hand*; *It doesn't seem to matter*; para 4 – *So … by being …*; *In the end*

Exercise B10 Exam practice Page 101
(students' own answers)
See also Appendix 3 on page 205

WRITING SECTION B UNIT 9

Exercise B1 Page 102
Example 2
1 a college student
2 college authorities or the video librarian
3 because the college is setting up a video library and they need the information in order to decide whether to include the film in the library
4 what the film is about, the level of the language, who might like it
5 the name of the film
6 either present or past for summary of film; present or past for comments on level of language; *will* or *would* for who it would appeal to

Example 3
1 employee at tourist office
2 your boss
3 want to know whether tour is suitable for international visitors
4 description of tour, good and bad points and your recommendation
5 Tour of … (name of factory)
6 past tenses

Example 4
1 member of fitness club interested in getting new skill
2 other members of the club
3 to report on the usefulness of the course
4 details of course and how useful it is
5 name of course
6 past; probably *will* or *would* for comments on its usefulness

Exercise B2 Page 103
(possible answers)
Example 2
Report on: 'Jurassic Park'
Description:
Language:
Appeal:

Example 3
Subject: Tour of Unwins Plastics Company
Details of tour:
Comments:
Recommendation:

Example 4
Subject: Helping the Elderly to Keep Fit
Course details:
Comments:

Exercise B3 Page 103
(possible answers)
Size: it's surprisingly big
Type of entertainment: various styles of music
Atmosphere: very lively
Cost: drinks are more expensive than a normal bar

Exercise B4 Page 104
Version 1
Some details are included but not enough for new students. Where in the city centre? When does it open? No reason given for Saturday being the best night to go.

Version 2
Lots of factual detail which will help a new person. Would make reader want to continue reading.

Version 3
Again, not much detail. Too much opinion, which is not what a report should contain. 'Chatty' language.

Exercise B5 Page 105
(possible answers)
1 all three places named
2 answer was short of details – no information about where these restaurants were
3 yes, in all three
4 Black's had no best feature mentioned
5 not really a report, more of an article you might read in a magazine; clear paragraphs but no headings
6 too chatty, personal, e.g. *I should know, because I'm always short of cash!*; *The first place I want to tell you about*; *I really like it!*
7 no, not really, because the information and the style it's written in are not appropriate
8 not completely: apart from the style problems, and some missing information (see above) there's also some inappropriate information, e.g. all day opening, but task wanted places for the evening; emphasis on cheapness not appropriate for business people; emphasis on young people not appropriate

Exercise B6 Page 105

Candidate A's answer corresponds to the second report from the examiner and Candidate B's to the first.

Candidate A
Language corrections
was being held – was held
inclusive – including
accomodation – accommodation
persons – people
spent to learn – spent learning
make – do
suggestion – suggestions
learn – learnt
worth – value
informations – information
have be – have been
to visit – to visiting
going – to go
Other points
good detail: dates, prices, number of participants and teachers, what happened on each day
clear organisation: good headings, good linking devices: although; at the same time; however
style: informative, not too personal, neutral language

Candidate B
Language corrections
to training – to train
elderly – the elderly
some people very friendly – some very friendly ...
a lots of – a lot of/lots of
I'm not too keen – I was not keen on
I'm suppose is necessary – I suppose it is necessary
what I'll – which/that I'll
laught – laugh
Other points
range of structure/vocabulary: *The aim of ... was to*; *It was organised by ... and held*; *gentle stretching exercises*;
lack of detail: nothing about dates, cost, numbers etc. but sentence at beginning of para. 2 excellent
organisation: no headings; no clear separation between facts and comments
chatty style: *To be honest, I'm not too keen on*; *you know*; *we had a good laugh*
danger of missing purpose: no recommendation about future participation

Exercise B7 Exam practice Page 106

(students' own answers)
See also Appendix 3 on page 205

WRITING SECTION B UNIT 10

Exercise B1 Page 108

(possible answers)

1	Disagree	7	Disagree
2	Agree	8	Agree
3	Disagree	9	Agree
4	Disagree	10	personal decision, but authors disagree
5	Agree	11	Agree
6	Agree		

(reference to most of these answers will be found in 'suggested procedure')

Exercise B2 Page 110

(students' own answers)

Exercise B3 Page 111
(possible answers)
Sample question 1
1 yes
2 three things named in introduction, and reasons given
3 yes, approximately right length (190 words)
4 yes, detail about moor and Sherlock Holmes show this
5 – work divided into logical paragraphs and ideas are linked together quite well (*so, also, because, in fact*)
– the last paragraphs seems a bit of a jump in style, as if the writer is talking. Also the conclusion (just a six-word sentence) needs a little more
6 good range of structures:
good modals – *lots of horrible things could happen*; *I would want to meet*; *how a dog could kill*
other structures: *without anyone finding out*; *I didn't know if there was*
reasonable vocabulary: *described as ... a wild and mysterious place*; *get the impression that*; *cold and unemotional*; *friendly towards* etc.
7 yes, the writer gets across his/her enthusiasm

Sample question 2
1 no title
2 task achieved – person named, reasons given and relationship mentioned
3 right length – 180 words
4 yes: the question asks you to imagine the relationship, so some of the answer cannot show as much factual detail
5 no paragraphs, so a bit difficult to follow
good linking (*but, However, First of all, And then, She might, of course*) stops a bit suddenly, but not bad
6 good structure: modals – *could, to have been, might*
good vocab: *badly treated, legal powers over her, doesn't have much self-confidence*
7 yes, the writer enjoyed reading the book and was interested in the character of Laura Lyons

Chapter 3 Use of English

USE OF ENGLISH UNIT 1

Familiarisation exercise Page 114
1 C   2 D   3 D

Exercise 1 Page 115
4 Category 3: B   5 Category 1: C   6 Category 3: B
7 Category 2: D   8 Category 3: D   9 Category 3: B
10 Category 3: A   11 Category 1: C   12 Category 2: A

Exercise 2 Page 116
(possible answers)
2 reached   3 hope   4 check   5 pouring   6 guess/imagine
7 avoid   8 notice/see   9 hurt/injured   10 happy/pleased
11 puddle   12 spent/wasted

Exercise 3 Page 117
(possible answers)
2 receipt/invoice/ticket   3 pause/space/gap   4 scenery/sight
5 build/expand/increase   6 meaning/idea   7 gain/win

Exercise 4 Page 117
2 As   3 and   4 so as to   5 Since   6 Although   7 particularly
8 if

Exercise 5 Page 118

Really cold places
2 D   3 B   4 A & B

What causes colds
1 C   2 A & B   3 B, C & D   4 B   5 A & C

The power of tornadoes
1 A & B   2 B & C   3 A & B   4 B & D

Exercise 6 Page 119
2 B   3 D   4 B   5 A   6 B   7 C   8 D   9 B   10 D   11 B
12 C

Exercise 7 Page 120
2 D   3 C   4 A   5 C   6 D   7 B   8 D

Exercise 8   Exam practice Page 121
1 D   2 D   3 B   4 A   5 C   6 B   7 C   8 A   9 D   10 B
11 C   12 C   13 A   14 A   15 B

USE OF ENGLISH UNIT 2

Familiarisation exercise Page 122
1 they   2 others   3 which   4 for

Exercise 1 Page 122
2 read   3 Although   4 all   5 The   6 enough   7 been
8 where   9 Everyone/Everybody   10 can; less

Exercise 2 Page 123
2 *hardly* is a negative word, therefore doesn't fit with *no*;
correct answer: any
3 need a relative word here to connect the two sentences
together; correct answer: which
4 sentence means there are several answers, so a number is
needed; correct answer: one
5 *arrived* is followed by prepositions *at* or *in*, not *to*; correct
answer: got
6 incorrect form of auxiliary verb; correct answer: have
7 *like* means he worked in a similar way to a bank clerk, but
actually he was one; correct answer: as
8 *closer* is already a comparative word so if you want to make it
strong you can't add another comparative structure; correct
answer: much
9 *an increase* is not followed by *of*; correct answer: in
10 *and* makes you think there's going to be something positive
in the second half. A contrast is needed; correct answer: but
11 wrong choice made as a result of not reading to the end of
the sentence; correct answer: nothing
12 *much* makes the second sentence contradict the first; correct
answer: little

Exercise 3 Page 124
2 where   3 when   4 which   5 What   6 which   7 whose

Exercise 4 Page 124
2 were   3 been   4 will   5 would   6 been   7 was   8 has

Exercise 5 Page 125
2 another   3 In   4 either   5 despite   6 other

Exercise 6 Page 125
2 another   3 it   4 themselves   5 them   6 these   7 they
8 their

Exercise 7 Page 125
2 anywhere; Somebody; something   3 everywhere
4 somebody   5 any   6 None   7 some   8 few   9 many
10 little

Exercise 8 Page 126
2 when   3 those   4 as   5 result   6 to   7 if   8 far   9 There
10 anything   11 a

Exercise 9 Page 127

Albert Schweitzer
2 as   3 way   4 as   5 at   6 had   7 his   8 helped/enabled
9 which   10 next   11 after   12 Although   13 in

Train journey to work
1 with   2 would   3 not   4 that   5 an   6 none   7 have
8 and   9 there   10 allowing   11 first   12 nobody/no one

Exercise 10   Exam practice Page 128
1 as   2 the   3 of   4 was   5 whose   6 by   7 would   8 all
9 It   10 or   11 in   12 own   13 let   14 often/commonly/
frequently   15 such

USE OF ENGLISH UNIT 3

Familiarisation exercise Page 129
1 I **wasn't interested in** the lecture.
2 Frank asked me to **take care of his cat** for him.
3 Steve's feet **are so big (that) / are such big ones (that)** it's
almost impossible to get shoes for him.

Exercises 1 and 2 Pages 129 and 130
(possible answers)
2 What do you **think** of his work?
3 Do you know **why** she left the company? *or* Have you any
idea why she left the company?
4 You're not **allowed** to smoke in here. *or* You must not
smoke in here. *or* Smoking is not allowed in here.
5 I don't **want** to tell you the answer. *or* I'd prefer not to tell
you the answer.
6 I think **everybody**/everyone will (probably) pass the exam.
or I don't think anyone will fail the exam.
7 Whose book **is** this? *or* Whose is this book?
8 **Why** don't we go swimming this afternoon? *or* Shall we go
swimming this afternoon? *or* Do you fancy going swimming
this afternoon? *or* How about going swimming this
afternoon?
9 I'm **not** interested in art. *or* Art doesn't appeal to me. *or* Art
doesn't interest me.
10 Anne **didn't** look at her notes when/while she was speaking.
11 Greg **plays** tennis very well. *or* Greg is a good tennis player.
12 There's no **point** (in) asking Jim the answer. *or* Don't bother
asking / to ask Jim the answer.
13 The students **found** the lesson boring. *or* The students
thought the lesson was boring.
14 Their new car **cost** (them) a lot of money. *or* Their new car
was very expensive.
15 It takes **me** two hours to travel to work every day. *or* My
journey to work takes (me) two hours every day.
16 You'd **better** go to the doctor. *or* I think you should go to
the doctor.
17 The **only** person I don't know in the village is my neighbour.
or My neighbour is the only person in the village I don't
know.
18 Ella has spent **almost** all her money. *or* Ella has almost no
money left. *or* Ella has very little money left.
19 I decided to stay at home in **case** Jo rang. *or* There was a
possibility that Jo might ring so I decided to stay at home.
20 In **addition** to playing the piano, Penny also plays the
guitar. *or* Penny plays both the piano and guitar. *or* Penny
not only plays the piano, she also plays the guitar.

Exercise 3 Page 131
1 A lot of different goods **are exported by** the Japanese.
2 Since I last went to her house, Pam's **study has been painted** pink.
3 Donald **is being taught chess by** his sister.
4 I had the feeling that **I was being** followed.
5 The hostages **are going to be freed** at midday.

Exercise 4 Page 131
1 All this work **should be finished** before lunchtime.
2 Your name **ought to have been** added to the list before you left the building.
3 I'd like **to be woken** up at 8 o'clock, please.

Exercise 5 Page 132
1 The President **is believed to have** a huge private fortune.
2 The world's climate **is believed by** many scientists to be changing.
3 Apes are said **to be able to** understand human speech.
4 The palace **was thought by** local people to be haunted.
5 Florence **is considered to be** a very beautiful city.

Exercise 6 Page 132
1 I'm **going to have my** knee X-rayed on Friday.
2 The garage think I ought to **have my car serviced** soon.
3 I don't know the time because I'm **having my watch repaired** at the moment.

Exercise 7 Page 133
(possible answers)
1 Oscar **was not allowed to leave the room**.
2 The **police officer wouldn't/didn't allow him to leave the room**.
3 The **police officer wouldn't/didn't let him leave the room**.
4 The **police officer made him stay in the room**.
5 Oscar **was made to stay in the room**.

Exercise 8 Page 133
1 Our dog would **not let the postman** deliver the letters.
2 We **were not allowed** to enter the country by the border guards.
3 Why **didn't/wouldn't he let you** have the day off?
4 My mother **made me keep** my own room tidy.
5 When I was younger, I **was made/obliged/forced/expected to** look after my baby sister.

Exercise 9 Page 134
1 Cars **must not be parked** here.
2 Because yesterday was a national holiday, we **didn't need to go** to college.
3 We really **shouldn't have bought** such a large dog.
4 Does **the car have to be** repaired this week?
5 You **must have been delighted** to see her again after such a long time.
6 Linda **could (easily) have been injured** in the fall.
7 I saw Frank in the city centre yesterday, so he **can't be (living)** in America.
8 You **ought to be working**, not watching TV.

Exercise 10 Page 135
1 Paula **apologised for causing/having caused** me a problem.
2 Lois **offered to carry Clive's** case for him.
3 Mandy **denied breaking/having broken** the plate.
4 Don told **Meg (that) she had** beautiful hair.
5 Jan **advised me not to do** that.
6 Zoe asked Jo **if/whether she felt like** seeing her room.
7 Helen **warned her son not** to play with matches.

8 I asked Daniel **if/whether he knew** the way to the football stadium.
9 Mrs Honeybone **offered to make** Paul a cup of tea.
10 The travel agent **advised us to** fly on a weekday.

Exercise 11 Page 136
1 If you don't **say 'please'**, I won't give it to you.
  If you **say 'please'**, I'll give it to you.
  Unless you **say 'please'**, I won't give it to you.
2 If it doesn't **stop raining soon**, I can't go for a walk.
  If it **stops raining soon**, I can go for a walk.
3 If you **promise to keep it a secret, I'll tell you**.
  Unless **you promise to keep it a secret, I won't tell you**.
4 If Debbie was/were **shorter**, she could be a ballet dancer.
  If Debbie wasn't/weren't **so tall**, she could be a ballet **dancer**.
5 If I **had enough time, I could start again**.
6 They would **have understood the film if they hadn't missed the beginning/had seen the beginning**.
7 If Sam **had remembered to set his alarm clock, he wouldn't have overslept this morning**.
  or If Sam **hadn't forgotten to set his alarm clock, he wouldn't have overslept this morning**.
8 You wouldn't **be cold if you had remembered to bring a sweater**.
  If you hadn't **forgotten to bring a sweater, you wouldn't be cold**.

Exercise 12 Page 136
1 If **we hadn't had** your support, we couldn't have won the competition.
2 If **I were you, I'd/I would** ring Chris today.
3 You **won't understand him unless** you listen to him carefully.
4 Maria would have got lost **if she hadn't had** a map of the town.
5 We'd be hungry **if you hadn't brought** some sandwiches.
6 If Ian had listened to Clare's advice, **he would be working** here now.
7 Polly **would understand if somebody had** explained the situation to her.

Exercise 13 Page 137
1 John wishes **he had a car**.
2 I regret **not going/having gone to the party last night**.
3 Zoe wishes **she lived in a hot country**.
4 If only I **hadn't told them the truth**.
5 I wish **I hadn't come to work today**.
6 I wish someone **would answer that phone**.

Exercise 14 Page 137
1 Helen **wishes she had gone** to bed early last night.
2 David wished **he had been able** to have a holiday.
3 I wish **I still saw** him.
4 I **wish I were/was** rich!
5 Jill **regretted resigning/having resigned** from her job.

Exercise 15 Page 138
1 Brian **has worked here for** two and a half years.
2 It's **ages since I saw** my cousin.
3 Clare **became a politician** 20 years ago.
4 I **haven't seen Margaret since** 1984.

Exercise 16 Page 138
1 Ms Craig **still hasn't** sent in her application form.
2 The house **hasn't been/isn't sold yet**, I'm afraid.
3 The kidnapper **hasn't left the house** yet.
4 I think Bob **is still eating/having** his meal.

Exercise 17 Page 138

1 This is the best example of Dali's work **I've (ever) seen**, I'm quite sure.
2 Is this the **first time you have (ever)** visited Tibet?
3 Howard **has never run faster** than that!

Exercise 18 Page 139

1 Emily said she **preferred listening to** talking to people.
2 John claimed **(that) he would rather listen** to the radio than watch TV.
3 Marilyn **would rather drink** Scotch whisky than Irish whiskey.
4 **I'd/would prefer you not** to talk to me like that!
5 Sonja **would rather not** talk about it just now.
6 **I'd/would rather you didn't** throw all that food away.
7 Mel told Fred that **she'd prefer him to** stay away from her.

Exercise 19 Page 139

1 The door handle was too high for Pam to reach.
2 Pam was not tall enough to reach the door handle.
3 The door handle was so high that Pam couldn't reach it.
4 It was such a high door handle that Pam couldn't reach it.

Exercise 20 Page 140

1 It **was such terrible news** that nobody believed it.
2 Martin **walked so slowly** that he got left behind.
3 The room **was so crowded/full (of people)** that I couldn't see anything.
4 It was **such cold weather that nobody** went out.
5 Wendy **is not old enough** to vote in the elections.

Exercise 21 Page 140

1 This computer **used to work better than** it does now.
2 People don't **have as many children as** they used to.
3 I'm **(much) worse than Geoff (is)** at chemistry.
4 Not **as much money is spent** on education as on defence.

Exercise 22 Page 140

1 I live **quite near (to)** my office.
2 Oxford **is not (very) far (away) from** London.
3 Is Paris **a long way from** the Channel Tunnel?

Exercise 23 Page 141

1 There **isn't anything that is** too much trouble for him.
2 There **is nowhere in the world** that I haven't visited.
3 The party was successful because **nobody forgot** to bring a present.
4 There **was no food left / wasn't any food left** on the table.

Exercise 24 Page 141

2 It was a **difficult decision for David to make**.
   David had **difficulty in making the decision**.
3 I broke **your porcelain dish by accident**.
   I broke your porcelain dish **accidentally**. or I **accidentally broke your porcelain dish**.
   Breaking **your porcelain dish was an accident**.
4 When **I was a child I lived in India**.
   During **my childhood I lived in India**.
5 Anne **didn't intend to say that**.
   Anne had **no intention of saying that**.
6 It's difficult to **explain the accident**.
   It's difficult to find **an explanation for the accident**.
7 I've never **succeeded in beating Tom at tennis**.
   I've had **no success in beating Tom at tennis**.
   I've never been **successful in beating Tom at tennis**.
8 Nick **apparently refused to leave**.
   It **appears that Nick refused to leave**.
9 Joe hasn't **chosen whether to study history or politics**.

Joe hasn't made **a choice about whether to study history or politics**.
10 The committee **agreed what to do by the end of the meeting**.
   The committee reached **agreement about what to do by the end of the meeting**.
11 The PM made **an apology about the financial scandal**.
   The PM **apologised for the financial scandal**.
12 What are you **planning to do for Bernard's birthday**?
   What are **your plans for Bernard's birthday**?
13 Walter **complained about the way he was spoken to**.
   Walter made **a complaint about the way he was spoken to**.
14 Would it be **possible for you to lend me some money**?
   Could you **possibly lend me some money**?
15 The princess **quickly kissed the frog's nose**.
   The princess gave **the frog's nose a quick kiss**.
16 Sam **applied for a visa by filling in a form**.
   Sam wrote/made **an application for a visa**.
17 Why do you always **blame me**?
   Why do you always put **the blame on me**?
18 You must be **responsible for what you do**.
   You have to take **responsibility for what you do**.
19 Colin and Jill **are very similar**.
   Colin is **very similar to Jill**.
   There's a lot **of similarity between Colin and Jill**.
20 Kevin found **it surprising to see all his friends in the restaurant**.
   To Kevin's **surprise, all his friends were in the restaurant**.

Exercise 25 Page 142

2 The boat **is in danger of** sinking.
3 Her sudden **appearance took me** by surprise.
4 I think **you must have made a / there must have been a / there must be some** mistake.
5 It's difficult **not to be/feel anxious / not to feel anxiety** when your children are late home.
6 There is **no time for (a) discussion** of that problem now.
7 Barry **gave his face a quick** wash.
8 I suggest you **give Tony a call** and tell him the news.
9 Their **marriage/wedding took place** 20 years ago.
10 Everyone's opinions must **be taken into account/consideration** before deciding.

Exercise 26 Page 143

2 Alex and I **get on (well)** together.
3 Barry **told me off for** damaging his bike.
4 No one has **come up with an idea** for a long time.
5 I **have gone off (watching)** horror movies.
6 You must **stick/keep to** what you've already decided, I'm afraid.
7 I **was put off (seeing)** the film by the publicity.
8 We **saw/waved Jim off** at the airport.
9 I **can't work out what** she meant.
10 The older generation used **to be looked up to** by the younger generation.

Exercise 27   Exam practice Page 144

1 I didn't realise that the train station was **such a long way** from the city centre.
2 Amy **wishes she had told** her brother the truth.
3 It's not possible **to make a comparison between** the two tax systems.
4 Lisa **warned Roger not to** sail too close to the rocks.
5 I think **you had better give** David your answer.
6 Jack **must have had** a good reason for leaving his job.
7 It was **thanks to/due to/owing to/down to Carol's generosity** that the club managed to survive.

8 It is **with great pleasure that** I announce the opening of Connell's new supermarket.

9 The weather **made it impossible for** the concert to go ahead.

10 The salesman told me that my printer **would have to be replaced** soon.

USE OF ENGLISH UNIT 4

Familiarisation exercise Page 145
1 to   2 ✓   3 which   4 also   5 ✓   6 own

Exercise 1 Page 146
to
3 ✓   4 ✗   5 ✗   6 ✗   7 ✓   8 ✗
for
1 ✗   2 ✗   3 ✗   4 ✓   5 ✗   6 ✓
of
1 ✓   2 ✗   3 ✗   4 ✓   5 ✓   6 ✓   7 ✗   8 ✗
about
1 ✓   2 ✗   3 ✓   4 ✗   5 ✗   6 ✓   7 ✓   8 ✗

Exercise 2 Page 146
the
1 ✓   2 ✓   3 ✓   4 ✗   5 ✗   6 ✓   7 ✗
a
1 ✗   2 ✓   3 ✓   4 ✓   5 ✗   6 ✓   7 ✗   8 ✗
9 ✗   10 ✓

Exercise 3 Page 147
it
1 ✗   2 ✓   3 ✓   4 ✓   5 ✗   6 ✓

Exercise 4 Page 147
will
1 ✗   2 ✓   3 ✗   4 ✓   5 ✓   6 ✓
be
1 ✓   2 ✗   3 ✓   4 ✓   5 ✗
been
1 ✓   2 ✗   3 ✗   4 ✗   5 ✓   6 ✓

Exercise 5 Page 147
much
1 ✓   2 ✗   3 ✓   4 ✗   5 ✓   6 ✗   7 ✗   8 ✗
all
1 ✗   2 ✓   3 ✗   4 ✗   5 ✗   6 ✓   7 ✓
one(s)
1 ✗   2 ✓   3 ✗   4 ✓   5 ✗   6 ✓   7 ✗   8 ✓
so
1 ✗   2 ✓   3 ✗   4 ✓   5 ✗

Exercise 6 Page 147
quite   then   more
1 ✓   2 ✗   3 ✗   4 ✓   5 ✓   6 ✗
had   being
1 ✗   2 ✗   3 ✓   4 ✓
rather   own
1 ✗   2 ✓   3 ✓   4 ✗   5 ✓   6 ✓   7 ✗   8 ✗
it   itself
1 ✗   2 ✗   3 ✓   4 ✓   5 ✓   6 ✓   7 ✗   8 ✓
even   also   always
1 ✗   2 ✓   3 ✗   4 ✗   5 ✗   6 ✓   7 ✓   8 ✗   9 ✓
10 ✓   11 ✗   12 ✗

Exercise 7 Page 148
3 ✓   4 much   5 what   6 of   7 a   8 so   9 also   10 ✓
11 are   12 ✓   13 yourself   14 ✓   15 the   16 for
17 already   18 ✓

Exercise 8   Exam practice   Page 149
1 ✓   2 a   3 have   4 to   5 them   6 do   7 ✓   8 was
9 which   10 so   11 ✓   12 ✓   13 for   14 ✓   15 there

USE OF ENGLISH UNIT 5

Familiarisation exercise Page 150
1 unemployed   2 engineer   3 knowledge   4 profitable

Exercise 1 Page 151
2 present; *presence* is an abstract noun
3 interest; *interestingly* is an adverb
4 own; *ownership* is an abstract noun
5 survive; *survival* is an abstract noun
6 courage; *encourage* is a verb
7 get; *getting* is a gerund
8 usual; *unusually* is a negative adverb
9 depend; *dependent* is an adjective
10 feel; *feelings* is an abstract noun in the plural
11 system; *systematic* is an adjective
12 company; *accompany* is a verb

Exercise 2 Page 151
2 must be an adjective describing the size or quality of the part of the coast, probably positive or neutral; possible answers: beautiful, rocky
3 must be a plural noun – people because they come here to make films; possible answers: directors, producers
4 must be a noun after pronoun *their*, and is followed by *they find* so whole phrase must mean when they get there; possible answer: arrival
5 must be an adjective to describe air, must be positive, and it supports *a wonderful climate*; possible answers: fresh, healthy
6 must be a noun because you can check it. Need to read to end of sentence to realise it's a reference to people who want to take part in the courses; possible answer: applicants, candidates
7 must be an adjective describing *people*; must be negative because they don't want to waste their time training these people; possible answers: useless, inappropriate

Real answers: 2 sunny   3 producers   4 arrival   5 unpolluted
6 applicants   7 unsuitable

Exercise 3 Page 152
2 correct
3 correct
4 wrong, should be plural noun because of the word *ones*; correct answer: similarities
5 wrong, no change has been made – has to be an adjective to describe the interior; correct answer: mountainous
6 correct
7 wrong, right form of word (adjective) but needs to be negative; correct answer: undiscovered
8 wrong, it should be a plural noun because it's followed by *believe*; correct answer: scientists
9 wrong, right form of word (adjective) but needs to be negative; correct answer: unlikely
10 correct

Exercise 4 Page 152
2 advisable   3 inadvisable   4 tourism/tour   5 to tour
6 visitor(s)   7 visit(s)   8 foreigner(s)   9 behaviour
10 tourism   11 behaviour   12 visitors

Exercise 5 Page 153

2 scientific 3 unscientific 4 dismissal 5 (un)employment
6 to employ 7 employed/employable 8 unemployed/
unemployable 9 to decide 10 decisive 11 indecisive
12 employment 13 indecisive 14 unscientific

Exercise 6 Page 154

2 pianist 3 Brazilian 4 pollution 5 generosity 6 kindness
7 musical 8 skil(l)ful 9 misunderstand 10 impractical
11 homeless 12 neighbourhood 13 sweeten 14 to dislike

Exercise 7 Page 155

2 poverty 3 anxiety 4 lengthen 5 explanation 6 daily
7 height 8 strength 9 proof 10 flattens

Exercise 8 Page 155

2 inexpensive 3 inaccurate 4 irregularly 5 disappeared
6 uninjured 7 unexpectedly 8 illegal 9 immature
10 impatience 11 unlocked 12 disapproving

Exercise 9 Exam practice Page 156

1 attractive 2 communication 3 terrified 4 visitors
5 secretly 6 furniture 7 equipment 8 weight
9 unhealthily 10 unhappy

Chapter 4 Listening

LISTENING SECTION A UNIT 1

Exercise A1 Page 158

1 hills, 30 minutes' drive, coast
2 six, house, quite big
3 best thing, garden
4 huge
5 lot, time, evenings, barbecues outside
6 kids, go, sea
7 every morning, took, there, John, I, took, turns, stay, beach

Exercise A2 Page 159

When either John or **I** were not on **duty** we **went off** and
explored the **town**. Then we'd all **meet** for **lunch**. The **food**
there was **wonderful**, especially the **fresh fish**. And the **kids**
couldn't believe their **luck** with the **ice creams**. They came in
huge dishes with **lots** of **fruit**, and little **umbrellas** in, and on
the **last day** we were there, the ice creams came **lit up** with
sparklers. That was the **highlight** of the **whole** two weeks for
Jamie, I can tell you!

Exercise A3 Page 159

2 He thought someone should know what to do in an
   emergency.
3 the practical bits like dealing with people when they faint, or
   when people cut themselves
4 a weekend
5 he'd know what to do; he wouldn't panic
6 a first aid course
7 He wasn't very keen to go on the course. He was surprised to
   find he was quite interested in some bits. He's glad he went
   on it because he thinks it'll be useful.

Exercise A4 Page 160

Extract 1

1 maybe a travel agency or a tourist information office
2 a tour guide and a tourist, maybe
3 The coach is full so Mr Carstairs can't go on the excursion.
4 The woman apologises and offers him a refund.

Extract 2

2 Africa 3 humans began living together 4 the ancient
Egyptians 5 tail 6 make their tail look bigger (fluff up their
tail) 7 sit and stare 8 I'm here

Extract 3

Illustration 1: Robert before
Illustration 2: Robert now
Illustration 6: Paula before
Illustration 5: Paula now

	Before	**Now**
Robert	*Fatter* *Long hair, tied back* *Big earring*	*Slimmer* *Going bald* *Smaller earring*
Paula	*Big front teeth* *Curly hair* *Ears not pierced* *Thin*	*A bit fatter* *Big earrings* *Looks great*

Exercise A5 Page 161

2 couldn't see the point
3 handed over
4 I'm not very hopeful
5 unemployed
6 dreaded
7 it was tempting
8 did the washing up
9 not bothering to do things
10 jump at the chance
11 doing his bit
12 what was just around the corner
13 got him down
14 grabbed

LISTENING SECTION A UNIT 2

Exercise A1 Page 162

Description	Extract
general conversation	2
weather forecast	7
lecture or talk	10
interview	3
telephone conversation	5
news bulletin	12
telephone information line	4
extract from film/book/play	6
public announcement	1
advert	8
commentary	11
speech	9

Exercise A2 Page 162

(possible answers)

Extract 2
1 in a café or restaurant, or at the dinner table somewhere
2 pass the salt
3 friends
4 they both seem to know the situation and Gary well; they use informal spoken language with each other, e.g. *pass the salt*

Extract 3
1 not that well, as the man asks questions that a friend would know the answer to
2 she's probably quite strong – she says her parents didn't try to influence her decision because they knew she'd make up her own mind

Extract 4
1 to get some information about bus times, probably

Extract 5
1 someone who's called to speak to another woman
2 take a message for her

Extract 6
1 on the radio, maybe
2 very embarrassed – it felt like the longest walk ever, and in silence and with everyone looking at him

Extract 7
1 anyone who wants to know what the weather is going to do that day
2 key words: umbrellas, soaking, north and west of country, set to stay that way

Extract 8
1 that you can eat these mints at any time. He's making a joke about the unsuitability of the product's name

Extract 9
1 there's been some kind of party or celebration
2 by saying *so far*, which could mean that they're not going to be great in the future

Extract 10
1 some students

Extract 11
1 a tour guide
2 one of the people listening to him (a tourist, perhaps)

Extract 12
1 he might talk about the proposed drastic measures or about the current situation that cannot be allowed to continue

Exercise A3 Page 163
(possible answers)
Extract 2
1 in a shop / talking about clothes
2 pleased
3 I'm happy with it.

Extract 3
1 a man who's short of money
2 worried
3 I don't know how long he can carry on like this.

Extract 4
1 a man complaining
2 annoyed
3 … in the first place … I wouldn't have … would I?

Extract 5
1 her reactions to a film or show etc.
2 disappointed
3 I was expecting more, actually.

Extract 6
1 a man who's regretting something he said
2 sorry
3 I shouldn't have … I feel bad about it.

Extract 7
1 a woman who has failed something
2 surprised
3 I don't believe it.

Extract 8
1 a woman about to do some kind of performance
2 nervous
3 it'll all be over in … then I can relax a bit.

Exercise A4 Page 163
1 in a queue
clues: *you can come in here*; *join my friend*; *how many ahead of us*; *any movement up front*; *we're moving*
2 waiting for a shop, or something similar, to open so they can go in and get something like a book signed
3 probably the woman behind who's standing in the queue
4 buses
5 a book
6 because he thinks she always does the sensible thing
7 He's famous, because he's surrounded by body guards; and he's the person everyone is waiting for.
8 She's organised and sensible.
9 He's more disorganised. He didn't have time for breakfast and he'll take longer in the shop because he hasn't bought the book yet.

LISTENING SECTION A UNIT 3

Exercise A1 Page 164

Extract 1
The rhinoceros beetle digs out large amounts of earth and big stones in order to make its nest.
The cockroach would win the 100 metres race. It runs on its back two legs (it can run at 5.4km per hour) in order to escape from its enemies (rats and spiders).
The cat flea would win the high jump. It is able to jump 130 times its own height.

Extract 2

Bettina:	all the stuff to make spaghetti; they've just invited friends for dinner and they've got nothing in the fridge
Carol:	some nappies; her babysitter had just told her they'd run out. She was on her way home from having dinner with a friend
George:	some steak and salad; he's a night worker and he's going to make his dinner sometime during the night
Stella:	coffee; also working nights
David:	a light bulb; he'd just got up to go to work and he couldn't shave in the dark
Anna:	a carton of fruit juice; she's on her way home from a club

Exercise A2 Page 165
Tasty Fish
no spicy fish recipes
traditional recipes

Something Fishy
lots of colour pictures
£17.99
has Thai recipes in
a bit muddled
organised season by season
good index at back

Worldwide Fish
has spicy fish recipes
she doesn't like it
looks like a reference book
not many pictures
organised fish by fish
he likes it
£12

1 Tasty Fish
2 Worldwide Fish
3 Tasty Fish and Something Fishy
4 Something Fishy
5 Something Fishy

Exercise A3 Page 165
1 and Jack
2 Sarah
3 Jack, Sarah and Maria
4 Jack and Maria
5 Jack
6 Sarah
7 Jack
8 Maria
9 Maria

LISTENING SECTION B UNIT 4

Familiarisation exercise Page 166

1
B is right
A is wrong (she wanted to be a doctor when she was young)
C is wrong (her parents wanted her to work in a bank, like them)

2
C is right
A is wrong (the man saw him, but they're not friends)
B is wrong (the man was coming out of a shop)

Exercise B1 Page 167
Extract 1
3 a bit after 7.30
4 after work

Extract 2
1 to tell his wife he's going to be late
2 pick him up at the station
3 ring her again
4 a suit

Extract 3
1 (new?) receptionist/staff
2 one of the porters
3 entertainment officer

Extract 4
1 by the phone
2 in the fridge
3 in the right-hand cupboard

Extract 5
1 by getting rid of some people
2 on the basis of assessment tests
3 not very optimistic

Extract 6
1 to make an appointment
2 he's at the other surgery
3 for people who work

Exercise B2 Page 167
(possible answers)
Extract 2
I was hoping to return her ticket to you to sell.

Extract 3
… they were too tight …
… I'd never have been able to wear them …

Extract 4
… if you could come down to the station to give us a full report …
… makes, serial numbers and so on

Extract 5
I thought it was meant to be a comedy.
Do you think anyone has such a bad time as that?

Exercise B3 Page 168
(possible answers)
Extract 2
B is right (current statement, straight from my account)
A is wrong: they met at the gym last night
C is wrong: she pounds the streets for her morning training

Extract 3
C is right (… explain the mysterious things we see;
… unexplained sightings)
A is wrong: he has published 12 books
B is wrong: his ideas are based on historical information

Extract 4
A is right (it wasn't me who forgot to …)
B is wrong: he was rude this time but this is unusual for him, not fair to assume she doesn't like him
C is wrong: she doesn't feel like facing him again, but that doesn't mean she'll never see him again

Extract 5
B is right (I hope I don't see too many interesting sights today because I haven't got a spare film; the man hid it in the bag so it must be something valuable)
A is wrong: he still has the bag
C is wrong: he was feeling about in the bag, under the towel

Exercise B4 Exam practice Page 169
1 C 2 A 3 B 4 A 5 B 6 C 7 A 8 A

LISTENING SECTION B UNIT 5

Familiarisation exercise Page 171
1 (an) open-top bus
2 (the) castle
3 (the) (old) royal palace
4 four (other) languages
5 the (Central) Library
6 the (City) Museum
7 eight o'clock/8.00/8.00 am
8 £10/ten pounds/10 pounds

Exercise B1 Page 172
2 *is* should be followed by a noun or an -ing verb; probable answer: playing tennis or tennis
3 plural verb, so answer must be *problems*
4 *too* needs an adjective after it to describe the weight of the table. This phrase was probably exactly what the candidate heard on the tape; probable answer: heavy
5 *at* needs a particular place, not a city; probable answer: college in Chicago
6 *make* needs a verb, without the infinitive; probable answer: feel positive

Exercise B2 Page 172

Possible answers	Real answer
2 her desk/display	a chain
3 many/strange	science
4 a long time/a few weeks	15 years
5 has increased/is decreasing	is increasing/growing/getting better
6 the morning/surgery hours	their/the first visit
7 energy/money	time
8 & 9 games/magazines	video games and TV
10 drugs/equipment	the drill
11 more equipment/a better place	the latest technology

Exercise B3 Page 173
1 0123 77978   2 9.00 to 5.30   3 10.00 to 12.00
4 0171 0396418   5 October 14th   6 23547   7 50, Leisure
8 AJ4 3GY   9 3rd to 13th May   10 16th to 27th May
11 6.15 (pm) Friday, (the 20th)

Exercise B4 Page 174
1 People and Places   2 9   3 £100   4 (the) front   5 (a) waitress   6 5   7 King's Hotel   8 10   9 Past and Present
10 30th June

The questions that were affected by distracting information were numbers 4, 5, 7, 8, 9 and 10.

Exercise B5 Exam practice Page 175
1 lampshades   2 on the floor   3 never   4 a London engineer
5 the cost/price   6 air   7 a cat's eyes /cats' eyes   8 a mirror
9 a/one year   10 rich (and) famous

LISTENING SECTION B UNIT 6

Familiarisation exercise Page 176
1 D   2 A   3 C

Exercise B1 Page 176
(possible answers)
2 first day at school / accident / fighting with brother / 5th birthday party / learning to swim
3 train times / how to get to somewhere / what there is to see in a town / how much something costs / how to send flowers by post

4 the music / the food / the people / the funny clothes the people were wearing / the place where it was held
5 cleaning the Departure Lounge / waiting for an in-coming flight / waiting for a delayed flight to New York / working at the check-in desk / buying some duty-free perfume
6 over-priced / unusual food / tables are too close together / staff are friendly / too noisy
7 noisy neighbours / quality of goods / delayed trains / behaviour of a colleague / cost of something

Exercise B2 Page 177
2 A: 'the setting was what made the film'; 'it looked marvellous, made me want to go there'; 'beautiful sandhills and … glorious sunsets over the mountains in the distance'
3 D: 'what appealed to me most was the relationships'; 'the scene when … was so sad'; 'she wasn't the only one in tears'; 'hardly a dry eye in the house'
4 E: 'it was the unknown actors that were the stars'; 'it's amazing what he got out of them'; 'the scenes between … were really exciting'
5 B: 'Rupert Everett's performance was head and shoulders above the rest'; 'if this does turn out to be a big hit, it'll really all be down to him'

Exercise B3 Page 177
2 'I always like watching Ralph Fiennes' (statement B)
   'I found it very moving' (Statement D)
3 'there was lots of action' (statement C)
   'some spectacular camerawork in the mountains' (statement A)
4 'the main actor is a professional' (statement B)
5 '… and the setting was quite attractive' (statement A)
   'I want to be moved or excited' (statements C and D)

Exercise B4 Page 178
1 D   2 C   3 B   4 E   5 A

Exercise B5 Exam practice Page 178
1 F   2 C   3 D   4 E   5 A

LISTENING SECTION B UNIT 7

Familiarisation exercise 1 Page 179
1 F   2 T   3 F   4 F

Familiarisation exercise 2 Page 179
1 Carol   2 Tom   3 Tom   4 Shop assistant

Exercise B1 Page 180
2 'we've had the heating on much more than usual'
3 '… last year and the bill was nothing like as big as this one'
4 'I'm going to ring up and ask about it'
5 'don't forget they put up electricity charges last month'
6 'about what I was expecting'

Exercise B2 Page 180
1 F: The interviewer mentions exactly what he earns. He says he doesn't know what he's *worth*.
2 F: The interviewer says that the company is going to cut 1,000 jobs.
3 F: Mr Teacher says he doesn't enjoy making unpleasant decisions, which is not the same as saying he doesn't enjoy making *any* decisions.
4 T: ('What I don't understand is how somebody can be worth about £660,000 more than me.')
5 F: Mr Johnson acknowledges that Mr Teacher has a responsible job, but he says his own is more responsible.
6 T: (Both of them are on duty at the weekends.)
7 F: Mr Teacher said he started at BritElectric *after* college – 'straight out of college'.

8 F: He says his lifestyle hasn't changed that much, so it must have changed a bit.

9 T: Mr Teacher thinks he earns a good salary for an honest, hard day's work. Mr Johnson thinks Mr Teacher is overpaid, not that he himself is underpaid.

Exercise B3   Exam practice   Page 181
1 Yes 2 No 3 Yes 4 Yes 5 No 6 No 7 No

Exercise B4   Page 182
(possible answers)

		Multiple choice answers
1	been to Australia	B
2	small	C
3	surf or go spearfishing	C
4	during the day / in clear water	A
5	shout (at them)	A

Exercise B5   Page 183
Extract 1:
7 (suggestion) David

Extract 2:
1 (encouragement) Woman
6 (promise) Man

Extract 3:
3 (denial of accusation) Mike
2 (apology) Helen

Extract 4:
8 (reminder) Woman
5 (regret) Man

Exercise B6   Exam practice   Page 184
1 Martinez School   2 Goya Academy
3 Goya Academy   4 Iberia International
5 Martinez School   6 Iberia International
7 Martinez School

Chapter 5 Speaking

SPEAKING UNIT 1

Exercises 1 and 2   Pages 189 and 190
(possible answers)
1 Where do you come from?
   What's it like?
   How long have you lived there?
   Do you like living there?
2 What do you do?
   Do you think you'll always work there?
   When did you leave school?
   Do you enjoy it?
   What does your work/study involve?
3 Have you got a large or small family?
   Which person in your family are you most like?
   Do you live with your family?
4 What do you do in your free time?
   What kind of music do you like?
   How much free time do you have?
   Do you prefer cinema or theatre?
   Have you always liked …?
5 When did you start learning English?
   How do you think you'll use it in the future?
   How long have you been learning English?
   What do you like or dislike about it?
   Why are you learning it?

6 What do you want to do in the future?
   Are you looking forward to your next holiday?
   Have you got any plans for the future?
   How do you feel about going to …?

Exercise 3   Page 190
(students' own answers)

SPEAKING UNIT 2

Exercise 1   Page 191
(possible answer)
This photo shows a group of people looking at a statue in a gallery or somewhere. They are all looking very closely at it. Some are taking photos. I think it's a famous statue and they look very impressed.

Exercise 2   Page 192
(possible answers)
Similarities
They're similar because they both show some kind of art. *or* There are things to do with art in both of them.
Differences
The one above is more active. In the gallery the people are only looking, not taking part.
The gallery photo is not as lively as the other one.
The girl looks as if she's enjoying herself more than the people in the gallery.

Exercise 3   Page 192
(possible answers)
1 The girl looks as if she's really enjoying painting, but the people in the gallery look very serious.
2 They look quite happy – especially the girl who's doing the painting.
3 I'm not really aware of art in my daily life – except perhaps for some posters in the street, or CD covers.
4 I'm not really very interested in art. I prefer doing more active things, like sport.
5 The thing I enjoy most about art is photography. I think there are some wonderful photographs.

Exercise 4   Page 192
(possible answers)
2 Yes, sometimes, it depends what's on. There's a good gallery quite near my house.
3 Last month. I went to a local art gallery which has got some modern art in.
4 Unfortunately not. I'd love to be able to paint, but I'm hopeless.
5 The one with the child in. It looks much more fun to be doing something.

Exercise 5   Page 193
1 Candidate A gave too much detailed description of the first photo particularly. She did compare/contrast the two very well, but didn't have time to say what kind of sport she preferred.
2 Candidate B kept his answer short and answered the question well. He said more than just 'yes' or 'no' and said why he liked team sports.

Exercise 6   Page 194
(students' own answers)
For further practice: (students' own answers)

SPEAKING UNIT 3

Exercise 1 Page 196

1 all six of the classes
2 yes, all of them
3 yes: 65-year-old: Learning Chinese; 35-year-old: Painting;
  17-year-old: Using the Internet
4 In all cases they discussed the subjects during the
  conversation, and summarised their conclusion at the end.
  The final decision about the 17-year-old was made at the last
  moment.
5 Yes, they said more or less the same amount each.
6 Yes. He said to her:
  Which course are we going to talk about first?
  Yes, OK.
  And what else?
  All right, OK, that's fine.
  No, you're right.
  She said to him:
  You decide.
  Why?
  That is useful for all of them, isn't it?
  Yes, that's true.
  What about the 'Cooking for Beginners'?
  What do you think?
  Would you actually consider learning Chinese?
  So, what do we say?
7 It would have been better to ask the question before the
  discussion started. The examiner really doesn't want to take
  any part during your three minutes' talking time. Unless the
  instructions tell you something specific like 'talk about some
  of the …' or 'choose two or three to discuss …', then it's part
  of the test to negotiate with your partner how best to do the
  activity. The examiner, if asked in the middle of the activity,
  will probably just say the instructions again.
8 (possible answer)
  I really liked the way they involved each other and kept the
  discussion going, particularly the woman.

Exercises 2 and 3 Pages 198 and 199
(students' own answers)

Exercise 4 Page 199
(possible answers)
Which poster design did you choose?
Do you think posters are a good way of attracting people's
attention?
In your country, what are the worst environmental problems?
Do most people care about the environment/ the world around
them?
What can individuals do to help?
What do you think will be the most serious problem in the
future?
How can city life be improved?

(The answers to the questions above, and to those in the 'further
practice' section, are students' own.)